MW01250981

DISCOVER

THE

SOUTHWESTERN
ADIRONDACKS

WILD LAKES &
INDEPENDENT RIVERS

DISCOVER

THE

SOUTHWESTERN
ADIRONDACKS

WILD LAKES &
INDEPENDENT RIVERS

Bill Ingersoll & Barbara McMartin

WILD RIVER
PRESS

WWW.HIKETHEADIRONDACKS.COM

An Invitation to the Reader

Over time, trails can be rerouted and signs and landmarks altered. If you find that changes have occurred on the routes described in this book, please let us know so that corrections may be made in future editions. The authors welcome other comments and suggestions, too. Address correspondence to:

Editor, Discover the Adirondacks Series
7123 Trenton Road
Barneveld NY 13304
contact@HikeTheAdirondacks.com

ISBN 978-1-888374-32-2
Library of Congress Control Number: 2013936415

First edition, 1987
Second edition, 1993
Third edition, 2002
Fourth edition, 2013
© 2013 Bill Ingersoll

Published by
WILD RIVER PRESS
7123 Trenton Road
Barneveld, NY 13304

Printed in the United States of America by McNaughton & Gunn
Distributed by North Country Books, 220 Lafayette Street, Utica, NY 13502

All photographs by Bill Ingersoll.

Photographs
Front Cover: *Campsite at Middle Settlement Lake*
Back Cover: *Trail to Cedar Pond*
Frontispiece: *Independence River at Gleasmans Falls*
Page 6: *Little Woodhull Creek*

Acknowledgements

THIS FOURTH EDITION of *Discover the Southwestern Adirondacks* is more than just an updated hiking guidebook. Because this is an area so close to where I live, I had for several years taken it for granted — both as a recreational resource and as a wild area with its own distinctive history. Therefore when I began this revision process, I decided to use the opportunity to renew my relationship with the region by not only updating the trail information, but in many cases rewriting it — and at the same time challenging my assumptions about the area's history.

My research efforts were enabled by the wealth of historical documents that are starting to appear as online resources, making the Internet just a bit more like a library, and much more useful than its traditional role as a repository of opinion and generalized information. The website *www.fultonhistory.com*, for instance, was not only fun to navigate, but its searchable archive of regional newspapers was an invaluable tool. I am not a historian by profession, and my goal was not to write an historical treatise on the southwestern Adirondacks; rather I hope that the sketches provided herein will entertain some, and inspire others to ask more probing questions to help develop the back story even further.

As with any of the *Discover the Adirondacks* guidebooks, a large amount of collaboration was involved with this one as well, and there are several people who deserve credit.

Dick Cox, a resident of South Lake, offered some tips on little-known landmarks near the Black River headwaters.

Amber Bay assisted me with matters concerning the Mohawk language.

Paul Repak and Paul Sirtoli read all of the chapters and provided notes on the rewritten text. Paul Kalac also provided feedback.

I sought the opinions of a number of people while redesigning the front cover, and their input pointed me in a direction I might not have considered on my own. Sarah Richard provided a design element that proved to be the key to the graphic puzzle I encountered while reimagining the back cover.

While there is much about the fourth edition that differs from the previous three, it is still faithful in concept to what Barbara McMartin created with her original contributors in 1987. Those people included W. Alec Reid, Lee and Georgie Brenning, Scott K. Gray III, Stanford Pulrang, Willard (Bill) Reed, Ron Canter, James C. Dawson, and many others.

To everyone who has assisted with this project, your contribution has greatly enriched the final product. Thank you.

Contents

Introduction

THIS GUIDE COVERS a region that for many people is the gateway to the Adirondack Park. It is traversed and bounded by several major state highways, each of which carries thousands of visitors every year into and out of the mountain country. To many of these travelers, the woods that flank those highways may be little more than scenery, something pleasing to look at on the journey to someplace else. But if you are someone who likes a good outdoor adventure, you will probably note the numerous trailhead signs and side roads promising access to state land. You may note that while there are no large mountains to be seen, there are nevertheless plenty of large rivers winding through the area, and a wealth of wild lakes to explore as well. The forest will seem vast and inviting, with no lack of secluded nooks to investigate. If you become seized with the curiosity to see what lies down one of those little-used trails, then this book is for you.

The southwestern Adirondacks are a place for nature lovers: those who want to be close to wildlife; who delight in a sphagnum bog or a pine-crowned sandy ridge; who like long, level trails or well-groomed routes for hiking; or who want to feel as if the whole forest is theirs to enjoy in solitary quiet. Weekend hikers will only occasionally meet others on the trail, and those fortunate enough to walk in midweek will encounter only deer and birds and, rarely, signs of a bear. The majority of the walks are gentle, mirroring the gentle blue hills you see as you approach the region. Much of the forest floor is open, lacking the denser growth of the central Adirondacks.

The state lands of the southwestern Adirondacks cater to a wide variety of recreational uses, from backpacking to snowmobiling. Hunting is one of the most popular uses, and the region's deep snows make it an ideal choice for cross-country skiing as well. The area contains only one state campground, but many of the back roads provide opportunities for free camping on a first-come basis. The hiking trails range from short and very easy to the long and adventurous. Some are rarely used, and others are quite popular. Many of the snowmobile trails are excellent hiking routes, while certain others only have nominal value for hikers. This guidebook will help you sort through the multitude of options to find the hikes that suit your skills and interest.

Three blocks of state land lie within the region: the Black River Wild Forest, which extends from Nobleboro to Old Forge; the Ha-de-ron-dah Wilderness, which lies between Old Forge and Brantingham Lake; and the

Snowmobile trail near South Lake

Independence River Wild Forest, which extends from Brantingham Lake to the region's northern boundary near Stillwater. The State Land Master Plan, which defines these designations, suggests that the areas classified as "wild forest" will seem less remote and more crowded than the lands designated as "wilderness." It *is* true that there is greater leniency toward motorized access in the two wild forests, in the form of snowmobile trails as well as forest access roads that penetrate deep into the distant reaches, whereas in wilderness there is no legal motorized access.

But regardless of the official designation, there are large pockets of outstanding wildness to be found throughout the southwestern Adirondacks, including the cores of both wild forests. In fact, one large section of the Black River Wild Forest near North Wilmurt has been identified as fully meeting the requirements for a wilderness designation. A proposal has been advanced to reclassify this section as the Cotton Lake Wilderness, which would permanently protect it as a haven for solitary exploration.

How to Use the Discover Guides

The regional guides in the *Discover the Adirondacks* series will tell you enough about each area so that you can enjoy it in many different ways at any time of year. Each guide will acquaint you with that region's access roads and trailheads, its trails and unmarked paths, some bushwhack routes and canoe trips, campsites, and ski-touring routes. At the same time, the guides will introduce you to valleys, mountains, cliffs, scenic views, lakes, streams, and a myriad of other natural features.

Some of the destinations are within easy walking distance of the major highways that ring the areas, while others are miles deep into the wilderness. Each description will enable you to determine the best excursion for you and to enjoy the natural features you will pass, whether you are on a summer day hike or a winter ski-touring trek. The sections are grouped in chapters according to their access points. Each chapter contains a brief introduction to that area's history and the old settlements and industries that have all but disappeared into wilderness. Throughout the guides you will find accounts of the geological forces that shaped features of the land. Unusual wildflowers and forest stands also will be noted.

It is our hope that you will find this guide not only an invitation to know and enjoy the woods, but a companion for all your adventures there.

MAPS AND NOMENCLATURE

The best source for navigating the back roads of the Adirondacks remains DeLorme's *New York State Atlas and Gazetteer*, which is widely available at bookstores and local shops.

This guide contains maps showing all the routes mentioned, located at the back of the book. These maps are for *location purposes only* and should not be the only maps you carry in the wilderness. Detailed topographic maps are essential for finding your way through the woods, especially for bushwhacks.

Many people use the Internet as a source to obtain topo maps, or mapping software that allows them to print portions of maps at home as they are needed. If you are a frequent visitor of the woods, however, you will want a sturdier map. One useful Internet service is *www.MyTopo.com*, a site that allows users to center their own topo maps, joining all of the adjacent USGS quadrangles—even those with different scales—on one water-resistant sheet.

There are also a number of good commercial trail maps available, including National Geographic's *Trails Illustrated* series, which show state land boundaries as well as state-maintained trails and lean-tos.

All of these maps are ultimately based upon the USGS topo maps, which are available locally in some sporting goods stores. The USGS metric 7.5-minute maps for the southwestern Adirondack region include the Brantingham,

Crystal Dale, Honnedaga Lake, McKeever, Morehouseville, North Wilmurt, Number Four, Old Forge, and Thendara quadrangles.

DISTANCE AND TIME

Distance along the routes is measured from the USGS survey maps, and many have been verified using GPS receivers. They are given in miles, feet, or yards. Distance is a variable factor in comparing routes along paths or bushwhacks. Few hikers gauge distance accurately even on well-defined trails.

Time is given as an additional gauge for the length of routes. This provides a better understanding of the difficulty of the terrain, the change of elevation, and the problems of finding a suitable course. Average time for walking trails is 2 miles an hour, 3 miles if the way is level and well defined; for paths, 1½ to 2 miles an hour; and for bushwhacks, 1 mile an hour.

Vertical rise usually refers to the change in elevation along a route up a single hill or mountain; *elevation change* generally refers to the cumulative change in elevation where a route crosses several hills or mountains.

A line stating distance, time, and vertical rise or elevation change is given with the title of each section describing maintained trails, but not for less distinct paths and bushwhacks for which such information is too variable to summarize. Distance and times are for *one way only*, unless otherwise stated. The text suggests how to put together several routes into a longer trek that will occupy a day or more.

TYPES OF ROUTES

The southwestern Adirondacks contain hundreds of potential wilderness destinations, and an almost endless variety of ways to get there. This guidebook describes a variety of routes, ranging from well-marked trails to rugged bushwhacks. Former logging and mining operations have left a legacy of abandoned woods roads, many of which make useful trails even though they may not be signed or marked. Often all that is needed is a sense of adventure and a curiosity to see what's out there.

Each section of this guide generally describes a route or a place. Included in the descriptions is such basic information as the suitability for different levels of woods experience, walking (or skiing, paddling, and climbing) times, distances, directions to the access, and, of course, directions along the route itself. The following definitions clarify the terms used in this book.

A route is considered a *trail* if it is so designated by the New York State Department of Environmental Conservation (DEC). This means the trail is routinely cleared by DEC or volunteer groups and adequately marked with official DEC disks. Foot trails are generally marked with red, blue, or yellow disks.

The DEC has marked some trails for special types of travel. *Ski trails* and *horse trails* are marked with yellow disks bearing the emblem of that activity. Likewise, red disks bearing *snowmobile* or *mountain bike* emblems denote trails designated for those sports, which are limited to some portions of Wild Forest areas.

Snowmobiles are permitted on designated trails in winter when there is sufficient snow cover. This guide indicates trails not heavily used where skiing and snowmobiling may be compatible, but a skier must always be cautious on a snowmobile trail. Hikers can enjoy both ski and snowmobile trails.

A *path* is an informal and unmarked route with a clearly defined foot tread. These traditional routes, worn by fishermen and hunters to favorite spots, are great for hiking. A path, however, is not necessarily kept open, and fallen trees and new growth sometimes obliterate its course. The paths that cross wet meadows or open fields often become concealed by lush growth. You should always carry a map and compass when you are following an unmarked path and you should keep track of your location.

There is a safe prescription for walking paths. In a group of three or more hikers, stringing out along a narrow path will permit the leader to scout until the path disappears, at which point at least one member of the party should still be standing on an obvious part of the path. If that hiker remains standing while those in front range out to find the path, the whole group can continue safely after a matter of moments.

The terms *logging road* or *woods road* refer to routes constructed before the land was acquired for the Forest Preserve, and they are used frequently throughout this book to describe the nature of certain trails and footpaths. Some of the more ancient logging roads have reverted to beautiful woodland paths, and indeed many of them form the basis of today's hiking trail network. Hikers may find some of the more recent logging roads to be unsightly, however, since they were often constructed with gravel surfaces to accommodate mechanized equipment. Nevertheless, many of them provide excellent access to worthwhile destinations. Following them will require that you pay careful attention to your map, because misleading side routes may be frequently encountered.

Hikers in the North Country often use the term *bushwhack* to describe an uncharted and unmarked trip through the deep woods, where no trails or paths exist. Sometimes bushwhacking literally means pushing brush aside, but it usually connotes a variety of cross-country walks.

Bushwhacks are an important part of this regional guide series because of the shortage of marked trails throughout much of the Adirondack Park and the abundance of little known and highly desirable destinations for which no visible routes exist. Although experienced bushwhackers may reach these destinations with not much more help than the knowledge of their location, we think most hikers will appreciate these simple descriptions that point out the easiest and most interesting routes and the possible pitfalls. In general, descriptions for bushwhacks are less detailed than those for paths or trails; it is assumed that those who bushwhack have a greater knowledge of the woods than those who walk marked routes.

"Bushwhack" is defined as any trip on which you make your way through the woods without a trail, path, or the visible foot tread of other hikers and without markings, signs, or blazes. It also means you will make your way by following a route chosen on a contour map, aided by a compass, using streambeds, valleys, abandoned roads, and obvious ridges as guides. Most bushwhacks require navigating by contour map and compass, as well as an understanding of the terrain.

Bushwhack distances are not given in precise tenths of a mile. They are estimates representing the shortest distance one could travel between points. This reinforces the fact that each hiker's cross-country route will be different, yielding different mileages. Some of this guide's shorter bushwhacks are calibrated in yards traveled, hopefully making them more suitable for the novice bushwhacker.

A bushwhack is said to be *easy* if the route is along a stream, a lakeshore, a reasonably obvious abandoned roadway, or some similarly well-defined feature. A short route to the summit of a hill or a small mountain can often be easy. A bushwhack is termed *moderate* if a simple route can be defined on a contour map and followed with the aid of a compass. Previous experience is necessary. A bushwhack is rated *difficult* if it entails a complex route, necessitating advanced knowledge of navigation by compass and reading contour maps and land features.

Compass directions are given in degrees from magnetic north and in degrees from true north. The text will usually specify which reference is used, but if no reference is given the degrees refer to magnetic north.

The guide occasionally refers to old *blazed* lines or trails. The word "blaze" comes from the French *blesser* and means to cut or wound. Early loggers and settlers made deep slashes in good-sized trees with an axe to mark property lines and trails. Hunters and fishermen have also often made slashes with knives, and although they are not as deep as axe cuts they can still be seen. *It is now, and has been for many years, illegal to deface trees in the Forest Preserve in this manner.*

In the twenty-first century, it is more common to find a *flagged* route—one that has been marked by colored ribbons. Marking a trail in this manner on public land is just as illegal as blazing and just as unsightly to many hikers. Nevertheless, following an old blazed path—whether it be blazed by old axe blazes, daubs of paint, or flagging—for miles in dense woods is often a challenging but good way to reach an otherwise trailless destination.

You may see *yellow paint daubs on a line of trees.* These lines usually indicate the boundary between private and public lands.

All *vehicular traffic*, except snowmobiles on their designated trails, is *prohibited* in the Forest Preserve. Vehicles are allowed on town roads and some roads that pass through state land to reach private inholdings. Most old roads referred to here are town or logging roads that were abandoned when the land around them became part of the Forest Preserve. Now they are routes for hikers, not for vehicles.

There has been an increase in the use of four-wheeled off-road vehicles, even on trails where such use is prohibited. New laws have gone a long way toward stopping this in the Forest Preserve, ensuring that some of the old roads remain attractive hiking routes. However, some short routes may be opened to controlled ATV use by people with disabilities.

Also, it is important to note that in the southwestern Adirondacks there are numerous private inholdings buried deep within state land, and some trails that lead to these properties have been designated as motorized access routes. This is an exception to the ATV policy noted above. The condition of these trails may be impaired by large mud wallows and other evidence of motor vehicle use, and they are generally identified as such in the text.

Enjoying the Backcountry: Responsible Use

The wilderness areas and wild forests of the Adirondack Park are an outstanding resource, and it is the responsibility of all users to treat that resource with respect. The failure of just a few people to do so can leave a lasting impact, infringing on the rights of other people to enjoy a pristine, wild environment.

Compared to other parks and wild areas, Adirondack visitors are relatively unburdened by the need for backcountry permits and excessive regulations. The emphasis here is self-reliance, mutual respect for other backcountry travelers, adherence to state regulations, careful trip planning, and the practice of low-impact camping and hiking techniques. These are the basic principles of wilderness travel, and abiding by them will help ensure that the freedom of the outdoors will remain available for generations to come.

This section outlines the basics of what you need to know to enjoy the Adirondacks safely and responsibly.

PUBLIC VERSUS PRIVATE LAND

Most of the land described in these guides is in the *Forest Preserve*, land protected by the state constitution from logging, resale, and development. All of it is open to the public. The *Adirondack Park Agency* has responsibility for the Wilderness, Primitive, Canoe Area, and Wild Forest classifications into which the various Forest Preserve tracts have been assigned. Care and custody of these state lands is left to the *Department of Environmental Conservation (DEC)*, which is in the process of producing Unit Management Plans for the roughly 130 separate Forest Preserve areas.

Private lands are generally not open to the public, though some individuals and organizations have granted public access across their land to state land. It is always wise to ask before crossing private lands. Be very respectful of private landowners so that public access will continue to be granted. Never enter private lands that have been posted unless you have the owner's permission. Unless the text expressly identifies an area as state-owned Forest Preserve, a public easement, or private land whose owner permits unrestricted public passage, the inclusion of a route in this guide does not imply a public right-of-way.

Easements are parcels of private land where the state has purchased certain rights, such as for recreation and development. The public can often use these lands the same as the Forest Preserve, although special restrictions may apply. You may encounter small camps on easement lands; these are exclusive leases to which there is no public access. Some easements are closed to the public seasonally. Details for specific easements are outlined elsewhere in this guide.

CAMPING AND CAMPFIRES

Backcountry camping is permitted throughout the public lands of the Adirondacks except within 150 feet of water and trails and above 4000 feet in elevation. Camping within the 150-foot zone is permitted only at designated campsites, marked by yellow "Camp Here" disks. In certain fragile areas, camping is restricted to specific locations, and the state is using a "No Camping" disk to mark sites closed for regeneration. Since designated sites are subject to closure or relocation, this guide mentions the specific location

Lean-to at Middle Settlement Lake

of only a few prominent sites.

Lean-tos are three-sided log shelters that are available on a first-come basis. They are scattered throughout the wilderness and make handy shelters in inclement weather. Most of them are quite popular, being among the first campsites to be filled on weekends. It is illegal to set up a tent inside them, and backcountry etiquette requires that smaller parties leave room for late-comers, up to the shelter's capacity (generally 8 people). Solo campers and small groups seeking solitude are advised to avoid lean-tos, especially during the summer and fall seasons, because many are located in relatively promi-nent, high-traffic locations.

In most cases, *permits* for camping on state lands are needed only for stays in one location that exceed three nights, or for groups of more than eight campers. Permits can be obtained from the local rangers, who are listed on the New York State Department of Environmental Conservation website, *www.dec.ny.gov*.

Only dead and downed wood can be used for *campfires*. It is illegal—and in poor taste—to cut any standing timber, even if it is dead. When gathering firewood around a campsite, it is best to range out a short distance rather than deplete the supply closest by. This will help ensure that a supply will remain for other campers, and it will help prevent the forest floor from becoming trampled and denuded of vegetation.

Many modern hikers and paddlers do not build campfires at all, noting the potential impact they could have on the forest. Stoves are far superior for cooking, and many small, lightweight, and efficient models are available specifically for backpacking.

Most of the forest floor is covered by a layer of duff, an organic soil made of decaying plant matter. A campfire built on this type of soil can cause it to combust and smolder long after the actual fire is extinguished. A duff fire can expand well beyond the original fire ring—burning a pit in the ground, charring roots, and even igniting trees—long after you have left. Therefore build fires only at designated campsites, or on bare rock or mineral soil (which will feel sandy or gravelly to the touch). *Never build a fire anywhere else.* Douse all fires with water and stir the ashes with a stick before you leave. This means not just extinguishing the flames, but ensuring that all pockets of heat have been thoroughly drowned.

If you are spending the night in a place where there is no established campsite, it is your responsibility to practice *low-impact camping techniques.* This means that the next person who comes along should see no indication that you stayed there, such as trampled vegetation, fire rings, and waste. Allow future visitors to enjoy the same unblemished landscape that you have enjoyed, and choose your campsite carefully. Organizations such as Leave No Trace (*www.LNT.org*) provide excellent resources on this topic.

Carry out what you carry in. Always check your campsite before leaving to make sure all litter has been picked up and no personal items have been left behind.

SAFETY IN THE WOODS

It is best *not to walk alone.* Make sure someone knows where you are heading and when you are expected back.

Carry water or other liquids with you. Not only are the mountains dry, but the recent spread of *Giardia* makes many streams suspect. Durable plastic water bottles are readily available in most gear shops. Each hiker should carry at least two quarts with them at any time of the year. If you are camping, you will definitely want to treat any potential drinking water you get from a lake or stream, either with a filter, sterilizer, iodine tablets, or by boiling for two minutes.

Always wear *non-cotton clothing* when exploring the backcountry. Cotton—

including denim—dries slowly and loses its ability to insulate when wet, making it an unreliable material for wilderness recreation. The significance of wearing the proper outdoor clothing increases as the weather becomes cooler and wetter, when keeping dry and warm becomes of paramount importance. However, wearing non-cotton clothing is recommended at any time of the year, in any kind of weather.

Carry a small *day pack* with insect repellent, flashlight, first aid kit, emergency food rations, waterproof matches, jackknife, whistle, rain gear, and a wool sweater, even for summer hiking. Wear layers of wool and waterproof clothing in winter and carry an extra sweater and socks. If you plan to camp and are unsure of what to expect and what to bring, join a hiking and camping club in your area to learn the essentials.

Always carry a *map and compass*. The ideal map will show not just your specific route, but the larger area as well.

Wear *glasses* when bushwhacking. The risk to your eyes of a small protruding branch makes this a necessity.

Carry *binoculars* for birding as well as for viewing distant peaks.

Most *wildflowers and ferns* mentioned in the text are protected by law. Do not pick them or try to transplant them.

Bears have become a problem throughout the Adirondacks in areas where campers have concentrated. In some places bear-resistant canisters are required for all backcountry campers, although this regulation has not been extended to the southwestern Adirondacks. The alternative to bear canisters is to keep all food in sealed containers and hang it overnight in "bear bags," suspended on a rope thrown between two trees at least 15 feet apart, with the bear bag at least 10 feet from the ground. Do not keep food in your tent. Bears are not usually a problem during the daytime and only at night if they detect food. If bears do come near your campsite, loud noises may scare them away. Remember they are not there for you, only your food. Be sure to report an encounter with an assertive or habituated bear with the local ranger.

Use great care near the *edges of cliffs* and when *crossing streams* by hopping rocks in the streambed.

Never bushwhack unless you have gained a measure of woods experience. If you are a novice in the out-of-doors, join a hiking group in your area and participate in their trips to the North Country. As you get to know the land, you can progress from the standard trails to the more difficult and more satisfyingly remote routes. Then you will really begin to discover the Adirondacks.

North of Nobleboro

IN 1787, A man by the name of Arthur Noble acquired over 87,000 acres of land in two patents flanking the West Canada Creek. His goal was to establish a settlement along the banks of this small river, perhaps dreaming that someday it would grow to be a city. He named the patents Arthurboro and Nobleboro, and built a sawmill and gristmill near where the creek's South Branch joins the main branch. Some logging did occur in 1790, and the lumber was reportedly exported all the way to Ireland, but the enterprise did not succeed. Within a few years, only Noble's name remained on the map.

A full century passed before logging really took root in the region, when lumbermen built dams at Mud Lake and at two stillwaters downstream along the creek to regulate its flow. According to Harvey Dunham's classic book, *Adirondack French Louie*, the largest log drive on the West Canada occurred in the spring of 1895, when over 20 million board feet of lumber followed the seasonal floods out of the woods.

At about the same time, the Adirondack League Club formed as a large private preserve that encompassed all of Jocks Lake, the site of Dut Barber's Forest Lodge, and a section of the West Canada Creek. The club renamed the lake Honnedaga and took over Forest Lodge, retaining Barber and many of his guides as employees. The members dedicated the club (founded two years before the creation of the Adirondack Park) to the proper protection of game and fish, an improved system of forestry, and the maintenance of an ample preserve for its members' enjoyment. Some of their rules regarding the taking of fish and game were stricter than the state's regulations at the time.

Today, Nobleboro is noteworthy as being the place where the West Canada Creek first meets a paved highway after its long journey out of the backcountry. The bridge that carries NY 8 toward Hamilton County offers a classic view of the confluence of the two branches, where in 1942 a crib dam and a debarking drum with a 20-cord capacity were built for a resurging pulpwood operation. Both are gone now, but once this was the place where pulp logs were stripped of their bark and loaded onto trucks. Some of these operations were captured on camera by Frank Reed, the traveling minister famous for the book and video called *Lumberjack Sky Pilot*. The last lumber drive on the West Canada was in 1949.

Jocks Falls

Waypoints along Haskell Road

Miles	
0.0	Intersection with NY 8 in Nobleboro
0.05	Scenic view parking area, **section 1**
0.2	Mill Creek Lake trailhead immediately before bridge over Mill Creek, **sections 2 & 3**
0.5	Driveway to camping area on West Canada Creek
1.4	Green Clearing trailhead, **section 4**
2.7	Gate, end of town-maintained road, **sections 5-8**

Today, Nobleboro is a quiet residential hamlet that still seems perched squarely on the edge of the wilderness. Much of the land between Nobleboro and the original holdings of the Adirondack League Club are now part of the Forest Preserve, and this is the setting for the hikes described in this chapter. Hidden within these woods are several attractive ponds, a wild stretch of the West Canada Creek, and the tallest waterfall in the southwestern Adirondacks.

If the area has a drawback—at least from a hiker's perspective—it's that none of the trails in the woods north of Nobleboro are maintained expressly for foot travel. All of the state trails are snowmobile trails, and some are used by motor vehicles to access private inholdings. As a result, the hiking experience is not always pristine. But if an unblemished landscape is what you seek, then consider these routes merely as springboards to the wild, trailless expanse of country to the west, which encompasses the headwaters of Big Brook.

All of the adventures in this chapter begin on Haskell Road, which is easy to find because it is the only public road in Nobleboro other than NY 8. It begins near the west end of the bridge over the creek and quickly leaves the houses behind as it climbs into state land. Ordinary vehicles can follow it at any time of the year to a large parking area 2.7 miles north of town.

1 West Canada Creek at Nobleboro

Path, fishing, picnicking, camping

In 1998, the state built a new highway bridge to carry NY 8 across the West

Canada Creek. At the approximate location of the old bridge, they also built a scenic parking area overlooking the creek and Fort Noble Mountain. As you turn onto Haskell Road from the state highway, this is the very first driveway on the right. It provides the best public access to the creek in Nobleboro, where you can still see the foundation of the old dam in the creek bed when the water is low. If you are looking for an opportunity to stretch your legs on a short walk, then there are two options.

From the parking area you can walk along a short gravel grade to a spot just upstream from the dam site where it is possible to put in a canoe, but there is limited flat water here. The path continues to a clearing where people have camped, and ends 300 yards from the parking area at the well-blazed end of state land. Another path leads from the parking area back to Haskell Road, passing some interesting remnants from the old lumber operations off in the woods.

The other option involves crossing the creek, using the pedestrian bridge that was built as an attachment to the main highway bridge. The parking area is at the northwest corner of the bridge, but at the northeastern corner you will find an unmarked path on state land leading 0.3 mile to the delta-like confluence of the south and main branches of the West Canada. The path passes several campsites located on high banks over the water, and at its far end you can easily step out onto the rocky delta and get quite close to the South Branch.

Note that the parking area is not plowed in winter.

2 | Mill Creek Lake and Black Creek Lake

Snowmobile & motorized access trail, hiking, bushwhacking
2.1 miles, 1¼ hours, 375-foot vertical rise to Mill Creek Lake
6.2 miles, 3¼ hours, 650 foot vertical rise to Black Creek Lake

The two largest backcountry lakes in the woods north of Nobleboro are Black Creek and Mill Creek lakes. Both are similar in size and—as their toponyms suggest—are the sources of namesake creeks. They are both nestled in valleys at the feet of steep ridges, and they are both accessed from the same trail. Both have clusters of private camps on their southern shores, but otherwise fall entirely within state land. In fact, the two lakes have many things in common except their watersheds: Mill Creek flows into the West Canada, which is part of the greater Mohawk-Hudson watershed, but Little Black Creek is a tributary of the Black River, which flows toward Lake Ontario.

This trail serves multiple purposes. In addition to hiking, it is used by snowmobiles in the winter and by the camp owners in summer for motorized access. This is not a pristine wilderness footpath, but it is the most prominent route to the lakes, and with its connections to two other snowmobile trails it does present some interesting trip-planning opportunities. Although the tendency is to use the word "road" to describe this route, it is really only suitable for ATVs—and only for the purpose of reaching one of the private inholdings.

Note that short bushwhacks are required to actually reach the shorelines. The private parcels block the most direct approaches.

This route begins as a private road on Haskell Road 0.2 mile from NY 8, on the left immediately before the bridge over Mill Creek. The recommended parking area is at the scenic view.

NOBLEBORO TO MILL CREEK LAKE

On foot, follow the private road for 0.1 mile, bearing left onto the snowmobile trail. At 0.9 mile you come to a large clearing overlooking a small flow. Another route comes in from the left, this one originating near NY 8. To reach the lakes, bear right.

You begin a steady, gradual climb on a northerly course. The trees are quite tall here and you may see bear "nests" in the upper limbs of the beeches. These are made when black bears climb the trees to reach the tasty beechnuts, and pile the broken branches underneath them as they sit and eat. On the trunks you may also see scars in the pattern of the bears' claws, made as they climbed powerfully upward.

The road eventually levels off, and at 2.1 miles the snowmobile trail from Green Clearing, section 4, enters to the right, on the road leading to the private camps on Mill Creek Lake.

In the next ten minutes, you will see several yellow-blazed lines and pipes on the right indicating the boundary of the private parcel on the lake's southeastern shore. You will also pass two driveways leading to camps on the lake. Beyond the second driveway, a yellow-painted state land boundary pipe marks a property line heading 34° magnetic. An easy five-minute bushwhack along this line will take you to the brushy shore. Patches of weeds break the water's surface; spruce, balsam, and hemlocks line the lake's edges. Wetlands lie to the west along a major inlet and to the east near the outlet. A ridge rises steeply to the north, with the wooded dome of Lawson Top behind to the right. Two rock outcrops can be seen on the ridge; the eastern one is the destination of the bushwhack described in section 3.

A footpath marked with painted can covers leads west from the camps to a point on the dirt road just south of where it crosses the lake's major inlet. It roughly follows the line at which the hardwoods meet the conifers around the lake's edge. To get back to the main trail you may follow this path westward or return along the state land boundary. Either way will take about fifteen minutes, but the path is more level and interesting.

MILL CREEK LAKE TO BLACK CREEK LAKE

If you do not bushwhack to the shoreline, the main trail keeps far enough to the south that it offers no views. After crossing the inlet on a long plank bridge, the road leads through a dense stand of spruce and balsam. It then rises, passes an old road heading off to the right, and comes to a junction where a snowmobile trail heads west to Mad Tom Lake, section 11. This junction is 3.5 miles from Nobleboro.

You now begin a long, gradual ascent through a beautiful hardwood forest dominated by tall maples and beech. The road soon splits. The left fork parallels to the west, ending in a little over a mile later at a private parcel, so bear right. The road becomes more rugged and there are occasional rutted, muddy areas. The terrain then becomes rolling, markers are rare, and a wetland is visible through the trees to the west.

At 5.2 miles you reach a junction with the Round Top Mountain snowmobile trail described in section 7. The old roadway is plagued with mud wallows, and when the land rises you will see an old truck on the left. Given the current state of the road, it seems improbable that anyone would drive a highway vehicle this deep into the woods; but in the days before ATVs it was common practice to use old junkers like this for off-road travel. This one once belonged to a lumber company in Dolgeville, as the door lettering still boldly announces.

At about 5.8 miles you reach the well-marked boundary with private land, and the end of the public trail. This point is still 0.4 mile shy of Black Creek Lake, and the old road continues on private land directly to the cluster of camps on the south shore.

Therefore, as with Mill Creek Lake, the best public access is to follow the yellow-blazed property line left, northwest, and then north as you round a corner. This is a bushwhack route, but Black Creek Lake is very scenic and very much worth the trouble. When you reach the shoreline, you will find that the camp owners maintain their own trail system around the lake and to various other local landmarks. One path follows the beginning of Little Black Creek west toward Crosby Vly, and another loops around the north-

Abandoned truck on the trail to Black Creek Lake

ern shoreline. Yet another makes a detour up a steep hillside to visit boggy Burp Lake. Once off the rutted ATV trail the woods in this area quickly immerse you in natural beauty. Indeed, the region beyond the lake is part of the proposed Cotton Lake Wilderness.

3 Mill Creek Lake Lookout

Bushwhack

In a region with so few large mountains and prominent cliffs, the presence of any open view is worth noting. One of the area's best is located on a ridge above Mill Creek Lake, and it can be accessed most easily from the trail between Mill Creek and Black Creek lakes, section 2.

Hike to Mill Creek Lake as described in either section 2 or 4, following the road-like trail around the south and west ends of the lake and past the Mad Tom trail junction. About twenty minutes after crossing the inlet you will have gained 250 feet. The road levels into a wet, grassy stretch at this point, and a small stream approaches to within 15 yards on the right. Leave the road and cross the stream on a bearing of 120° magnetic, east-southeast. This will take you to the ridgeline. Following it east, and in ten minutes you will come to a small, scrubby, bedrock summit where there are limited views through the trees. Continue east, dropping down off the summit and reaching a second high spot. After another minute's walk, head straight for the lake.

The outcrop is just below you, and from the top of the rock all of Mill Creek Lake and its wetlands are visible. A ridge beyond the lake blocks views to the south, but to the southeast the hills north of Jerseyfield Lake stretch to the horizon. Fort Noble Mountain rises to the east-southeast, and behind it stands Bethune Mountain and the country surrounding the South Branch of the West Canada Creek.

4 Mill Creek Lake via Green Clearing
Path

This route approaching Mill Creek Lake from the east was once a designated snowmobile trail, but it is now effectively abandoned and receives very little, if any, attention. This is a shame, because as a hiking route it would be far more preferable than the primary trail described in section 2. This route, despite its wetness and lack of maintenance, is distinctly more trail-like. Perhaps in a future management plan a decision will be made to reestablish it has a foot trail, but until then it can only be recommended for people seeking a wilderness-style excursion in a little-used patch of forest.

The trail begins at a small pullout on the northwest side of Haskell Road, 1.4 miles from NY 8. There is enough room for two or three cars to park, but the signage marking the spot is minimal.

The trailhead area is called Green Clearing because it was once a cleared area—by all appearances, the site of a small farm—even though the forest has long since reclaimed most of it. The path begins as an old road grade, swinging north past a cellar hole and climbing west through a narrow draw. It then climbs gently through a coniferous section, which was almost certainly a part of the clearing. You pass the remains of a low stone fence, and soon the conifers swiftly give way to open hardwoods.

The path is generally easy to follow to this point, but as you cross and follow a small stream beginning at 0.7 mile the path begins to show its age. The footing begins to get wet and you cross a second, larger stream. Heading north-northwest, you pass through a very wet section and then turn west, paralleling the stream flowing just out of sight on your left. The trail meanders northwest, and occasionally north. When it turns west, it passes through a stand of tall hemlocks. Through the trees on your right you see a wetland along Mill Creek.

At 2.1 miles you reach the creek. Keeping a bridge in place at this site had been a continuing problem, and this was no doubt a factor in the abandonment of the snowmobile trail. Hikers may need to ford the creek if no logs or beaver dams are handy.

Once across Mill Creek, the trail swings south near a dense alder thicket. After a short ascent and a zigzag southeast then south, the trail makes a wide swing to the west through mixed tree cover. A final turn south leads shortly to a dirt road. To the right, this road leads in 0.2 mile to the private land on Mill Creek Lake. Turn left onto the road and begin to ascend away from the lake. In 0.1 mile, or 2.6 miles from the trailhead, the road joins the dirt road coming in from NY 8, section 2.

5 Beyond the Gate on Haskell Road

Primitive road, cross-country skiing
6.1 miles, 3 hours, rolling terrain

It may seem odd that a hiking guidebook would recommend an excursion along more than 6 miles of rough road, but since this one provides such good access to the West Canada Creek it is worth at least a brief mention.

This is the primary access road for the scattered small private camps south of Honnedaga Brook, as well as for the large tract known as Miller Park further north near West Canada Mountain. As such, it is routinely used by motor vehicles, but only the very first section is maintained as a graded road. The remainder can be quite rough, and due to its deteriorating condition it has been closed to public motor vehicle use for several years. But in the winter, with a good snow cover, all of this is moot. Given the right conditions, this could make a good intermediate ski route.

Follow the town-maintained portion of Haskell Road north from Nobleboro all the way to its end at 2.7 miles, where you will find a large parking area. The road is gated at this point, although the gate is often open to accommodate private traffic.

Setting off on foot, you will find that the first portion is well maintained, and sometimes even plowed in winter. You pass the Herkimer Landing Trail at 0.8 mile (section 6), and then the end of the good maintenance after about 1.5 miles, where a driveway leads to an unseen camp near the creek.

The remainder of the road is unimproved, and plowing depends on whether there is logging activity at Miller Park. Long sections of the road are located quite near the creek, with plenty of opportunities for views. The valley is a truly beautiful place, and if the conditions are right you won't mind that you are walking or skiing a road past an occasional camp. Polack Mountain is the primary landmark across the river.

You cross Seabury Brook at 2.7 miles, and then Honnedaga Brook at 5.2 miles. Look for an unmarked footpath along the south side of Honnedaga Brook, on the right side of the road. It leads in 0.2 mile to a scenic bend on the West Canada, where it appears that the river once burst through a gravel ridge crossing its path. Polack and Spruce mountains are the backdrops to this impressive scene.

You can follow Haskell Road all the way to the end of state land at 6.1 miles. Beyond, the road continues into Miller Park as a private way.

6 Herkimer Landing Trail

Snowmobile & motorized access trail, hiking, camping, snowshoeing, cross-country skiing
6.2 miles, 3 hours, 1420-foot elevation change

Jock Wright served in the Revolutionary War and hunted and trapped throughout New England. In 1796, he moved to Norway, New York, and spent the rest of his life hunting and trapping in the headwaters region of the East and West Canada creeks. Among his favorite fishing haunts was a lake he discovered in 1805. It was known as Jocks Lake until the late nineteenth century when the Adirondack League Club renamed it Honnedaga. It has also been called Transparent Lake because of the extraordinary clarity of its deep blue waters.

Jock frequently visited both his lake and Little Salmon Lake, which lies to the south of Jocks Lake. He caught trout throughout the year to take back to

Big Brook from the Herkimer Landing Trail

settlements in the valley. In the years before he died in 1826 at the age of 75, he had a hunting cabin at Rocky Point on Jocks Lake. It is sad to note that both lakes, which lie close to 2200 feet in elevation, were so susceptible to acid rain that for many years they were devoid of fish.

Logging roads were pushed towards Jocks Lake from Nobleboro in the middle of the nineteenth century. Just after 1880, Dut Barber built a hotel called Forest Lodge near Rocky Point. Guests reached the establishment traveling by train from Utica to Prospect Station, then by stage to Wilkinson's at Nobleboro, where they spent the night and prepared for the arduous last leg of the trip. The last ten miles was over "one of the worst roads in the north." It was all "ups and downs . . . said to be uphill either way you traveled it. There were hard pulls up Town Camp and Thunder Brook Hills and past

Whiskey Springs." The point where it reached Jocks Lake's shoreline was called Herkimer Landing. Hence, its name was Herkimer Landing Road.

By modern standards, this route is more trail than road, although it is still commonly referred to as a road and motor vehicles still use it to reach a small private inholding. It was never designed as a motor vehicle road, though, and it has long since been eclipsed as the primary access route to Honnedaga Lake. Even snowmobile traffic is remarkably light, perhaps because it would take a generous amount of snow to cover its imperfections. Today it is a little-used trail with an unusually rich history.

Follow the town-maintained portion of Haskell Road north from Nobleboro all the way to its end at 2.7 miles, where you will find a large parking area. The road is gated at this point, although the gate is often open to accommodate private traffic. The Herkimer Landing Trail is located 0.8 mile beyond the gate. If you choose to walk this portion of Haskell Road, then be sure to factor the added distance to the figures given below.

HASKELL ROAD TO BIG BROOK

The Herkimer Landing Trail begins by heading uphill, gradually at first. There are some mud wallows within the first mile, but otherwise the trail surface on this first section is relatively good. After winding through the foothills, the trail emerges into the valley of Big Brook, benched high up on the hillside. Tall hardwoods grace the slopes above and below you.

The net elevation gain from Haskell Road to the highest point is over 400 feet, although there are several smaller ups and downs in between. Soon after reaching the height-of-land, the trail makes a sharp 100-foot plunge to cross an unnamed stream on a wooden bridge at 2.1 miles. Hills like this make the Herkimer Landing Trail a challenging ski route. Incidentally, this stream is the outlet of a prominent pond only about 0.4 mile to the south, which will certainly appeal to some curious bushwhackers.

At 2.3 miles, or 3.1 miles from the Haskell Road gate, you reach the junction with the Round Top Mountain snowmobile trail, section 7, which comes in on the left. Just beyond this junction, the trail enters an open area with a concrete bridge over Big Brook. Rarely will you see such a substantial bridge so deep in the backcountry, and it would seem at odds with the wild setting except for the fact that it is quite ancient. The concrete is crumbling, and the abutments are eroding, but it is perfectly safe for pedestrians and it makes a good place to take a break. The view upstream along Big Brook is attractive, and while you are here be sure to look for the USGS benchmark that is embedded in the railing.

Just beyond the bridge, at 2.4 miles, there is a prominent campsite to the left of the trail.

BIG BROOK TO LITTLE SALMON LAKE

Beyond the bridge, the trail takes a northeasterly course that is generally parallel to the outlet of Whiskey Spring Vly. You can see why old-timers complained about the hills: in the next 3 miles, the trail will climb a net total of 690 feet. The climbing is for the most part at a moderate grade, but portions are highly eroded, and others are very wet. Be alert to tracks in the trail surface. Moose do inhabit this area, and you may see evidence of one's passage.

Shortly after passing the South Lake snowmobile trail (section 31) at 5.3 miles, you pass side trails to the right that lead to a private camp. Note that the northernmost of these paths is the recommended starting point for the hike to Jocks Falls, section 8. Immediately afterward, the Herkimer Landing Trail begins a 220-foot descent where, at 0.5 mile past the camp, a handmade sign marks a side route to the left.

This side trail, sparsely marked with old snowmobile markers, leads in 0.4 mile toward a campsite near Little Salmon Lake. For many hikers, this small pond 6.2 miles from Haskell Road (7 miles from the gate) will be the logical destination. Little Salmon is a very secluded location, and the side trail dwindles to little more than a herd path before it reaches the shoreline. The campsite is useful, if not handsome; it is set several hundred feet back from the shore, and the shallow water at the nearest edge of the pond makes it difficult to obtain sediment-free water.

The Herkimer Landing Trail does continue past this junction to eventually cross into the posted lands of the Adirondack League Club, but it becomes too wet for walking where it crosses an extension of Mile Vly, about 1 mile away. There is no public access to Honnedaga Lake.

7 Round Top Mountain Trail

Snowmobile trail, hiking, snowshoeing
2.4 miles, 1¼ hours, 500-foot elevation change

Little needs to be said about the Round Top Mountain trail, which connects the Herkimer Landing Trail (section 6) with the trail to Black Creek Lake (section 2). It was cut as a snowmobile trail, but machines seem to rarely use it, perhaps because a substantial amount of snow would be required to make the lumpy northeast end passable. It begins 2.3 miles along the Herkimer Landing Trail, rises 335 feet to a height-of-land below the summit of Round Top Mountain (labeled "Round Mountain" on USGS maps), follows a ridgeline, drops down the south side, and descends a total of 160 feet to a junction with the trail to Black Creek Lake, just 0.6 mile before that route enters the private parcel on the lake's south shore.

If your intent is to reach Black Creek Lake, this route via Round Mountain is 0.3 mile longer than the main route via Mill Creek Lake, and substantially hillier. It is, however, a more pleasant hiking route, with a greater likelihood for solitude.

There is a shortcut to Black Creek Lake from Round Mountain, but it is not easy to find. As you climb the snowmobile trail up from Big Brook, the route straightens as it traverses directly below the round summit of Round Mountain. It is in this section, at a point 1 mile from Big Brook, that a faint footpath leads northwest toward the lake. It is lightly used, lightly maintained, with several vague sections, making it unsuitable for novice hikers. But if you can find the path—which may be marked only by old flagging, if at all—it leads 1.1 miles on a direct route from Round Mountain to the southeast corner of Black Creek Lake. From the gate on Haskell Road, it is 5.2 miles to the lake using this route.

You will find a path circling the shoreline. The way left leads in 0.2 mile along the southern shoreline to the private inholding, but the way right leads through the handsome wetlands on the east shore to circle around the north shore. Additional paths loop northward to Burp Lake. There is essentially a network of footpaths around Black Creek Lake and its environs, presumably made and maintained by the camp owners. The lake is one of the most attractive in the region, and certainly worth overcoming the challenges of reaching it.

8 Jocks Falls

Path and bushwhack

Jocks Falls is perhaps the most secluded of all the destinations hidden in the woods north of Nobleboro. Alternately known as High Falls or Baby Lake Falls, this is a thirty-foot cascade located high on Honnedaga Brook, not far from the Adirondack League Club boundary. A wide footpath leads tantalizingly close to it from the Herkimer Landing Trail, but the final approach to the falls requires a short bushwhack through thick woods.

The start of the path is located near a private camp on the Herkimer

Landing Trail, 5.3 miles from Haskell Road and 6.1 miles from the gate. (Alternately, if you approach via South Lake, it is 6.7 miles along the snowmobile trail described in sections 30 and 31.) Several trails lead between the Herkimer Landing Trail and the cabin, which sits on a very small patch of private land surrounded by state land. Find the northernmost of these routes, skirt around the property, and look for the prominent (but unmarked) path heading into the woods from the northeast corner of the parcel.

If there is one thing that can be said about this path, it's that it is rarely straight for more than a few yards at a time. Its course from the cabin is generally east, keeping to the hills north of Threemile Vly, although it meanders quite a bit in the process. Its highest point is a broad hilltop at about 2560 feet in elevation, but then it begins a prolonged descent into the valley of Honnedaga Brook. By the time you reach the brook at 2.1 miles, you have lost more than 530 in elevation—which, of course, you will need to regain on the return trip.

Your arrival at Honnedaga Brook marks the end of the obvious path. A rustic camp once stood beside this bend in the creek, with plenty of metal bits and pieces remaining to give you a flavor of what life was like here. Its owners reached it by following an old road up from Haskell Road along Honnedaga Brook, and that was also once the preferred route for hikers seeking the falls. But when the owners sold the camp to the state no one was left to maintain the route, and it has long since fallen into disrepair.

Unfortunately, there is no reliable path to lead you north from the cabin site to the falls 0.5 mile away, so you must find your own route. Do not try to follow the banks of the brook north, for the wetlands along it make it difficult for walking. Instead, bushwhack along the base of the hill that lies to the west, just high enough to avoid the floodplain. This bit of elevation will help when you try to cross the first stream you meet, for to the east is all wetlands. Continue along the base of the hill to the falls, which is a double stream that cascades down nearly 30 feet from a vly just upstream.

Note the linear jumble of rock lining the brook below the falls. Logging crews would build barriers such as this to straighten the course of a stream, reducing the chances of a logjam. Imagine the sight of logs spilling over this already impressive cascade in a spring flood!

Wilmurt

THE TOWN OF Wilmurt was once the largest town in New York State. It was established in 1836 and originally encompassed all of the northernmost lands in Herkimer County, including what are now the hamlets of Wilmurt, Old Forge, and Stillwater. It was also very sparsely inhabited, with an 1865 population of 148 residents spread over more than 244,000 acres. The primary occupations of those inhabitants according to census records from that era were logging, farming, and whatever odd labor was available.

In 1896, the residents of the northern half of the town successfully petitioned the county for their own township, which they named Webb. The remaining portion of Wilmurt was still quite large, with its territory extending from the West Canada Creek to the South Branch of the Moose River. Most of its residents lived in the southern part of the town, near the hamlet of Wilmurt.

David H. Beetle, in his 1946 book *West Canada Creek*, cites several unverifiable tales about the mismanagement of the town's $70,000 in tax revenue, which was mostly funded by a handful of large landowners such as the Adirondack League Club. It was apparently no secret at the time that the town's officials were engaged in a variety of fiscal shenanigans, such as billing the state for the maintenance of roads that no longer existed. Perhaps it was resentment on the part of the neighboring towns that led the Herkimer County Board of Supervisors to petition the state to abolish Wilmurt—at the

Waypoints along NY 8 through Wilmurt		
NY 365 to Nobleboro		Nobleboto to NY 365
0.0	Intersection with NY 365, beginning of Hooper Dooper Ave, **section 11**	5.4
1.0	Intersection with Remonda Road, **section 11**	4.4
2.1	Ledge Mountain trailhead, **section 10**	3.3
2.8	Intersection with Gray-Wilmurt Road, **section 9**	2.6
5.4	Intersection with Haskell Road in Nobleboro	0.0

objections of some of its residents. The state sided with the board, and in 1918 it dissolved the town, dividing its territory between neighboring Ohio and Webb.

Today, the hamlet of Wilmurt is little more than a quiet residential area along the West Canada Creek. Its post office, school, and service station are long gone, but from a hiker's perspective there are several interesting places to stop and explore. State land looms close to the north and south, and this chapter describes the routes that can be found along the NY 8 corridor between Nobleboro and the NY 365 intersection. Although they are not well signed, there are three trailheads located on dead-end roads branching off from the main highway. The Ohio Gorge, which is perhaps Wilmurt's most distinctive feature, requires a short bushwhack.

9 Ohio Gorge

Bushwhack

The Ohio Gorge is a 0.4-mile-long chasm on the West Canada Creek that lies very close to NY 8, but generally out of sight of it. Once, a service station located on the north rim allowed travelers a free glimpse into the gorge. Private residences now block access from that direction, but state land occupies the majority of the south rim. So if you are game for a short bushwhack, you will find the gorge to still be very accessible.

To reach the start of the bushwhack, turn south onto Gray-Wilmurt Road, which intersects NY 8 at a sharp bend 2.8 miles from NY 365 and 2.6 miles from Nobleboro. Bear right at the intersection immediately south of the bridge over the West Canada. The road is quite close to the creek, but this section is emphatically posted against public access. Private land extends to the head of the gorge, but state land begins immediately after a camp on the right side of the road at roughly 0.7 mile, where it begins to curve south away from the creek. Look for the yellow paint blazes and signs marking the boundary. The road ascends a small hill at this point, and at the very top of the rise, at 0.8 mile, look for an old driveway on the right. This is the recommended starting point.

This clearing was, according to maps, the site of a small camp. From its right side an old road extends northwest into the woods. It soon angles almost due west, parallel to the creek; and while it will not lead you into the gorge it is a useful starting point. You can leave the road at any time and head due north, downhill, to reach the south rim, which is never more than a few hundred feet away. The woods are very open and present few obstructions.

The woods along the rim also allow for relatively easy walking. The easiest place to get to the side of the creek is near the mouth of the gorge, where the terrain slopes gently down to the water. If you follow the rim upstream, you will find there is no way into the bottom of the gorge without making a very steep scramble. This may be feasible in the summer, but in the winter it might not be an option without ice climbing equipment. However, when the leaves are off the trees you can see just enough from the edge to appreciate the rock bluffs on the north side and the rapids in the mighty creek below. The gorge invites you to respect its ruggedness from afar.

You can follow the south rim upstream all the way to the well-blazed end of state land, and then follow the boundary line for about 100 yards back to the road. All in all, for the short amount of time it takes to explore the gorge, it is well worth the effort.

10 Ledge Mountain

Hiking, snowshoeing
0.6 mile, 20 minutes, 350-foot vertical rise (summer)
0.9 mile, 30 minutes, 350-foot vertical rise (winter)

Ledge Mountain is the local name for a small ridge located less than a mile north of NY 8. A short foot trail takes you to the summit with its wonderful view over the vast landscape to the south. It is not frequently used but it is pleasant to walk. It was originally developed as a local resident's Eagle Scout project in conjunction with the DEC.

The hike begins on a dirt track road on the north side of NY 8 in Wilmurt, 2.1 miles east of the intersection with NY 365, and 3.3 miles west of Nobleboro. Without signage it will not resemble a typical DEC trailhead. Look for the entrance to a large gravel pit, with the two-track dirt road leading into the woods to the right. This road leads to an interior parking area 0.3 mile from the highway. It is passable by ordinary cars in the summer, but vehicles with a higher ground clearance are favored. There is ample room for parking near the highway if you choose not to drive it. The access road is not plowed in winter, but the roadside parking area is routinely cleared.

Leaving NY 8, the access road forks about 100 yards from the highway, where you should bear left. The road rises up a few short grades before reaching a small grassy clearing on the left, 0.3 mile from NY 8. This is the place to park, and the trail, marked with yellow disks, leads from the clearing through the shrubs. The access road continues into private land.

The trail leads north from the clearing, and then turns left at the foot of the hill. After a short level stretch you hook right and quickly begin to climb. The slope is not very steep. Sugar maples predominate in this hardwood forest, but there is a wealth of other trees as well, such as yellow birch, black cherry, white ash, striped maple, beech, and basswood. You pass close to a corner of the small cliffs as you step across one small wet spot, and then climb into a draw just to the east of them. After one final ascent on the north side of the summit, you follow along the ridge over to the small ledge on the south side.

The view south covers much of the West Canada Valley below Ohio Gorge, but you can only see one short stretch of the creek itself. The unbroken forest appears to extend all of the way beyond the Blue Line to the hills that define the northern edge of the Mohawk Valley. Since much of this region is forested with hardwoods, the view is particularly special in the fall.

11 Mad Tom Lake

Snowmobile trail, hiking, mountain biking
3.4 miles, 1¼ hours, 430-foot vertical rise (from Remonda Road)
3.6 miles, 1½ hours, rolling terrain (from Hooper Dooper Ave)

Mad Tom Lake is a small, boggy pond located at the source of a brook with the same name. When you see it on a map, it appears to be a mere speck compared to other nearby destinations—a rather long walk to a tiny body of water. Certainly, numerous other ponds and lakes described in this guide offer far more appealing features. Mad Tom does not offer spectacular scenery, but it *does* offer a good excuse to visit a part of the woods that you might not have visited before, and this *is* a good trail for stretching your legs in a quiet forest setting. Some people may even find it to be a good mountain bike route, too.

There are two trailheads servicing Mad Tom. Both routes converge in less than a mile and are essentially the same in terms of scenic quality. The route from Remonda Road is slightly shorter but includes a steep initial ascent; the route from Hooper Dooper Ave is slightly longer but presents a somewhat less hilly profile. Both are well-used snowmobile trails in winter. In the summer, any evidence of ATV use that you may see is strictly illegal.

THE HOOPER DOOPER AVE APPROACH

Hooper Dooper Ave is a town road that begins on NY 365, less than 0.1

mile from its junction with NY 8. The road's name is said to have been the favorite curse words of a former resident. Follow it for 1.1 miles, where signs indicate a snowmobile trail on state land to the right. There is room to park on the shoulder.

The trail leads generally east through an open hardwood forest. At 0.2 another snowmobile trail turns right, south, to cross private land back toward NY 8. Continue east, dipping through a ravine at 0.6 mile with a bridge over a small stream. At 0.8 mile you reach the junction with the trail from Remonda Road on the right. Mad Tom is to the left.

THE REMONDA ROAD APPROACH

Remonda Road is a residential dead-end spur extending northwest from NY 8, 1 mile from the NY 365 junction. It ends just 0.2 mile from the highway, with homes on both sides. There is no formal parking area, so you need to take care not to block access to either property. Also, do not block the continuing trail, because it is used for access a hidden camp a short distance into the woods.

The trail begins as a woods road past the gate, bending northeast into a small valley. In 0.2 mile the public trail bears right off the road, which continues straight ahead to the camp. The trail climbs steeply, ascending roughly 120 vertical feet in the next 0.1 mile. But once at the top of this hill, the grade quickly eases and it remains gentle all the way to the junction with the Hooper Dooper approach at 0.6 mile. Mad Tom Lake is straight ahead.

MAD TOM LAKE

From the junction, the trail gradually climbs over rolling and unchanging terrain as it winds northeast to Mad Tom Lake. The height-of-land is a broad hilltop at about 1775 feet in elevation, where the route swings more easterly. The woods are deep and unbroken on either side of the trail, but wilderness explorers may want to take note that the area to the northwest (everything to the left of the trail) is a wide-open expanse that has been seen by very few people. After the height-of-land, the trail descends to a wet area with many conifers. Five minutes later you will see a small grassy clearing on the right; it contains old stove parts and a midden area.

At a point 2.6 miles from the junction—a distance that some hikers may easily cover in an hour—a sign marks the spur trail to Mad Tom to the right. Follow this rougher, more primitive trail as it descends into evergreens and out to the edge of the lake, 0.2 mile away. Mad Tom Lake is only about three acres in size, but it is surrounded by a much larger wetland where many tamaracks grow intermixed with dead standing timber. Sweet gale, sheep laurel, low-bush cranberries, and pitcher plants abound, but illegal ATV use has damaged some of the vegetation near the trail entrance.

The main snowmobile trail does not end at Mad Tom, but instead continues for an additional 0.9 mile northeast to a junction near Mill Creek Lake. This section has no major hills and can be walked in about 20 minutes. The well-used trail to the left and right is the motor vehicle access route to Black Creek Lake described in section 2.

Along the path to Cotton Lake

Wheelertown & North Wilmurt

WHEELERTOWN AND NORTH Wilmurt are rural crossroads too small to be considered hamlets. Wheelertown, located at the intersection of Wheelertown and Hughes roads, was mostly farmland in the late nineteenth century; by the late twentieth century the junction was vacant and reforested. North Wilmurt, located at the intersection of Farr and Withers roads, used to be called Farrtown after Ed Farr and his family of three sons. They ran a "hotel" there (probably little more than a roadside saloon) and made shingles. North Wilmurt today is a collection of modest camps.

The roads that connect these two locales, and the state lands they access, form the basis of this chapter. Wheelertown Road, which is mostly residential in nature, starts at a junction with NY 365 north of Hinckley Reservoir and extends for 5.7 miles to an intersection with Reeds Mill Road, better known as Farr Road. This road, which leads in 7.2 miles to a junction with North Lake Road at Reeds Pond, was part of the original route to North Lake. Today, it is a fair gravel road that is open year-round.

The residential properties on Wheelertown Road restrict state land access to a few specific entry points. Farr Road, however, has miles of state land frontage. Its course roughly parallels a remote section of the Black River that lies to the west, but the primary attraction for most hikers will be the large block of state land to the east. This is a sprawling area with myriad hills, streams, vlies, and small ponds. Much of it is trackless, or else tracked only by old woods roads that have essentially reverted to footpaths over time. The only official trail is the route to Twin Lakes.

All of the state lands surrounding Wheelertown and Farr roads are currently part of the Black River Wild Forest, although in this instance there are no active snowmobile trails or other facilities to justify that designation. A proposal has been advanced to reclassify most of the state land to the east of Farr Road as the Cotton Lake Wilderness. This action, if adopted by the state, would affect the way the region is perceived, but not necessarily the way it is currently used, because this low-key area has for generations been a resource mostly for local hikers, hunters, backpackers, fishermen, snowshoers, and skiers. Few people probably know the entire area well.

In the Adirondacks, there are currently 20 separate tracts of state land

Waypoints along Wheelertown & Farr Roads

NY 365 to Reeds Pond		Reeds Pond to NY 365
0.0	Wheelertown Road begins at intersection with NY 365 near north shore of Hinckley Reservoir	12.9
2.6	Intersection with Jim Rose Road, **section 12**	10.3
4.1	Bridge over Little Black Creek, with state land access at northeast corner	8.8
4.4	Wheelertown, intersection with Hughes Road	8.5
5.0	Intersection with Lite Road	7.9
5.5	Bridge over Maple Lake's outlet, no public access	7.4
5.7	Intersection with Enos Road. *TURN RIGHT* onto Reeds Mill Road	7.2
6.4	Russia-Ohio town line. Reeds Mill Road becomes Farr Road	6.5
8.4	Driveway, start of path to Ash Ridge, **section 13**	4.5
10.7	North Wilmurt, intersection with Withers Road, **sections 14-15**	2.2
10.8	Bridge over Twin Lakes Stream	2.1
12.1	Driveway, site of small cemetery plot on state land	0.8
12.4	Twin Lakes trailhead, **sections 16-17**	0.5
12.8	Bridge over the Black River	0.1
12.9	Farr Road ends at intersection with North Lake Road at Reeds Pond	0.0

formally protected as Wilderness Areas by the Adirondack Park State Land Master Plan (SLMP). Such protection ensures that these places will remain wild and rugged for generations to come—places where motorized and mechanized access is forbidden, but where people are free to enter under their own power. Several deserving tracts meeting all of the guidelines were either overlooked or passed over due to other considerations when the SLMP was first adopted in 1972. The proposed 25,000-acre Cotton Lake Wilderness is one of them.

The region's relative obscurity, despite its proximity to civilization, can be traced to a lack of a developed trail system and a scarcity of highly attractive features with mass appeal, such as open summits or large lakes. The scenery is far more intimate here compared to some of the more popular places elsewhere in the Adirondacks, and perhaps this same subtlety is why the area was overlooked by the authors of the original SLMP. Rather than being a hindrance to access, some people view the lack of a trail network as an invitation for personal exploration and discovery.

Our hope with this chapter is that you will explore these routes, visit these small places, and agree that although the Cotton Lake region lacks the grandiosity of other, better-known areas, it possesses many of the same intrinsic values and warrants the same recognition.

12 Little Black Creek via Jim Rose Road

Path

Jim Rose Road is a dead-end spur that leads from Wheelertown Road to a collection of camps. Most of the surrounding land is private, but its beginning touches a parcel of state land that provides excellent access to a secluded section of Little Black Creek. Although not an official trail with signs and markers, it is an obvious route that is reasonably easy to follow.

Follow Wheelertown Road north from NY 365 for 2.6 miles. Here, the road swings rather sharply to the north while Jim Rose Road continues east. Just 0.1 mile from the junction, look for a trail on the left side of the road. There is room to park on the shoulder.

Setting off on foot, the trail immediately intercepts a cross trail. Left leads to a private residence, so bear right. The route is very prominent, and it leads northeast on an arrow-straight course through scrubby forest growth. Old maps reveal that this was once a road, and that the surrounding area was once cleared. At 0.5 mile it bends left, north, and descends gently to a clearing beside the creek where there had once been a building. The total distance from your car is 0.6 mile.

The clearing is not an exciting spot, but that's not the point. The benefit of this short route is the access it provides, not the destination it reaches. Little Black Creek is like a natural boundary dividing the recovering farmland near Wheelertown Road from the wild country to the northeast. If you ford the creek (it can be quite shallow in the summer) you will find a continuation of the road leading northward into the woods. If you bushwhack upstream for about 0.4 mile you will reach a scenic waterfall where Little Black spills over a ledge that is much wider than it is tall.

13 Ash Ridge

Path

As you follow Farr Road north from its junction with Wheelertown Road, look for a rough driveway-like trail on the right (east) side of the road at 2.7 miles. The spot is marked by a plantation of even-aged white pine, which stands out in this otherwise hardwood forest. People sometimes drive the first 0.1 mile of this trail to a campsite further back in the pines, although the route is relatively rough and narrow.

The campsite is spacious, but there is more to see. Look for a footpath leading southeast from the rear right corner. It dips to a crossing of Muskrat Brook, a small stream where you may find a primitive bridge leading to the far side. The path continues past the brook on a southeasterly course. It is used lightly and probably maintained less, but because it was once a woods road experienced hikers should not have much trouble finding it.

The path ends 0.9 mile from Farr Road in a nondescript area northeast of Ash Ridge. The primary motive for walking such a route is to use it as a springboard for deeper explorations into the backcountry. It is suggested here as a substitute for the Forty Mountain Trail, which lies a short distance to the south. Public access to that route has been curtailed since a landowner on Lite Road has emphatically posted the trailhead against public access. Anyone who wishes to explore the area around Forty Mountain and Big Brook can still do so from this route, albeit with the need to do some additional bushwhacking.

14 Cotton Lake

Path

Cotton Lake is a mere 3 acres in size and contains no fish. Its circular shape means that you can stand at any point along the shore and take in the entire view. However, the pond's remote setting and collection of weathered snags gives it a wild character, and the route leading to it passes through miles of handsome forest, with subtle variations as it crosses from hilltops into valleys. Cotton Lake will never be a crowd pleaser, but for wilderness connoisseurs

Cotton Lake

this hike is surprisingly good. It can be enjoyed at any time of the year.

The best route to Cotton Lake begins in North Wilmurt. The majority of it follows old woods roads that may have been created during timber salvage operations after a 1950 hurricane blew down about 25 to 50% of the forest cover. The way is clear, for the most part, but navigation requires close attention to detail. Experienced off-trail hikers will find nothing especially difficult about this hike, but novices are routinely confused.

The hike begins on Withers Road in North Wilmurt, which turns east from Farr Road at a bend 5 miles north of Wheelertown Road and 2.2 miles south of North Lake Road. Follow Withers Road for 0.6 mile, where it makes a sharp bend to the left. Look for the start of the woods road on state land to the right, just before the bend. There is no parking area, but traffic is so light on Withers Road that leaving your vehicle on the shoulder is unlikely to be a problem.

Setting off on foot, follow the old road south into the woods. It climbs gently for the first 15 minutes through tall hardwoods, and even if you encounter the occasional blowdown the wide trail should be clear enough to follow. At 0.6 mile it begins to swing left, east, and you reach a junction where another prominent woods road turns right. That route continues south and can be used by bushwhackers to reach an attractive beaver flow at the foot of Forty Mountain.

Continue east on the main trail, dipping through a glen and rising again to traverse a broad hillside. The woods are quite young here, and you pass some hardware from former logging operations, including a metal barrel. Soon afterwards, at 1.1 miles, the road forks. The route to the left is the path to Twin Lakes Stream described in section 15.

Bear right for Cotton Lake. You can see an open wetland to the left, and the trail dips south to pass wide around it. The trail becomes more winding as it avoids several similar vlies—the so-called "Constellation Meadows," since there is a tight cluster of them arranged like stars in the sky. The mixed woods are quite handsome, with little evidence of the hurricane damage that reportedly befell this area in 1950.

The trail angles southeast through a beech forest (note the bear claw scars on some of the trunks) and then begins a 140-foot descent into the valley of the North Branch of Little Black Creek. This descent occurs in two phases, with a wet area in between. You reach the North Branch at 2.7 miles. It is a small brook, and usually easy to cross at any time of the year. Its source, North Branch Lake, is only 0.5 mile upstream. It has been reduced in size in recent years due to the loss of a beaver dam on its outlet.

Across the North Branch, the trail continues on a course that is generally east-southeast. After circling wide around another small wetland on the right, it begins to rise slightly near the foot of a larger hill on the left. At 3.6 miles (less than a mile from the brook) the old road ends with little fanfare. This is the section that seems to cause the most confusion. Look for a continuing footpath veering left. It may be marked with old flagging, a sawed-off log, or nothing at all. The remaining 0.4 mile of the path is very faint and is easily lost by hikers unfamiliar with the area. It continues along the foot of the large hill before angling left, uphill, for a brisk climb onto the small plateau where Cotton Lake is nestled. It passes a large rock, and when the pond appears ahead through the trees the path soon fades completely. The total distance from Withers Road is 4 miles.

Alternately, if you come to the end of the woods road and can find no trace of the footpath, simply bushwhack due east. This course will take you at an angle up the hill, which is forested with open hardwoods.

There are no campsites at Cotton Lake, although the openness of the surrounding woods would allow you to pitch a tent practically anywhere. Because the pond is so small, it is reasonably easy to bushwhack around it. The multi-tiered beaver dams on the outlet are worth checking out.

Topographic maps show a trail leading toward Cotton Lake from the

Remains of the dam at Twin Lakes

south, originating from a maze of private roads near Hooper Dooper Ave. This is actually an access route to a tiny inholding near the Middle Branch of Little Black Creek, but because it begins on posted private land it is of little use to hikers.

15 Twin Lakes Stream

Path, canoeing

This hike begins the same as Cotton Lake, section 14, and is very similar in nature to that route. Beginning at Withers Road, follow the old woods road as described above for the first 1.1 miles, where the road forks. Bear left, coming to the breached beaver dam of a drained pond in 0.2 mile. The dam serves as a suitable causeway for hikers. A short distance beyond, note the side trail coming in from the left. This is a shortcut used by camp owners at the end of Withers Road, and it leads to their private property.

As the old road winds northeast, watch for a large rock at 1.7 miles that is sometimes used by hunters as a natural deer stand. The route traverses a hill so gentle that you may not realize you are climbing, and it reaches a height-of-land at 2 miles and about 1940 feet in elevation. The descent is more noticeable, but it is far from steep. Like the Cotton Lake trail, the road vanishes and is replaced by a faint path. Your arrival at Twin Lakes Stream is preceded by a transition from hardwoods to conifers. The trail ends at the side of an open wetland that flanks a stillwater on the creek. The total walking distance from Withers Road is 2.7 miles, or 1.6 from the fork with the Cotton Lake trail.

Just a short distance downstream, the remains of an old stone dam can be found in the creek, of the kind used by lumbermen to augment spring stream flows.

In this age of lightweight pack canoes, some people will find a viable paddle route upstream. The initial flow where the trail ends is very brief, but after about 0.25 mile of either vigorous paddling, lining, or rough portaging, you reach the ample waters of Twin Lakes Marsh. There, the navigable waters extend upstream to the northwest, as well as along a spur to the southeast where the broadest part of the marsh lies. There are at least two sites on these stillwaters where camping would be attractive.

16 Twin Lakes

Hiking, camping, snowshoeing, cross-country skiing
3.1 miles, 1½ hours, rolling terrain

In the nineteenth century, the commission in charge of the state's canal network built dams throughout the Black River headwaters region to ensure

a steady supply of water. Some of the dams were remote and not well tended, and when water shortages were experienced in the canals an investigation revealed that lumbermen had been secretly opening the valves at these dams to enhance their log drives.

One of these reservoirs was at Twin Lakes, a sprawling wetland complex with two small natural ponds. The selection of this site is interesting since it is bounded by few large hills; if the dam had been built too tall, water would have leaked westward to the Black River. Therefore the Twin Lakes Reservoir had a large surface area, but it was very shallow, with an average depth of only 9 feet.

Today, only a portion of the dam remains and the natural conditions have been largely restored. The former access road is now technically a snowmobile trail, although in the decade between the third and fourth editions of this guide snowmobiles have rarely been observed here. The Twin Lakes Trail is most commonly used for foot travel, with most of that use in the winter. Even though this is the only marked trail beginning on Farr Road, it is not very frequently traveled.

It begins at a small parking area on Farr Road 0.5 mile south of North Lake Road, or 6.7 miles north of Wheelertown Road. The trailhead is plowed in winter. The first 0.9 mile is nearly level as it passes through a hardwood forest; the first hill, though not large, is a noteworthy event. Thereafter the route is more rolling, with several more hills of comparable size in both directions. At 1.7 miles you reach the source of Vincent Brook, marked by a small wetland and a pool of water obstructing the trail.

After traversing another hill, the trail descends into a conifer-filled valley to reach a large beaver meadow at 2.5 miles. Formerly, it was possible to cut straight through this area and cross the stream on slippery logs, but twenty-first century beaver flooding has altered that. If necessary, seek out the long, curving dam downstream to the right.

The trail resumes on the far side and angles north to follow a small stream, with a rock outcrop pressing close on the right. Then it swings right, beginning a moderate ascent of about 175 vertical feet. After skirting the edge of the hilltop it descends to the outlet of the old reservoir, where the trail ends at 3.1 miles.

A side trail to the right leads to the dam. Much of it was an earthen structure, and this portion still survives. You can walk along it to a small campsite and then to the remains of the floodgate, which is now partly obscured by trees. Twin Lakes Stream flows freely past it.

You can also venture out into the old flowed lands. It is not too difficult to follow the channel northeast to the first pond, but beyond that the terrain becomes increasingly wet. Winter is an excellent time to visit, when you will feel exhilarated by all the open space that is available. There used to be a campsite at the north end of the upper pond, and while it is still easy to find, new growth has rendered it unusable. A major inlet enters from the east, and it is reportedly a good spot to fish.

17 Waterfalls on Twin Lakes Stream

Bushwhack

For a stretch of 0.4 mile downstream from the old reservoir, Twin Lakes Stream tumbles and slides over a series of ledges and ramps. Two of these drops are noteworthy cascades. They are accessed by a short bushwhack that can be added to a visit to Twin Lakes, turning an otherwise straightforward hike into a loop.

Follow the Twin Lakes Trail, section 16, as far as the beaver flow at 2.5 miles. After crossing the meadow, continue on the trail to the foot of a prominent hill, but where the trail bears left, north, you should bear right, south. The foot of the hill will guide you to Twin Lakes Stream while helping you avoid the wetlands that occupy much of the valley floor. It is only about 0.3 mile from the trail to the creek. As you draw nearer, the terrain gets very rocky and you may wish to cut a corner over the hill to avoid some of the worst entanglements.

You should hear the lower waterfall long before you see it, and that sound will guide you the rest of the way. November Falls is roughly 12 feet high, with angled slopes and a vertical finish. The woods surrounding the falls are tangled, but upstream the going is more reasonable. The various ledges and slides on the stream are good company, encouraging you never to stray too far inland lest you should miss something interesting on your journey upward.

The upper cascade, Hole-in-the-Wall Falls, is a fraction of the height of November Falls, but it is no less appealing. A barrier of solid rock extends across most of the creek, but the water has forced its way through a breach on one side as if by brute force.

Minutes later, you reach the remains of the dam at the outlet of Twin Lakes. The top of the embankment leads left to the terminus of the state trail.

North Lake Road

THE FIRST HALF of the nineteenth century saw the wilderness of the Black River Valley give way to intense development and colonization. The early settlers were quick to realize the river's potential, particularly at High Falls, Long Falls, and the Great Falls where Lyons Falls, Carthage, and Watertown are located today.

Textile, lumber, and paper industries, as well as the Black River Canal system, exploited the river's water, but their operations were plagued by inconsistencies in the water's flow. Spring floods damaged or destroyed many mills and factories, and summer droughts not only hindered canal navigation but so curtailed waterpower that some industries had to adopt steam as a backup power source. One by one, throughout the entire Black River watershed, dams were proposed and reservoirs constructed in an effort to regulate the flow. The net effect was beneficial to downstream communities, but the dam building process was slow and wrought with controversy and disaster.

Far up on the Black River, in a long valley where many streams converged, lay small Lake Sophia. The first dam built at this site on the Black River was completed in 1856, creating the North Branch Reservoir. That dam could not contain the spring floods of 1869 and the resulting torrent caused great destruction down the entire length of the river. An improved dam and spillway complex was constructed and North Lake, as we know it today, has changed little since then.

North Lake Road runs northeast through the center of the Black River Wild Forest and it provides access to many of the waters that received regulatory scrutiny. From the hamlet of Forestport, turn east off NY 28 at the exit for Woodhull Road, near the bridge over Forestport Pond. Continue east for 1.2 miles to Forestport Station, where the tracks of the Adirondack Railroad cross at an intersection. Ahead of you, past the Buffalo Head Restaurant, North Lake Road veers left and ascends toward the high plateau of the western Adirondack foothills.

From 1950 to 1998, one of the most unique features along the road was a red-and-white tower 1218 feet tall near the Forestport-Ohio town line. In the era before GPS, it was used by the Air Force and the Navy to test prototype radio navigation systems using low-frequency signals. The tower was brought down in April 1998, but the bunker still remains at the edge of the large clearing.

Outlet channel of Chub Pond

This chapter describes the outings available along the section of road from the Adirondack Park boundary to North Lake. The road is maintained year-round, although winter travelers should keep its remoteness in mind. It is wise to avoid this area during and immediately after a heavy snowfall, to give the plow crews a chance to clear the road.

18 Stone Dam Lake

Hiking, snowshoeing
3.3 miles, 1½ hours, rolling terrain

The well-marked hiking trail to Stone Dam Lake makes a delightful trek through a peaceful hardwood forest. Several intermittent streams are easily crossed, wet areas are few, and the woods are handsome. Although the ascent is steady, it is so slight as to be hardly noticeable. However, there are innumerable small ups and downs and twists and turns on the route, which winds generally a little east of north to the lake.

The trailhead is located on the north side of North Lake Road at the 6.6-mile point, 0.4 mile past Koenig Brothers' Sawmill. The small parking area is located below the shoulder of the road; it is fine in the summer, but it is not plowed in the winter. A brown DEC sign marks its location.

The yellow-marked trail begins as an old roadway. The trail reaches high ground above Little Woodhull Creek and parallels the eastern shore for 0.9 mile to a bridge, a twenty-minute walk from the trailhead. The tall forest along the creek is rich with hemlock and as handsome as you can find. Throughout this walk, much of the forest cover is open beneath a high canopy, sheltering a rich understory of ferns. Pause to enjoy views of the stillwater above the bridge, the small waterfall beneath it, and the lovely series of rapids downstream.

A fifteen-minute walk past the creek you will pass an erratic where you can still hear the creek—you are now following the valley of Stone Dam Creek, but far enough from this tiny stream to be unaware of it. After an hour of walking, you are beside a small rift with rock outcrops. Beyond there is a small wet area with few good stepping points. There is little variation in the scenery, but the distance passes quickly. You walk through an area where large tree trunks lie moss-covered on the forest floor, perhaps the results of a very old blowdown.

After ascending the slopes of a hill known as Stone Dam Mountain, the wetlands of Stone Dam Lake appear through the trees to the east. Soon, the

Waypoints along North Lake & South Lake Roads

Miles

0.0	Forestport Station. North Lake Road begins as left fork by Buffalo Head Restaurant, 1.2 miles east of NY 28 on Woodhull Road
5.0	Herkimer County line, Adirondack Park boundary
5.2	Forestport Tower site
6.6	Stone Dam Lake trailhead, **sections 18 & 19**
7.1	Mulchi Spring
9.5	Mink Lake, **section 20**
10.1	Intersection with Farr Road, Reeds Pond, **section 21**
13.3	Little Woodhull Lake trailhead, **sections 22 & 23**
14.7	Intersection with North Lake access road immediately before bridge over spillway, **sections 24-28**
15.1	Road crosses the top of first North Lake dam in Atwell, becomes South Lake Road
15.3	Second North Lake dam
16.9	South Lake snowmobile trail, **sections 30-33**
17.2	South Lake boat launch, **section 29**
19.0	Adirondack League Club gate, end of public road

main body of water comes into view 200 feet away, and you find yourself on a small spruce-lined rise, probably an esker. This is the closest the trail comes to the lake, and it is a good point to depart for explorations.

If your primary goal is only to see the pond, then it is a fairly simple matter to head down off the trail to the nearest spot on the shoreline. However, a peninsula extends out from the north shore and it is there, just inside the trees near the tip, that the remains of an old lean-to camp are found. The forest has grown quite thick on this peninsula, so there is now no easy way to find the site, and certainly no place to camp.

The lake occupies only a fraction of the area originally dammed; shores of the shallow body of water are lined with sundew, leatherleaf, and other bog plants. These meadows extend south along the sinuous outlet as well as to the north of the peninsula.

The trail continues northwest along the esker; there is a small, jet-black pool to the left just before the northern marshes come into view to the right. The continuing trail to Chub Pond is described in section 19.

19 Chub Pond from Stone Dam Lake

Hiking, camping
2.3 miles, 1 hour to southern lean-to
3.8 miles, 2 hours to northern lean-to

The yellow-marked foot trail that continues north from Stone Dam Lake to Chub Pond is one of the most lightly traveled routes in this chapter. Its remoteness no doubt contributes to that distinction. This route does not follow an old road, and it was cut expressly for hikers. Much of the route is through featureless terrain so that if you stray from the trail, it could be possible to recross it and never see it. Unlike most Adirondack trails, here you really need the markers to find the way.

From the inlet stream at the west end of the Stone Dam Lake marshes, 3.3 miles from North Lake Road as described in section 18, you climb a small rise, pass several small marshes, and cross and recross an intermittent stream. After twenty minutes of winding along ridges you reach a dense ferny valley with notably tall maple and beech. You cross a steep knoll, and at 1.5 miles, after a forty-minute walk, reach Big Brook.

The trail, still heading north, ascends to a height-of-land at 1.7 miles, and then begins the descent into the Woodhull Creek valley. Fifteen minutes after you cross Big Brook, you find yourself in a draw with an intermittent stream which the trail crosses and recrosses.

At 2.1 miles, about an hour from Stone Dam Lake, you reach a low-lying area that has been flooded by beavers. What was once a forested glen is now a scene of wild devastation, and it creates an interesting obstacle. The yellow-marked foot trail skirts the swamp's edge briefly, and then the markers lead *through* it, on a course that is more feasible than it first appears. Once on the far side, it leads for 0.1 mile more to intersect the snowmobile trail from Bear Creek Road described below.

However, if you don't cross the wetland then you may encounter an informal trail that keeps to the south side of the drainage. It leads directly to the southern lean-to at Chub Pond, one of the most architecturally distinctive shelters in the entire Adirondack Park. At one time, individuals could obtain a permit to build a lean-to on public lands with the understanding that it would be open to all who pass through. Such is the case here. This one was built in 1961, and repaired after it was struck by fallen trees from a 1984 windstorm. Today it is a most unusual sight to see this well-chinked log structure with all of its furnishings. Note, though, that despite its name the

Campsite at Chub Pond

lean-to is 0.2 mile from the nearest point on the shoreline.

This shelter is 2.3 miles from Stone Dam Lake. Another trail leads north-west from the shelter, leading through a wet area to the northern terminus of the yellow trail described above, 0.2 mile from the lean-to. Following blue foot trail markers and red snowmobile markers, it tunnels through an area devastated by the July 11, 1984 storm. On that date, heavy thunder and lightning storms accompanied by high winds hit the Forestport area. Moving east, the winds touched down at Chub Pond, leveling an area a half mile or more long and several hundred yards wide. The trail through the blowdown area has long since been cleared, and new growth shades the rotting, toppled trees. Scenes like this remind you of the great forces of nature.

The occasionally wet trail takes you through the center of the blowdown area to the outlet of Chub Pond, 0.6 mile from the lean-to. This was one of several reservoir sites in the Black River and Woodhull Creek watersheds used to supply the state's nineteenth-century canals with water, although this one was abandoned in 1896. A small wooden dam below the bridge still raises the water by a foot or so.

The trail loops around the northwest edge of the pond, reaching a junc-tion 1 mile from the southern lean-to. The trails in both directions are faint. Left is one of two routes to Bear Creek Road. Right is a foot trail that sticks close to the shoreline for 0.3 mile, reaching a good campsite and then the main trail from Bear Creek, section 35. Keeping right, it is just 0.2 mile further to the northern and more scenically located lean-to. This spot is 1.5 miles from the first shelter, 3.8 miles from Stone Dam Lake, and 7.1 miles from North Lake Road.

20 Mink Lake

Short bushwhack

Beyond the Koenig Brothers' Sawmill, buildings are few along North Lake Road; the woods grows thicker and the road begins to climb what is known locally as Mulchi Hill. Older folks remember a time when the roads were primitive and the descent of the two steep sections near Mink Lake and Reeds Pond were hazardous for horse-drawn carts or the early automobiles. The pavement of today makes travel much easier, but frost heaves and mud-dy washes in this area let you know this road is not yet completely tamed.

At the bottom of the first descent, look for Mink Lake through the trees to the left. A small, not-easy-to-spot turnout at 9.5 miles has enough room for one or two cars to park. From here it is a short bushwhack down the bank for 100 yards to the brushy shoreline. The vegetation here is typical of the shrub wetlands found throughout the Adirondacks, and many game and song birds reside here. Because it is so difficult to approach the shore, the best way to appreciate the marshes is from a canoe. The carry from the road is short, but good launching spots along the dense shore are hard to find.

21 Reeds Pond

Canoeing, camping, fishing

After a series of descents, North Lake Road reaches an intersection with Farr Road at 10.1 miles. On the left lies Reeds Pond, the outlet of which flows under the road and plunges into the Black River, 0.1 mile away. In the last half of the nineteenth century, a sawmill operated by the Reed family was located here. Today, the pond is a popular fishing and camping spot. There are large drive-in campsites with room for tents, trailers, and campers on both sides, the westernmost being the most desirable, and the most quickly filled.

It is an easy matter to launch a canoe on the western shore and paddle leisurely north to the pond's major tributary, Otter Brook, which flows in from the north. You cannot go far up the brook; after you encounter a few small beaver dams, alders close in and you must turn around. It is, however, a quiet place to be and there is a good chance of seeing beavers, muskrats, and otters.

22 Little Woodhull Lake

Hiking, snowshoeing, cross-country skiing
3.2 miles, 1½ hours, rolling terrain

The trail to Little Woodhull Lake is one of several in the region that is technically a snowmobile trail, but is far more often used by hikers and skiers. As late as 1998 it appeared to be effectively abandoned, with thick patches of hobblebush obscuring the furthest section. Since then there has been a modest resurgence in hiker interest, and maintenance of the trail has resumed. It is very pleasant for hiking and skiing, and botanically speaking Little Woodhull is one of the more distinctive ponds in the area.

The trailhead is on the left side of North Lake Road at 13.3 miles, just as the road pitches down a short slope. There is ample parking at a larger turnout 100 feet up the road on the right, which is plowed in winter.

Starting northwest, with a short ascent past trail signs and a campsite, the trail follows an old road through a tall hardwood forest. It levels, and then rises gently again after walking for ten minutes. Keep an eye out for an old iron culvert and some wooden corduroy along the way, which are signs of the trail's age.

At 1.3 miles, after about 30 minutes of walking, the trail makes a sharp turn to the right. Old blowdown in this area was likely caused by the same storm that hit Chub Pond in 1984. The old road continues straight for a short distance toward a wetland on Otter Brook, and if there weren't signs and markers to indicate the correct turn then this could be a confusing place.

Bearing right, you quickly pass out of the blowdown and cross Otter Brook, which is just a small woodland stream. Beyond, you begin to find huge hemlocks growing very close to the trail.

At 2.4 miles, or an hour from North Lake Road, the trail nears the edge of a wetland. Once, the trail led out through the marsh grass to follow this major inlet of Little Woodhull Lake for about 100 yards downstream. As scenic as that was, it was a poor location for a trail. Now, it keeps to the coniferous woods south of the wetland on a hilly detour that bypasses the wetland and merges with the old trail on the far side. The trail is narrow and winding for the next 0.6 mile to an intersection next to the creek, 3 miles from the road. A red-marked trail crosses the stream on rocks and continues on to the Sand Lake Falls Trail. See sections 26 and 27 for descriptions of these routes.

A yellow-marked foot trail continues to follow the inlet quite closely. It dips sharply to stream level and then winds through a dark spruce-fir forest before ending at 3.2 miles near the point where the inlet flows into the lake. There is an opening here which is a pleasant place to sit and picnic, but it is a poor place to camp.

From this vantage you will have a view over much of the lake. There is a large beaver lodge not too far away, and you will find that these waterways are a haven for a variety of aquatic plants and wildlife. Little Woodhull Lake is shallow, and in the summer months thick mats of vegetation rise to the surface. In July you will find colonies of pickerelweed in bloom, as well as white and yellow pond lilies. The latter are scattered all across the lake. When the weather gets colder much of this vegetation disappears, leaving behind an open expanse of water.

Bushwhacking around Little Woodhull Lake is difficult, but such a beautiful place deserves further exploration. The long, narrow outlet is surrounded by acres of varied wetlands with a sculpture garden of dead standing timber amidst the shrubs and grasses. Large rocks and bleached logs interrupt the swampy shoreline, and wildlife abounds. Winter travelers, of course, will find the going easier and may wish to go further and explore Lily Lake to the northwest. At their nearest point, the two ponds are separated by less than 200 feet of land.

23 Black River Access

Path, canoeing

A snowmobile trail once ran from North Lake Road to South Lake, crossing the Black River and passing close to its South Branch. Though the trail has long been abandoned, people still walk it as far as the Black River to canoe or fish. Only a few old markers survive, but the route is short enough that navigation is not difficult.

The trail begins from the rear left corner of the parking area for the Little Woodhull Lake trailhead, 13.3 miles along North Lake Road. While there are no directional signs, the beginning of the route should be obvious. It is only 0.2 mile to the Black River, but two diverging logging roads make the way a bit unclear. Bear right at both intersections and follow the obvious course heading southeast and you will be at the water's edge in five minutes. An elaborate wooden bridge, reinforced with cables and supported in the middle by a wooden pier, once allowed safe passage across the river. It now lies in ruin.

From the end of the trail, the Black River appears shallow but marginally navigable. Because the path is so short, it would be easy to carry a canoe here and enjoy an hour or two of exploratory paddling. You cannot go far upstream before the way becomes rocky, but with persistence you may find 2.5 miles of navigable water downstream.

North Lake

AFTER THE LONG and sometimes jostling drive up from Forestport Station, North Lake Road reaches its namesake lake at 14.7 miles. The previous chapter described the excursions available along the drive to North Lake, but this chapter focuses on those outings that begin along the narrow gravel lane that loops around the lake's west shore—called, appropriately, the Loop Road.

North Lake is a man-made reservoir that was first dammed in 1856 on the authority of the state's Canal Board, who sought a source of water for the Erie Canal. It serves that same purpose to this day. Along the twin earthen dams at the lake's southern end is the tiny hamlet of Atwell. Here you will find the State House, the name for the white wood-frame building that was the old dam keeper's residence and the site of the long-gone Atwell Post Office.

The Loop Road turns left from North Lake Road immediately before the bridge over the spillway, just as the woods part to reveal the view of the lake and Ice Cave Mountain beyond. For much of its length it remains close to the water. The majority of the west shore has uninterrupted public access, with the only exception being a single cluster of private camps midway up. There are several designated campsites for public use along the road, most of them located on or close to the water. Many are drive-in sites, but when these fill up (an event that occurs frequently in the summer) latecomers must vie for the handful of walk-in sites. There is no fee to camp here, and also no reservation system.

The north end of the lake, which lies in Township 6 of the Moose River Tract, was part of the original holdings of the Adirondack League Club when it formed in 1890. Old maps show that the club maintained a camp at their end of the lake, which was roughly the midpoint on a trail from Honnedaga Lake to the Bisby Lakes, two of the focal points of their vast holdings. The club sold most of Township 6 (all but the section containing Honnedaga Lake) to the J. P. Lewis Co. in 1941, but leased back this property for the next 30 years.

In 1990, the Adirondack Nature Conservancy brokered a deal in which the state and a Lewis County company called Lyon Falls Pulp and Paper purchased the land from J. P. Lewis. The paper company gained title to the land

View of Ice Cave Mountain

Waypoints along Loop Road around North Lake

Miles

0.0	Loop Road begins 14.7 miles along North Lake Road, immediately before bridge over spillway. Road is often unplowed.
0.05	Canoe & kayak access to North Lake, **section 24**
0.1	Path to Atwell Martin's "wigwam" site, **section 25**
0.3	Sand Lake Falls trailhead, **sections 26 & 27**
3.3	Parking area near Golden Stair Creek
3.4	Road passes large campsite at north end of North Lake
3.5	Parking area near Canachagala Mountain
4.4	Large parking area at end of road, **section 28**

and the right to harvest its timber, but the state received the development and public recreation rights, opening up what had been a closed domain for so many decades. Since the original purchase the private ownership has changed several times, but none of this has affected the public's right to use and enjoy the land.

The Loop Road is narrow and bumpy, but otherwise passable by ordinary vehicles all the way to its end. It is not plowed in winter, except when logging is being conducted, and it is gated in the spring. Areas where logging is actively occurring may be temporarily posted against public access.

24 North Lake

Canoeing, camping

North Lake is 3.3 miles long and on average only about a quarter-mile wide. It is not large enough to attract many high-powered motorboats, and its three narrowest points almost divide the lake into four pond-sized segments. With a canoe you can easily spend a day exploring, fishing, and watching ducks, loons, kingfishers, and other birds. For people wishing to stay longer, there are two lean-tos and eight primitive campsites located on the east shore, away from the Loop Road and its drive-in sites.

The best place to park and launch a canoe or kayak is at the very first turnout on the Loop Road, within 200 feet of its beginning by the North Lake

Road bridge. There is a register booth and space for a handful of cars.

The southern lake segment is the most populous, with private camps along most of the east shore and the popular Loop Road campsites on the west shore. There are half a dozen small islands, all but one too small to be inhabited. The lake briefly narrows at 1.1 miles, and then you enter the second segment. Here, you will find a smaller number of private camps on the west shore and the two lean-tos on the east shore. The construction qualities of the two shelters are worlds apart from one another. The southern one was once someone's woodshed, and probably attracts more curiosity than actual overnight use. The northern one was once a small, four-walled cabin; it became a lean-to when someone cut out the lake-facing wall. This one is used frequently. Look for it just inside the woods about 1.5 miles from the starting point.

The third segment, which sits at the foot of Sugarloaf Mountain, features the first three of the canoe-access campsites on the east shore, which are all small, cozy, and lightly used.

The fourth segment is one of the largest, and perhaps the most scenic. There are several bays to explore, two small islands, and views of Canachagala and Ice Cave mountains. The Middle and North branches of the Black River both flow into their own coves. The water is deep, black, and cold. Large rocks loom in the murky depths like eerie ghosts. Several prominent drive-in campsites are located on the west shore, but there are five primitive sites on the east shore. The two in the narrow cove where Ice Cave Creek and the North Branch flow in are the most secluded.

Because North Lake is a reservoir, some drawdown does occur in the fall, exposing a few shoals and a wider band of the gravelly shoreline.

25 Atwell Martin's Wigwam Site

Path to local historic site

Atwell Martin, "the hermit of North Lake," came to the area in the mid-1800s after an unhappy love affair led him to despise women. He built a bark shanty (he called it a wigwam) and decorated it with animal bones to ward off witches. Not completely shut off from society, he became the first gatekeeper of the new dam in 1855 and moved into the new structure built for the gatekeeper, the rustic precursor to the current State House. Atwell was uncomfortable in those surroundings, and, following his primitive heart, he moved back into his wigwam. For visitors of North Lake, the site has been a curiosity for over a century.

To find the site, go down the Loop Road for 0.1 mile. An unmarked path leads southwest another 0.1 mile along an old road to a clearing. The old metal sign that marked the site is now illegible, but it used to read: "Here . . . years lived Atwell Martin the North Lake Hermit in his wigwam cabin." When the settlement of North Lake got its own United States Post Office, it was named Atwell. The post office is long gone, but the name Atwell remains.

26 Sand Lake Falls

Snowmobile trail, hiking, camping, cross-country skiing
4.7 miles, 2½ hours, 210-foot initial vertical rise, rolling terrain thereafter

Sand Lake Falls and its lean-to are located along a remote section of Woodhull Creek, a mile below Sand Lake. The snowmobile trail leading there is also marked as a foot trail, and while it hardly resembles a wilderness footpath it is not without interest. Most of it was clearly a road at one point in its history; that road led not to Sand Lake Falls, but to the dams at Sand Lake and Woodhull Lake, which were also built to supply the canals. As a hiking trail, this section is relatively wide and straight.

However, the northwest end of the trail leaves the road and follows too close to the boggy edge of Woodhull Creek's tributaries to be enjoyable. In early spring or black fly season this hike could be a disaster. There are two approaches to Sand Lake Falls, and admittedly this is the poorer route for hikers because of the very real potential for flooding. The obstacles are not insurmountable, however, and locked in the frozen embrace of winter this may even be the preferred route for skiers. The trail is well-defined, snowmobile traffic is not too heavy, moderate hills provide some excitement, and the wetlands invite exploration.

The trailhead is located 0.3 mile along the Loop Road, although there is no dedicated parking area. (In the off-season you can commandeer one of the nearby vacant campsites for that purpose.) The trail begins by immediately climbing above the road. This is the steepest part of the whole trip, gaining more than 200 feet in the first 0.7 mile. Leveling off, the trail leads generally northwest through a tall hardwood-dominated landscape with gentle contours. Take time to search the tops of the mature beech trees for huge "nests." These are made when black bears climb up to feed on beechnuts and pile the broken twigs and branches underneath them. Claw-scarred trunks are further evidence.

As you continue northwest, you cross two small streams, Nelson and Hoxie brooks. Within an hour of hiking, you descend about 80 feet to cross a third stream, Clark Brook, and quickly climb again to your former elevation. During this ascent, at a point 2 miles from North Lake, a vague junction is reached with an old snowmobile trail coming in from the southwest. It leads in 1.8 miles to Little Woodhull Lake, section 27.

After cresting the hill, the trail begins a steady descent to a wetland surrounding Grindstone Creek, which you reach at 2.7 miles. Once across, the trail leads west, then north over a few ups and downs, reaching a junction at 3.6 miles. The old roadbed continues straight, but it leads in 150 feet to the posted boundary of the Adirondack League Club.

The snowmobile trail turns left, descending quickly toward the upper reaches of a large wetland. At 3.7 miles it reaches a bridge over the outlet of the Fourth Bisby Lake, where the approaches at both ends might be soggy. This is an odd place for both a trail and a bridge, but given the even wetter conditions downstream and the clearly marked League Club boundary upstream, this is the only viable site.

But that excuse only goes so far. Away from the bridge, the trail curves away from the boundary to follow the edge of the wetland, where there is no solid ground. The *better* place would be a bit further inland. The trail does cut through the woods at 3.8 miles, only to come to an even wetter place a moment later. The next trail markers are attached to stakes planted in the boggy growth; when the water is high, they are quite laughable. Forget them and make your own way through the woods to the right, keeping the wetland in view to ensure you remain on the right course.

At 4 miles you reach the bridge over Woodhull Creek. For the next 0.5 mile, the trail continues to pass through the open wetland, but except for a few short sections this part is noticeably drier—and at times it is even scenic and enjoyable. At 4.5 miles signs direct you inland for the last time, and the last 0.2 mile to the lean-to are passed in the woods away from the creek.

The lean-to is in good condition and the area around it is attractive, with room for tents nearby. Sand Lake Falls is not visible from the lean-to, but the creek is only 100 feet away. You can easily walk to the rock ledges at the top of the falls, or follow a herd path to the large pool at the base of the angled rock. This pool and others in the rocky stretch beyond afford good swimming, and the angling camper might want to try his luck at each one. In the springtime and during wet seasons, the water thunders through here, carrying the combined output of Woodhull Lake, Sand Lake, and the four Bisby Lakes.

Sand Lake Falls

27 Little Woodhull Lake Link Trail

Hiking, snowshoeing
1.8 miles, 1 hour, 140-foot vertical descent

This 1.8-mile link trail is part of an old snowmobile loop between North and Little Woodhull lakes, but while it is still technically available to snow-mobiles it has probably been many years since one has tried to navigate it. Hikers rarely come this way either, although no fault can be found with the route. Perhaps the direct route from North Lake Road, section 22, is so sat-isfactory that no one sees a need for this second approach.

From the trail to Sand Lake Falls, section 26, at a point 2 miles from North Lake, this red-marked trail leads off to the left, southwest. It leads through featureless terrain before gradually descending into the dense mixed-woods basin of Little Woodhull. There are markers, but the tread is faint in places and blowdown will likely be present.

Your first glimpse of the lake is through the trees to the right at approxi-mately 1.6 miles, near where an abandoned spur trail once led to the shore. At 1.8 miles the trail approaches Little Woodhull Creek. The last bridge built here has been gone for many years, but the markers lead down to the right where you can easily step across on rocks.

The junction with the main trail is just above the creek. Left leads to North Lake Road, and right leads to the lake, 0.2 mile away. From the Loop Road trailhead, the hike to Little Woodhull is a one-way total of 4 miles.

28 Ice Cave Mountain

Logging road and path

Ice Cave Mountain gets its name from a series of deep fissures that are so concealed from sunlight that they sometimes contain residual winter ice well into the summer. These fissures so impressed early residents that the name Ice Cave was also applied to a nearby creek and its surrounding valley. Today, there is no marked trail leading to the caves, but one of the logging roads northeast of North Lake leads to a well-used path. There are no signs or offi-cial markers, so attention to detail is required to find the correct route. Note that since this hike is located on the easement land where logging can occur, some landmarks are subject to change.

Follow the Loop Road all the way to the extremely large parking area at its end, 4.4 miles from North Lake Road. There are two continuing logging roads stemming from the northwest corner of the lot, both gated. The left road leads to Ice Cave Mountain, but if you have some time you may also want to make a quick side trip down the road to the right. In 0.3 mile it leads to a picturesque gorge on the North Branch Black River.

The road to the left is an obvious route, wide and easy to follow. At 0.4 mile a side road branches off to the left toward Ice Cave Valley. (This, too, is a recommended side trip. In 0.4 mile it leads an open wetland with good views of the mountain.)

To reach the caves, stay on the main road for 1.3 miles from its beginning at the parking area, about 30 minutes of hiking. At this point, you reach a small streambed flowing right through the road. The path begins to the left of the road at this spot, but it may only be marked by a bit of flagging. (The road continues for another 0.6 mile to a remote stretch of the North Branch.)

The footpath leads north, pulling away from the stream and leading through a patch of jumbled rock. The tread becomes better defined as it takes you nearly due north up the flank of the mountain. The short climb is tiring and steep. As the path levels off at the top, after 0.3 mile and more than 300 feet of climbing, it bears left, west, to traverse the ridgeline towards the largest fissure.

The "cave" appears as a gaping hole in the mountain, and the path passes close to a precipice with a view fifty feet down into the cool depths, 1.7 miles from the trailhead. You then circle around to an opening on its southern end where you can, with extreme caution, approach a ledge inside the cave. *This ledge is almost always wet and slippery, and a single misstep will prove disastrous.* The walls of the ice cave are nearly vertical, and a descent into it requires proper equipment and skills. The path circles around a few more feet to a safer view of the cave, and then passes very close to a second, smaller fissure in the forest floor. The path ends in a yard or two in a tiny clearing, with a vague view of S-shaped North Lake through the trees.

Bushwhackers will enjoy seeking out the mountain's other notable features. About 200 feet northwest of the end of the path there is a small set of jagged ledges, and although getting to them is not easy, one small opening does afford a spectacular view over Ice Cave Valley, down the length of North Lake, and all the way to Starr Hill in Oneida County. There is also a huge balancing rock about 0.3 mile northeast of the caves on the west side of the mountain. The numerous talus caves along the foot of the mountain can also be fun to explore.

South Lake

THE DAM AT South Lake was completed in 1859, creating a reservoir about 500 acres in size at the source of the South Branch Black River. It is the second largest of the Canal Lakes, behind only Woodhull Lake in terms of surface area; and with an elevation of 2018 feet above sea level, it is also the highest settled lake with public access in the southwestern Adirondacks. The hills to the east, which are the outermost fringes of the vast West Canada Lake plateau, may not seem like much when viewed from the water, but they are the highest summits in the Black River Wild Forest, surpassing even the fire tower mountains described elsewhere in this guide.

South Lake has a wild and undeveloped appearance not normally expected of reservoirs. This is largely because the state owns the majority of the shoreline, with most of the private camps clustered in just three locations near the west end of the lake. This has not always been the case, though. Once, only about 1.5 miles of the southern shoreline was in the Forest Preserve. The balance—most of the forest around the lake—was given to the state as a gift in 1965 by Hazel Northam, executrix of the Walter Pratt Estate. This gift was generous, and it has made South Lake an outstanding recreational resource, but it was not without controversy.

The title to the 4462-acre tract was transferred under the terms of a law enacted by the state legislature in 1925, which allowed the Conservation Commission (the precursor to today's DEC) to accept such gifts, with the caveat that they "shall be irrevocably dedicated to be used for the purposes of a public park or reservation." This law was expanded in 1960 to allow land to also be given "for use only for those purposes of silvicultural research and experimentation in the science of forestry." In both cases, none of the land was to be considered part of the Forest Preserve.

Of the acreage at South Lake, some 888 acres around the shore were granted for park purposes, while the balance was to be used only for silvicultural research. These conditions of land acquisition conflict with Article XIV of the New York State Constitution, the so-called "Forever Wild Clause" that is widely interpreted to mean that *all* state-owned forestland in the Adirondack Park, regardless of the acquisition method, is automatically part of the Forest Preserve, where logging and development are prohibited. According to this view, the law is invalid because the terms of the constitution supersede those of any statute.

South Lake

However, this legal contradiction has never been fully resolved. The law is still a part of the state's environmental conservation code, and signs identify the property as Pratt-Northam Memorial Park, in accordance with another deed stipulation. In every other respect, though, DEC manages these lands as part of the Black River Wild Forest, consistent with Article XIV. No logging, experimentation, or park-like development has ever occurred since the state took ownership.

South Lake can be found by following South Lake Road (as North Lake Road is renamed in Atwell) for 2.1 miles uphill past North Lake's twin earthen dams, for a total distance of 17.2 miles from Forestport Station. See the waypoint chart on page 57 for further details. There are two primary attractions: the lake itself, of course, as well as a snowmobile trail that opens up the vast wilderness landscape to the south.

29 South Lake

Canoeing, camping, fishing, swimming

North Lake and South Lake, because of their similar sizes, origins, and names, are often considered companions to one another. Indeed there are many similarities, but if the lakes are siblings, they are not twins. North Lake's water is deeply stained with tannins, but South Lake has some of the clearest water in the region. North Lake functions like a typical reservoir, with water drawdowns every fall, but at South Lake the water level isn't tinkered with very much. North Lake has its Loop Road to provide easy access all the way to uppermost end. South Lake only has a snowmobile trail.

South Lake is the perfect size for a day of paddling or a relaxing weekend of canoe camping. The main body of the lake is about 1.8 miles long, and about 0.2 mile to 0.5 mile wide. Because of its east-west orientation, it is perhaps more susceptible to headwinds and whitecaps than North Lake, although there are many calm days as well. The lake features the requisite loons and beavers, and motorboat traffic is light.

The best place to launch a canoe or kayak is next to a blue boathouse owned by the Canal Corporation, about 2.1 miles from Atwell and 17.2 miles from Forestport Station. There is plenty of parking to the left of the gravel landing.

If you are eager to get past the camps to the wilder parts of the lake, then the north shore is the shorter and more direct route to tour along. Here the water is generally edged by open hardwoods, and you will see two clearings where camps once stood on the former Pratt-Northam lands. Halfway down the lake there is a rocky bluff facing southeast that is popular among intrepid swimmers, and occasionally by campers, although the site is less suitable for that activity. At the east shore, the land rises steeply behind a shield of conifers before tapering to a rocky point.

Looping around the south shore entails a longer paddle, but the views are perhaps better. There are several coves to explore, including one that is actually the lake's second outlet. The woods are darker and more coniferous, seeming to conceal more mysteries. Eventually, near the southeast corner of the main lake, you reach the earthen dam. It is a 350-foot long strip of open ground with an outstanding view of the lake's rugged east end. There is a small dock where you can land your boat, and a trail leads inland to connect with the snowmobile trail, sections 30 and 31. If your intent is to extend your water-born explorations with a hike to Little Salmon Lake or elsewhere, this is the logical place to disembark and set off on foot.

Northeast of the dam, South Lake narrows into a channel that extends east before hooking north. It leads into what is locally known as Little South Lake, a wild body of water that seems more like a separate pond than an extension of the reservoir. A slant-rock waterfall splashes near the northeast corner of Little South, and there are several coves and a bog mat rich with pitcher plants to explore. Raymond Brook, the major inlet to the east, is navigable for a short distance. There is an informal campsite right at Little South's bottleneck entrance, where submerged slabs of bedrock indicate there was probably a waterfall before the reservoir was created.

On average, the one-way trip across the length of South Lake takes about one hour.

30 South Lake Dam

Snowmobile trail, hiking, mountain biking, cross-country skiing
2.7 miles, 1¼ hours, rolling terrain

This may be one of the most underappreciated trails in the southwestern Adirondacks. Perhaps many people are turned off by the fact that it is a snowmobile trail leading to an earthen dam, and not a wilderness footpath leading to a purely natural setting. But sometimes even the most dedicated hiker doesn't want to endure miles of mud, rocks, and roots. Sometimes we simply want a wide, clear route through attractive woods with little to slow us down. The dam, believe it or not, provides a pretty good view of South Lake's rugged east end. But for those people who really *do* want the wilderness footpath experience, there are some options to consider that stem from this route, as described later in the chapter.

The first mile of this trail was upgraded in 1999 to serve as a driveway for the group of summer camps on the south shore. It features a fair gravel surface that is even plowed in winter, though public automobile use is not permitted. As a snowmobile trail, the overall route receives just enough use that it often has a firm base, without an overbearing amount of traffic to discourage snowshoeing and skiing. In the summer, few people use the trail at all.

The trailhead is located 16.9 miles from Forestport Station, or 1.8 miles from Atwell along South Lake Road, just before the road reaches the lake. Signs mark the trail's beginning, but there is no formal parking area. Because it doubles as a residential driveway, hikers are asked to park to the side.

The trail begins at the west end of the lake, heading south. The first 1 mile is essentially a small road. You can see the lake through the trees to your left, but it is an "arm's length" view since the trail never passes closer than a hundred feet of the shoreline. If you are anxious to see South Lake you can pick your own way to the shore easily enough through the open woods.

Spillway outlet of South Lake

After angling eastward, you pass the cluster of camps at 1 mile and the end of the improved section. As remote as these properties seem, one of them is a year-round residence. The trail continues much further back from the water now. It climbs over one small knoll, dips through a slight valley, and then gently climbs a larger hill. As you begin this climb, there is a large, low-lying rock to the right of the trail at 1.5 miles, roughly forty minutes from the start. This rock is the best clue to start looking for the footpath to Carnahan Dam, section 32, which begins 50 feet further to the east.

The surrounding hardwood forest is quite handsome, and more mature than what you might expect along a former logging road—though it should be noted that this section is an older Forest Preserve parcel, and not part of the Pratt-Northam gift lands. The trail slowly descends from the hill, passing a narrow bay on the left. At 2.5 miles you reach a bridge over a sizeable creek. To the left, a low concrete dam creates a small cascade at the outlet end of another small bay. This is the lake's spillway, and the stream is one of two outlets that merge in a large vly to the south to form the South Branch Black River.

Just past the bridge, look for an unmarked side trail angling back to the left. It is less than 500 feet long and should not be missed. It leads to an opening on the shoreline with a very good view of the central portion of South Lake, including the set of rock bluffs on the north shore that is a favorite swimming area for boaters in the summer.

Back on the snowmobile trail, there is a second side trail only 0.1 mile later, 2.6 miles from the trailhead. The main trail bears right and begins to descend from this junction, as described in section 31.

Take the side trail instead. It isn't marked, but at only 0.1 mile in length it doesn't need to be. It leads straight to the west end of South Lake's main dam, a large earthen structure 350 feet long with an open view of the lake and the Raymond Hills beyond. If you have picked a calm, sunny afternoon for this hike, then you will not find a better spot for lunch.

31 South Lake to the Herkimer Landing Trail

Snowmobile trail, hiking, cross-country skiing
4.2 miles, 1½ hours, 720-foot elevation change

Beyond the South Lake dam, the snowmobile trail described in section 30 becomes a somewhat more rugged route. Whereas the first section follows an old road that is in good shape even though it is probably as old as the reservoir, this next section appears to be a Pratt-Northam logging road—a little rougher and a little wetter. It is also much hillier. The east end of the trail, just before its junction with the Herkimer Landing Trail, has the distinction of being the highest marked trail covered in this guidebook.

Few hikers use this trail in its entirety, although it could be combined with the Herkimer Landing Trail, section 6, for a satisfactory through-hike to Nobleboro. Instead, it is more likely that the few people who will hike, ski, or snowshoe this route will have their sights set on the wild terrain to the north and south. For those people, a few choice side excursions are called out in the text below.

From the side trail to the South Lake dam described in the previous section, 2.6 miles from the South Lake Road trailhead or just 0.1 mile from the dam itself, the trail descends and crosses the South Branch Black River, which is little more than a brook at this point. At 0.2 mile a side road branches east toward the valley of Raymond Brook, and at 0.5 mile you cross a small stream and enter a clearing where a lumber camp once stood. Some hardware still remains strewn about the site.

The trail swings east and begins to climb, topping out at about 2150 feet

Little Salmon Outlet

in elevation. At 1.3 miles you reach another small clearing where the trail swings right, south, to begin a gradual descent toward Little Salmon Outlet. Soon you can see the wetlands surrounding that creek through the trees to your right as the trail contours along the foot of a hill. At 1.9 miles, about 45 minutes from the dam, the trail swings right across a bridge over yet another small stream. Immediately after the bridge, note the side road forking left, uphill. This is the start of the path to Little Salmon Lake, section 33.

A moment later, at 2 miles, you cross Little Salmon Outlet. The trail then reaches a clearing at 2.2 miles where the remnants of another old lumber camp can be found. At this point the trail swings left, uphill, but to the right another, more obscure road leads right. Adventurous explorers can seek out a rough footpath extending eastward, parallel to Little Salmon Outlet, into the proposed Cotton Lake Wilderness—assuming, of course, that this rarely-used path continues to be maintained.

From this point forward, the snowmobile trail is rough and untamed enough that no groomer can tackle it. This may explain why so few snowmobiles use it, because even though it follows an old logging road, it was not a very good logging road. The surrounding forest is quite young as you climb into the high country in stages. One of these ascents is relatively steep, as snowmobile trails go. As you near the height-of-land the trail condition gets pretty bad; it appears that ATVs sometime stray this way off the Herkimer Landing Trail. You are on a broad hillside due south of Little Salmon Lake, topping out near 2540 feet before making the short descent to reach the Herkimer Landing Trail 4.2 miles from the dam, or 6.8 miles from the trailhead on South Lake Road.

Bearing left will take you to Little Salmon Lake in 0.9 mile, and right leads to Haskell Road in 5.3 miles.

32 Carnahan Dam

Path

It was common practice in the nineteenth and early twentieth centuries for logging crews to build small dams throughout the backcountry. Each spring they would strategically open the floodgates, floating their harvest to mill on the augmented stream flow. The remains of these structures are common-place throughout the Adirondacks.

One such dam exists a short distance south of the snowmobile trail described in section 30, on the South Branch Black River. It is a humble structure that was breached long ago, but local lore holds that it was built by Sol

Carnahan, a colorful and outspoken lumberman based in the Nobleboro area around the turn of the twentieth century. It is therefore called Carnahan Dam, and because of its proximity to the trail it is reasonably easy to find.

Follow the snowmobile trail around South Lake for 1.5 miles from the trailhead, or 0.5 mile past the end of the driveway. At this point, the trail has dipped through a small valley and is beginning to gently climb another, larger hill. There is a large, low-lying rock to the right of the trail, and 50 feet beyond a faint footpath turns right, south.

This path is 0.3 mile long and contours around the hill to the valley of the South Branch, barely flinching from its southerly heading. Should you fail to find it, bushwhacking through the open hardwoods should be an easy matter. Shady conifers fill the woods as you dip into the valley, and after 10 minutes the path ends beside the rock dam, which is located at the foot of a large vly surrounding the river.

All that remains of the dam are the two barriers of shot rock, one on each bank. There was typically also a crib structure in the middle of these dams, where the floodgate would've been located. That part of Carnahan Dam is long gone, but its foundation remains in the form of a few ancient logs embedded in the river's bottom.

In the summer, the river can be forded at this spot—an idea that might be appealing to people wishing to explore the trackless wilderness interior to the south of the river.

33 Little Salmon Lake from the West

Path

At a point 1.9 miles from the South Lake dam, or 4.5 miles from South Lake Road as described in sections 30 and 31, an ancillary logging road branches left, uphill. It is the beginning of a 0.7-mile route to the west end of Little Salmon Lake that has, from time to time, been unofficially maintained as a footpath. This is the shortest route to the pond, and probably no more or less obscure than the official route to the east end, section 6. The low interest in Little Salmon, historically, might be explained by its lack of fish due to acid rain. However, this is one of several acidified lakes that the state has resumed stocking with brook trout in recent years, to encourage its recovery.

From the snowmobile trail, follow the side road up the hill. The beginning is wide and easy to follow as it leads just a bit south of east. At 0.3 mile it crosses a small wet area, where old wood pallets make a crude bridge. The

Gull Lake

route climbs a hill and promptly grows faint, turning into a footpath for the remaining distance. It swings toward the foot of a large hill to the north and essentially follows it to the northwest corner of the pond. Should this last part of the path elude you, then bushwhack along the same general route, keeping close to the foot of the hill as you head east. The hill will guide you straight to the pond.

Bear Creek Road

LIKE THE BLACK River, the headwaters of Woodhull Creek were also dammed to provide water for the state's nineteenth century canals. Woodhull Lake, at the head of the creek, was the first to be dammed in 1860, and it added 781 million cubic feet of storage to the system. Sand Lake followed in 1872, First and Second Bisby lakes in 1880, and Third Bisby Lake in 1881. Gull Lake, Little Woodhull Lake, and Lily Lake were also surveyed in 1881, but no reservoirs were ever authorized there.

The sixth reservoir in the Woodhull Creek watershed was Chub Pond, or Chub Lake as it was called at the time, and its story is perhaps the most colorful of all the Canal Lakes. The site was first surveyed in 1855, and a contract to build the dam was awarded to John Uhle for $23,247.50, below the state engineer's estimate of $26,000. When the completion deadline of October 15 passed and no dam was constructed, the original contract was considered abandoned and a new bidding process began. The Canal Board awarded the new contract to Surramus Britton and John V. Townsend for $27,700 in April 1856, with work to be completed one year later.

Six months into that contract, however, an auditor for the board determined there were insufficient funds to cover all of the canal projects the board had approved, including enlargements to the Erie Canal and the completion of the Black River Canal. The shortage was projected at "several millions of dollars after the amount then provided for that purpose was expended." All non-essential projects were quickly halted. Work was suspended at Chub Lake on November 12, 1856 on the authority of Cornelius Gardinier, the canal commissioner who had approved the project. The contract was cancelled by the board in September 1857 after the expenditure of $9,317.96.

Despite several calls to complete the dam in 1862 when funds were once more available, the Canal Board took no action at Chub Lake until 1881, twenty-five years after the first dam had been abandoned. At this time the state took possession of the "Lumberman's Dam," an old timber structure built by loggers at Chub Lake's outlet during the intervening years. It was raised and brought into official service the following year, but it was not as big as the dam that had been planned in 1855, and the reservoir that it created never reached the capacity promised by the original engineering study.

Nor was it constructed to the same durable standards as the other canal dams. The aging wood structure failed in the spring of 1896, sparking yet an-

Waypoints along Bear Creek Road

Miles	
0.0	Bear Creek Road begins at intersection with NY 28 and Woodgate Road at blinking light in Woodgate
0.8	Tracks of the Adirondack Railroad
2.1	Adirondack Park boundary
3.1	Road ends at state land boundary, trailhead parking area, sections 34-41

other discussion on the fate of the Chub Lake Reservoir. The state engineer advocated for the construction of a permanent dam, but by this time there had been a shift in the Canal Board's policy. Frustrated by the inaccessibility of its numerous Black River and Woodhull Creek reservoirs, and "the constant use of the water surreptitiously, by lumbermen, for the purpose of floating logs down the stream," the state had abandoned by law several of the lakes in 1889, including all of the Bisby Lakes, in favor of a new reservoir in Forestport.

Therefore with no appetite to build another remote dam on Woodhull Creek, the site remained an unused asset in the canal system until 2006, when the Canal Board's modern successor, the Canal Corporation, finally transferred ownership of Chub Pond to DEC for inclusion in the Forest Preserve. Today, only the dams at Woodhull and Sand lakes remain active components of the modern Erie Canal system.

This chapter describes the network of trails that developed around the original road system built to service these reservoirs, beginning east of the hamlet of Woodgate. In most cases, those roads from the nineteenth century now serve as the area's backcountry snowmobile trails. Comparing modern maps to the first USGS sheets issued in 1912, it is remarkable how little some of these routes have changed. Many of the foot trails are not as old, but it seems as though nearly every hike leads to a site that was part of the canal system, considered for inclusion in the system, or known well to the men who tended the dams as they traveled from one lake to the next.

All of these excursions begin at a single trailhead at the end of Bear Creek Road. To find it, follow NY 28 to the blinking light in Woodgate, just outside the Adirondack Park. Turn east onto Bear Creek Road, which is primarily a paved residential road in nature. It leads across the tracks of the Adirondack

Railroad at 0.8 mile, and then the park's Blue Line at 2.1 miles. The road ends at 3.1 miles at a large DEC parking area. The continuing unimproved road is the start of all the hikes that follow.

34 Mill Creek Road

Snowmobile & motorized access trail, hiking, mountain biking
3.4 miles, 1¼ miles, rolling terrain

The inescapable component of this trail system is the primitive road leading northeast from the parking area, picking up where Bear Creek Road leaves off. Officially called Mill Creek Road because its primary purpose now is to provide access to an inholding near Mill Brook, it was once part of the most direct route to the dam at Woodhull Lake, and therefore called Woodhull Road. It is currently in poor shape, and far too rough for ordinary vehicles to drive. It is not always pleasant for walking, either, but since all of the other trails in this chapter stem from this one route it cannot be avoided.

The first half mile is not too bad. The road begins wide and straight, passing a designated campsite on the left and reaching the start of the trail to Chub Pond, section 35, at 0.3 mile. However, by the next junction at 0.5 mile mud wallows begin to appear. The route that forks to the left is the loop to Bear Creek, section 36, intended as a bypass for hikers and skiers. The primary reason why a hiker would choose to stay on Mill Creek Road and not follow the foot trail detour is because the road, despite its aesthetic shortcomings, is the shortest route into the interior, both in terms of time and distance.

At 2 miles it reaches a four-way intersection. Left is part of the Bear Creek loop, and right leads to Gull Lake, section 37. A fourth junction at 2.7 miles marks the end of the Bear Creek trail.

For the purposes of comparison, if you choose to bypass the road using the Bear Creek trail instead, these same two junctions would be at 2.3 and 3.1 miles, respectively.

There is no bypass for the last 0.7 mile of the road, which includes the only significant grade, a modest climb of about 100 vertical feet. The motor vehicle route ends at a junction at 3.4 miles, or 3.8 miles via the Bear Creek loop. The unmarked trail to the right leads to a private camp at the northeast corner of Gull Lake. Straight ahead is the snowmobile trail to Sand Lake Falls, section 39. Left leads through what a sign proclaims to be the "Village of Millbrook" to Bear and Woodhull lakes, sections 40 and 41.

The road is suitable for skiing, but it does receive a relatively high amount of snowmobile use in the winter.

35 Chub Pond

Snowmobile trail, hiking, camping, mountain biking, cross-country skiing

3.9 miles, 1¾ hours, rolling terrain, 180-foot descent at Chub Pond

Chub Pond is essentially a widening of Woodhull Creek, about 0.3 mile wide and nearly a mile long. Although it was one of the Canal Lakes as mentioned in the chapter introduction, the only dam there currently is a low wooden structure that raises the water by a mere foot. It is accessed by a snowmobile trail that is nearly level for the most part, until it drops 180 feet into the pond's valley. Depending on snowmobile usage it can be a good ski route in the winter, and for summer hikers it is an acceptable route with a few unfortunate pockets of mud wallows. One of the pond's chief attractions is the scenically perched lean-to on the north shore. Its other attraction may be its fishery.

From the Bear Creek Road trailhead, follow Mill Creek Road northeast for 0.3 mile to the first trail junction. The route to Chub bears right, leading to a bridge over Lot 8 Creek at 0.6 mile, and then Gull Lake Outlet with its lovely open wetlands at 1.3 miles. The trail cuts widthwise across this wetland, which is certainly one of the more striking landmarks along the route. At 1.9 miles you reach a junction with the trail that approaches Gull Lake from the south, section 38.

About 0.7 mile past this last junction, or after roughly 20 minutes of walking, you should notice a bog through the trees to the south. The trail continues to curve around the northern limits of the wetland for the next quarter mile. Buck Pond lies at its far end, and many pitcher plants grow there in thick clusters. Though it is not easy walking through the bog, it is worth taking a detour off the trail and risking a wet foot to view the lovely specimens of this carnivorous plant. If you walk to the edge of the pond, you can feel the bog quiver beneath your feet. Layers of dense peat and sphagnum mosses float on the water all around the pond in mats so thick they support shrubs and small trees—and, hopefully, curious explorers.

The trail continues on past Buck Pond, through a small wet area, to a fork at 3.3 miles. The right fork is a very faint trail that leads steeply down the hillside for 0.4 mile to Chub's north shore; few people seem to use it, and the only motivation to do so would be to get to the southern lean-to, section 19, in the shortest distance possible.

The left fork is by far the more prominent route. It begins a 0.4-mile descent to the shore, where at 3.7 miles you reach a campsite and another faint trail leading to the right along the shoreline, also described in section 19. Bear left for the lean-to, which you reach 3.9 miles from the Bear Creek Road trailhead.

This lean-to is designated Chub Pond #2. Sitting on a sandy bank overlooking the pond, it is a favorite destination of fishing and camping parties arriving by floatplane. The pebbly beach affords good swimming. If you have the means to do so, you will want to explore the wetlands along the northeast extension of the pond. With a pack canoe, you can paddle for a long way through quiet marshes watching marsh harriers glide low over the waving grasses. The place creates a deep sense of remoteness.

36 Bear Creek

Hiking, cross-country skiing
1.3 miles, 30 minutes, relatively level to Bear Creek
2.3 miles, 1 hour, minimal grades to Gull Lake trail
3.1 miles, 1½ hours, minimal grades to final junction with Mill Creek Road

This trail loop utilizes a network of lesser logging roads between Mill Creek Road and Bear Creek, providing access to the creek and offering an alternative to the main road. The three sets of measurements above suggest the three main ways this trail might be useful: as a short hike to an old bridge site on Bear Creek, as an approach to Gull Lake, or as a parallel route to Mill Creek Road. As a foot trail, it is not without its own issues: the middle portion can be quite wet, and the northernmost portion is apt to be lightly used and maintained.

Follow Mill Creek Road for 0.5 mile from the trailhead. Near a large mud wallow, the Bear Creek trail forks left. It follows a good roadbed through a shady forest, reaching a small clearing at 1.2 miles surrounded by spruce and balsam fir. A path leads left along an old road for 0.1 mile to Bear Creek, at a site where a bridge was once built atop the remains of an even older logging dam. A continuing roadbed can be seen on the opposite side, but both the dam and the bridge are long gone.

Just 0.2 mile from this spur trail, a second spur also leads left to another spot on Bear Creek, 300 feet away. This spot is attractive to people seeking to launch a canoe for an upstream paddle on the creek.

The next section of the foot trail pulls away from the creek. Portions of it are wet enough to require short detours. You reach the next junction at 2.1 miles, where a red-marked trail bears right, southeast, to reach Mill Creek

Gull Lake

Road in 0.2 mile, or 2.3 miles from the trailhead. The trail to Gull Lake, section 37, continues from this point.

The last section of the Bear Creek trail is 1 mile long, ending at 3.1 miles at a point on Mill Creek Road just 0.7 mile shy of its own terminus. Few people seem to use this section.

37 Gull Lake

Snowmobile trail, hiking, camping, cross-country skiing
1.3 miles, 40 minutes, 160-foot vertical rise from Mill Creek Road
3.3 miles from trailhead via Mill Creek Road
3.6 miles from trailhead via Bear Creek loop trail

In terms of surface area, Gull Lake is one of the larger water bodies in the area, although much of it is very shallow. Its north shore is a gem, with a variety of features to explore: a cluster of large rocks with good views, several tall white pines, and a handsome lean-to on its own isolated point. This is an excellent destination for a moderate day trip or relatively short overnight trip.

This section describes the 1.3-mile trail that leads to the lean-to from the junction 2 miles along Mill Creek Road, section 34. The road is the shortest approach route, and the one that is probably the most commonly used, but the Bear Creek loop described in section 36 is the more scenic alternative. That approach is 2.3 miles long.

Heading east from Mill Creek Road, the trail suffers from ATV erosion as it climbs a gentle hillside, passes close to a small stream, and traverses a hilltop with an unfortunate amount of rutting. These ills are short-lived, however. At 0.6 mile, about 15 minutes from Mill Creek Road, you reach a junction. To the right is the trail that leads south toward the Chub Pond trail, section 38. You can follow it for 0.1 mile to a place where boats and canoes are commonly launched.

Bearing left, you will find that it takes about twenty minutes to wind around the northern bays and marshes of the lake, descending over a series of ups and downs for a distance of 0.7 mile to the lean-to. The site is attractively nestled in the pine trees on the north shore of Gull Lake, with good views of the lake's eastern half. A path leads west behind the shelter to a handsome set of rocks on another part of the shore, where the view is extended to the rest of the lake. A rock ledge in front of the lean-to offers a good place for hikers and campers to take a swim on a warm summer day.

Woodhull Lake Lean-to

38 Gull Lake Outlet

Snowmobile trail, hiking, cross-country skiing
2.1 miles, 1 hour, relatively level

This trail connects Gull Lake, section 37, with the trail to Chub Pond, section 35. Rather than an alternate route to reach Gull, it is mostly used as part of a loop hike beginning and ending at the Bear Creek Road trailhead. This loop begins on Mill Creek Road, includes a side trip to the Gull Lake Lean-to, turns south along the trail described below, and exits via the Chub Pond trail for a total distance of 8 miles. People who like to hike longer distances will find this to be a good "leg stretcher."

From the junction near the northwest corner of Gull Lake, roughly mid-way between Mill Creek Road and the lean-to as described in section 37, this route turns right, south, coming to a site at 0.1 mile where a boat is routinely kept. (For people with pack canoes, this is the best place to access the water.) The trail continues along an old roadbed benched into the side of hill, with several opportunities for views of the water—although some of the best views are gained by taking short detours off the trail. At 0.4 mile there is a short herd path leading left to the beaver-dammed outlet, and at 0.5 mile you reach a tributary stream that doesn't appear on maps, but which is big enough to block dry passage in early spring.

You cross a bridge over Gull Lake Outlet at 0.7 mile, and at this point the trail briefly reverses direction, heading northeast back toward Gull Lake. At 0.9 mile you can see the lake again at a distance across a wide, grassy shore-line. The shore is too wet to approach here for summer hikers, but for skiers or snowshoers wishing to cut a corner across the frozen lake, this would be the logical place to reenter the woods and pick the trail back up.

At this point, the trail begins another 180° turn to resume its journey south. The remaining 1.2 miles pass through an open hardwood forest with no hills and few obstacles of any kind other than the occasional blowdown. When you reach the junction with the Chub Pond trail, left leads 1.8 miles to the northern lean-to, and right leads in 1.9 miles to the Bear Creek Road trailhead.

39 Sand Lake Falls from the West

Snowmobile trail, hiking, camping
3 miles, 1½ hours, rolling terrain, 275-foot descent to falls

Of the two routes leading to Sand Lake Falls and its lean-to, this may be the preferred route for hikers even though it is roughly 2 miles longer. The reason for that claim is that this approach is much drier than the route from North Lake described in section 26, which passes through the edges of wet-lands near the outlet of Fourth Bisby Lake. Factoring in the hike along Mill Creek Road, the one-way distance to the lean-to along the route described here is 6.4 miles. That may be a long way to walk with a full backpack, but Sand Lake Falls is certainly worth the effort.

From the end of Mill Creek Road, at the junction near the private in-holding nicknamed the "Village of Millbrook," continue following the blue-marked trail east. Its route matches a road that appears on the 1912 USGS

McKeever Quadrangle, which led to a camp deep in the woods south of Mill Brook. Little has changed, because at 1.2 miles, after 30 minutes of hiking, the modern trail enters a large, grassy clearing at the same spot marked on the old map as the cabin site. Legend has it that this was an old homestead where a family once hunted and farmed, and one version of the tale says that they starved during a severe winter. Some claim that they met a grisly fate at the hands of vengeful Indians. Yet another story describes a turn-of-the-century hermitage. All evidence, however, indicates that this was where a lumber camp once stood, and with a little exploration the site will yield its share of bottles, saw blades, barrel hoops, and horseshoes. While not as sensational a legacy as some would have it, such lumber camps were, in their own way, a colorful part of Adirondack history.

The trail follows along the right edge of the clearing, reenters the woods at its southeast corner, then crosses a stream. Heading east-southeast, you pass through a wet area and begin a gradual ascent. A half hour after leaving the clearing, at 2.2 miles, you reach the height-of-land at about 2030 feet and begin to descend into the Woodhull Creek valley. You may be able to hear the falls from here, and if you have found the distance tiring then this will give your spirits a lift. Moderate descents lead southeast over the course of the final 0.8 mile, ending at a clearing with the lean-to on the left and the falls on the right.

The lean-to is in good condition and the area around it is attractive, with room for tents nearby. Sand Lake Falls is not visible from the lean-to, but the creek is only 100 feet away. You can easily walk to the rock ledges at the top of the falls, or follow a herd path to the large pool at the base of the angled rock. This pool and others in the rocky stretch beyond afford good swimming, and the angling camper might want to try his luck at each one. In the springtime and during wet seasons, the water thunders through here, carrying the combined output of Woodhull Lake, Sand Lake, and the four Bisby Lakes.

40 Mill Brook to Woodhull Lake

Snowmobile trail, hiking, camping, mountain biking
3.5 miles, 1½ hours, 300-foot vertical rise

The snowmobile trail that extends northeast from the end of Mill Creek Road is a firm, smooth route and a satisfying (though long) approach to Woodhull Lake. The lean-to that it leads to is one of the largest in the Adir-

Bear Lake

ondacks and can easily accommodate a dozen campers with all their gear. Local tradition and some trail signs refer to the lake as "Big" Woodhull Lake, thus differentiating it from Little Woodhull Lake to the south. However, the official name of the lake has always been Woodhull Lake, dating back to the natural lake that existed before the construction of the first dam in 1849.

Beginning at the end of Mill Creek Road, section 34, bear left toward a private camp proclaimed by a sign to be the "Village of Millbrook." The trail passes to the left of the camps back into state land, and drops to cross Mill Brook. Heading generally northeast, you next begin a long, moderate ascent, broken by a few short, level stretches. The route is just east of north as you pass along the foot of Neejer Hill. At 0.9 mile you reach a junction with the foot trail to Bear Lake, section 41.

The snowmobile trail then angles north of east for the next 1.4 miles, reaching the height-of-land at about 1970 feet, as well as a few wet areas along the way. The road grade is dramatically evident here as ditches on both sides follow for a distance. A brief descent takes you to a small open area where the trail turns sharply to the left at 2.3 miles. At this point, an obvious but unmarked trail also goes right. That is the continuing route of the old Woodhull Road, which led to the dam at Woodhull Lake. A second road branched from it and led past Sand Lake to North Lake, linking many of the Canal Lakes together in a single road network. The dams at Woodhull and Sand now lie on the Adirondack League Club's posted property, and the middle portion of the road near Sand Lake has been abandoned. These two factors make the traverse to Atwell along this historic route impossible for modern travelers.

Bearing left, the marked trail leads northwest through an area of open vlies and scenic beaver ponds. The footing is apt to be wet, and you may be forced to seek a detour around some of the worst sections. You are still on an old roadbed, but one that is noticeably narrower than the Woodhull Road. This is a route that is used by very few people, except snowmobiles in the winter.

At 3.3 miles the trail descends to a junction. Ahead, the blue-marked trail crosses a bridge and leads to the Wolf Lake Landing Road, section 53. A muddy trail comes in from the right and it leads 0.2 mile to the lean-to.

The rocky shore and sandy bottom are just right for swimming, and the view across the lake is peaceful—good rewards for the long hike in.

41 Bear Lake via Neejer Hill

Hiking, camping
1.8 miles, 45 minutes, rolling terrain

Bear Lake has a charm of its own, as many of its visitors will tell you. Steep hills on the west, north, and east cradle the quiet waters that empty to the south, creating Bear Creek. Depending on beaver flooding, the upper half of this hourglass-shaped lake has sandy beaches that are ideal for swimming, sunbathing, and picnicking. Toward the outlet, the shores become brushy and the waters are filled with pickerelweed and water lilies. Tiny sundews can be found clinging to saturated wood lying along the shore. Many types of birds can be observed here, and the variety of animal tracks attests to the lake's popularity as a watering hole.

Even the three trails to Bear Lake offer a pleasant diversion. They are maintained only as foot trails and are a welcome change in an area groomed mostly for motorized travel. They converge at an intersection near the eastern shore, not far from a lean-to constructed in 2010. Tent sites with better views of the water can also be found on the east and north sides of the lake.

The approach from the south described here is the longest of all three routes, and the least used. To find it, you first need to follow Mill Creek Road to its end (3.4 miles) and then the Woodhull Lake trail, section 40, north to Neejer Hill (0.9 mile). Given that there are much easier ways to get to Bear Lake, this trail will mostly appeal to people making loops or through trips.

From the junction near Neejer Hill, the foot trail heads north through the open hardwoods. The tread is very faint, and without the blue trail markers much of it would be completely undefined. There are no hills of note, and only a few small stream crossings. You begin to pass through small clearings as you near the south end of the lake, and then the waters appear to your left. The intersection at 1.8 miles is on the south bank of the primary inlet, which flows in from the east. The trail to the right leads to Bloodsucker Pond, section 54, and the trail that crosses the creek leads to Wolf Lake Landing Road and McKeever, section 49. There is a campsite near the water, and the lean-to is located across the creek, on a short spur trail about 300 feet from the shore.

White Lake and Otter Lake

ONEIDA COUNTY'S PORTION of the Adirondack Park can be found in the northernmost reaches of the Town of Forestport, encompassing the communities of White Lake and Otter Lake. This region was not included within the original Adirondack Park in 1892, but was added almost forty years later in a major boundary expansion of more than a million acres. The lakes themselves are encircled by private camps, but state land lies close by to the east and west. Nearly all of the trails follow old logging roads, and while several of them are used frequently by snowmobiles they do provide peaceful hiking routes in the summer. Despite an occasional mud hole the trails are, as a rule, well maintained.

None of the destinations are very remote—any of these hikes can be done in half a day—but nevertheless you will find attractive campsites at each of the three backcountry ponds described in this chapter: Brandy Lake, Brewer Lake, and Round Pond. All three are stocked with brook trout.

The primary access to these lands and waters is along NY 28, which connects White and Otter lakes on its journey into the Adirondacks. Signs mark the access points along the highway, and additional trailheads can be found on the area's side roads.

42 Brandy Lake from Long Lake

Trail accessible by canoe, hiking, snowshoeing, camping
0.4 mile canoeing, 0.7 mile hiking, 45 minutes, rolling terrain

Brandy Lake is a 14-acre pond that is secluded, perhaps, but not remote. Trails approach it from several directions, but this route from Long Lake is the shortest. A canoe or kayak is needed to access the trailhead, since the trail starts on the far shore of Long Lake, which lies to the east of White Lake. But even with this slight complication the overall distance is only 1.1 miles. Of course in the winter, when the lake freezes, this trail becomes available to snowshoers.

Long Lake is often called "Little" Long Lake to distinguish it from the larger and better-known place with the same name in the central Adiron-

Round Pond

Waypoints along NY 28 through White Lake and Otter Lake

Woodgate to McKeever		McKeever to Woodgate
0.0	Woodgate, intersection with Bear Creek and Woodgate roads	7.6
0.6	Adirondack Park boundary	7.0
0.9	Intersection with Round Lake Road, **section 42**	6.7
4.3	Access road to state land, Granny Marsh, **section 43**	3.3
4.4	Brandy Lake trailhead, **section 44**	3.2
6.1	Access road to Brewer Lake trailhead, **section 45**	1.5
6.6	Intersection with Lakeview Road, **section 46**	1.0
7.5	Intersection with McKeever Road, **sections 48-54**	0.1
7.6	Moose River bridge at McKeever, intersection with Moose River Road, **section 47**	0.0

dacks. There is an active youth camp at its southern end, and dozens of private residences further north along the shore, but there is one strategically located access point on the east shore where the public can easily launch car-top boats.

To find it, turn off of NY 28 onto Round Lake Road at the sharp bend between Woodgate and White Lake. This road hooks left and leads to a fork at 0.5 mile. Bear right onto Long Lake Road, and follow it past Camp Nazareth for a total distance of 1.7 miles from NY 28. Here at the intersection with Capron Road there is a small parking area on state land to the right, with a short trail to the water on the left. The total carry—including the walk across the road—is only about 100 feet.

Paddle north across the lake, angling toward a set of islands that lies off the west shore. Curve around the northern tip of this little archipelago and look for the start of the trail in the bay that lies beyond. Following the most direct route, the paddling leg of the trip is only 0.4 mile long.

The foot trail, which may be faint at first, cuts inland and then angles north. It climbs at a slow ascent away from the lake, gaining no more than

100 vertical feet. At 0.6 mile a herd path forks left and leads to the nearest point on Brandy's shoreline, but the marked trail continues back from the water, reaching a spot where people have camped at the pond's northeast corner, 0.7 mile from Long Lake.

The continuing trail leads to the snowmobile trail described in section 44.

43 Granny Marsh
Path and bushwhack

This adventure begins as a road, narrows to a path, and ends as a bushwhack. Its destination is Granny Marsh, which is actually a 21-acre pond surrounded by an expansive wetland complex deep in the woods southeast of Otter Lake. In the nineteenth century, it was called Grannis Pond. The nature observer is sure to appreciate the varied vegetation and the signs of wildlife found here. It is best visited in the winter when snow and ice permit easier travel and offer protection for the boggy shore. The woods between it and NY 28 are mostly open hardwoods, and any bushwhack route with the proper compass bearing will get you there from the end of the path. The biggest challenge may be in finding a place to access the shore.

At a place 4.3 miles north of Woodgate on NY 28, and just 0.1 mile south of the well-marked Brandy Lake trailhead, a small DEC sign points to a state land access route leading east into the woods. This narrow driveway is called Cohen Road, and it can be driven with care in the summer. It passes a private residence on the left and crosses the active tracks of the Adirondack Railroad at 0.2 mile. An old gravel pit lies just beyond, and for the lack of anything better this is the place to park.

In the winter, none of this is plowed. The recommended parking area is at the Brandy Lake trailhead, meaning that snowshoers and skiers will need to walk 0.1 mile beside the highway and along the entire 0.2-mile length of Cohen Road.

Beyond the gravel pit, the continuing roadbed climbs a short grade to a fork. The main route to the left is a snowmobile corridor leading back to Otter Lake that can be ignored by hikers. The lesser route to the right, east, files through a young forest. Although it is in the process of slowly growing in, the road was built well and is easy to follow. It dips to a stream crossing at 0.2 mile near the tip of a long wetland, and then climbs back into the higher country. At 0.5 mile, a side road branches right, south. Bear left for Granny Marsh.

The road passes close enough to an attractive beaver flow to the south that it can be glimpsed through the trees. A moment later, at 1 mile, the road veers right and effectively ends. Look for a footpath to the left, continuing the eastward course. The route is unusually straight, but this is explained by the fading yellow paint blazes on the right side of the path: this was at one time the state land boundary. The path leads for 0.4 mile to a series of small clearings where a camp once stood. The established route ends here, 0.6 mile shy of Granny Marsh.

From this point forward, the route is a bushwhack. The open hardwood forest presents few obstacles other than one or two small swamps in low-lying basins. The coniferous forest barrier and boggy shoreline around the pond are the more formidable challenges. If you venture out onto the frozen surface, be mindful of the inlets and outlets, which are apt to be partially unfrozen.

44 Brandy Lake from the East

Snowmobile trail, hiking, camping, mountain biking
2.1 miles, 50 minutes, rolling terrain

This route to Brandy Lake begins at a prominent trailhead on the west side of NY 28, 4.4 miles north of the blinking light in Woodgate and 3.2 miles south of the Moose River bridge in McKeever. There is ample year-round parking, although in the winter the volume of snowmobile traffic on this route will discourage snowshoers and skiers.

The trail follows the bed of a relatively wide old road that winds through a forest of black cherry trees, gently descending into the valley where Purgatory Creek and Otter Lake Outlet flow together. Shortly after crossing the combined creek on a bridge, you reach a junction at 0.5 mile. The trail along Otter Lake Outlet, section 46, leads right.

Turn left on the main trail, which makes a broad U-turn over the next 0.5 mile, past a few wet areas, to another creek and a second junction. In this case the right turn leads to Round Pond, section 47. The old roadbed skirts high above the northernmost end of Long Lake, and at 1.7 miles a marked foot trail veers left off of the roadbed. That is the route to Brandy Lake, and it leads in 0.4 mile to a place where people have camped on the northeast corner of the pond, 2.1 miles from the highway.

The snowmobile trail, which veers right at the fork, continues for several more miles southwest toward Round Lake Road. This is the least desirable

Brewer Lake

approach to Brandy for foot travel, and so it is not recommended or described in this guidebook.

45 Brewer Lake

Hiking, camping
2 miles, 1 hour, 395-foot elevation change

Brewer Lake is perhaps the most attractive of the secluded ponds near Otter
Lake. It is accessed by a marked foot trail that, like most of the others in this
chapter, follows an old woods road. People have camped near the end of the
trail on Brewer's west side, but that spot is not a very good campsite. A better spot exists on the east side, near a distinctive grouping of large boulders.
Getting to that spot, though, entails either bushwhacking around the north

shore or gaining access to a canoe.

The trail begins at a trailhead within the hamlet of Otter Lake. At a point 6.1 miles north of Woodgate, or 1.5 miles south of the Moose River bridge, a sign indicates access to state land to the east. The nearby residence was once the Otter Lake General Store; the old parking area has been fenced off, so the current driveway jogs around it to cross the active tracks of the Adirondack Railroad. The trailhead is tucked inside the woods on the left. Be careful not to block the continuing driveway on the right.

From the trailhead gate, hike northeast on the red-marked foot trail, which climbs at a negligible grade. It begins a wide swing east, and then south as the climbing increases to something more noticeable, but never steep. The trail narrows, patches of bedrock appear, and the top of the ridge is reached at 1.8 miles. As you start to descend it becomes muddy and overgrown in places, making this likely to be the poorest part of the route that you will encounter.

The trail ends at 2 miles on the west shore. A herd path leads right, southeast, toward an attractive point. Brewer is small enough that you don't really *need* a canoe to see all that there is to see, but the rock ledges that dot the shore do invite further exploration. A winter visit would be another excellent way to spend a day. The terrain is very well suited to snowshoeing and skiing, but without a plowed trailhead access is not reliable during the snow season.

46 Otter Lake Outlet

Snowmobile trail, hiking, mountain biking, cross-country skiing
1.1 miles, 30 minutes, relatively level

Lakeview Road leads west from NY 28 at the north end of Otter Lake, just 1 mile south of the Moose River bridge in McKeever. It leads around the north and west shores of Otter Lake to a dead end near the state land boundary at 1.3 miles, with ample room for parking. This trailhead marks the start of a short but enjoyable trail that parallels the lake's outlet stream.

From the parking area, the trail continues as an extension of the road, leading southeast for 0.1 mile to the small dam that enlarges Otter Lake. This is also the place where the public can launch car-top boats. There is a bridge across the dam, with a trail on the opposite shore leading to Wood Road.

Just before the dam, the main trail turns right, southwest, to follow Otter

Lake Outlet downstream. This route, despite its occasional wet spots, offers an enjoyable springtime walk that keeps close to the creek for much of its length. It would also serve well as a ski trail in winter, if you arrive early after a fresh snowfall ahead of the snowmobiles. It leads to a junction with the Brandy Lake trail, section 44, 1 mile from the dam. Left leads in 0.5 mile to NY 28, and right leads in 1.6 miles to Brandy Lake.

47 Round Pond

Snowmobile trail, hiking, camping, mountain biking
0.3 mile, 10 minutes, rolling terrain to Round Pond
2.2 miles, 1 hour, rolling terrain to Brandy Lake trail

Round Pond is comparable in both size and appearance to Brandy Lake, but it is much easier to reach. A campsite on its northeast corner is only 0.3 mile up an obvious trail from Moose River Road. That same trail extends for a total distance of 2.2 miles to an intersection with the Brandy Lake trail, and this connection allows the possibility of hiking from point to point, with a second car parked near Otter Lake's outlet or on NY 28.

To find the trailhead, turn west onto Moose River Road from NY 28 immediately south of the Moose River bridge in McKeever. Drive 2.2 miles down this road to a point where the snowmobile trail enters from the south, left. Since there is no turnout here, you will have to park on the narrow shoulder.

From the road, it is a short ascent of 0.25 mile to an unmarked junction where a spur trail forks right. It leads in less than 0.1 mile to an informal campsite on the eastern edge of Round Pond. The shoreline is boggy and difficult to walk along. The pond is more rectangular than circular, but then few Round Ponds ever live up to their name.

The snowmobile trail continues south beyond Round Pond, climbing to a height-of-land in the next 0.4 mile. After a level stretch, you notice through the trees that the land to the east seems to drop away. You now begin a moderate descent and cross two streams. The trail levels off and 2.2 miles from Moose River Road intersects the trail to Brandy Lake, section 44. Right leads to the pond in 1.1 miles, and left leads to NY 28 in 1 mile.

McKeever

THE FIRST MILL at McKeever was built by the Moose River Lumber Company in 1891, a year before the site became a stop on the new Adirondack Railroad. It burned in 1893 but was replaced in 1895 by a larger one on higher ground above the river. The company was a partnership between Lemon Thomson and his son-in-law John Alden Dix, who clearly saw a lucrative opportunity in this intersection of the railroad and the river. By 1897 their facility was processing 25 million board feet of timber hauled all the way from Nehasane, about 39 miles away by train.

The company, which continued under Dix's management after the elder partner died in 1897, also owned land of its own along the Moose River. In 1903 it built a standard-gauge railroad extending east from the main line toward Remsen Falls, ending at a logging camp and allowing the company to harvest the area's enormous yellow birches. In 1907 a third mill was built at McKeever by Iroquois Pulp and Paper, a related enterprise with Dix serving as president. This facility converted softwood logs floated down the river into rolls of paper.

John Alden Dix's career path soon expanded from the realm of logging and paper manufacturing with a side trip into politics. He was elected governor of New York in 1910 and served in that role from January 1911 to December 1912. His administration replaced the Forest, Fish and Game Commission—which had advocated for the right to log the same Forest Preserve lands it had been charged with protecting—with the Conservation Commission, the agency that eventually grew into the modern Department of Environmental Conservation. Also in 1912, he signed legislation that defined the Adirondack Park as including all lands within its boundaries, including the private lands. Thus, in a brief span of time he laid the groundwork for the park's modern political structure.

After this stint in Albany, however, Dix's activities in McKeever began to wane. The Moose River Lumber Company went bankrupt in 1915. Its mill was closed and its railroad was abandoned. Iroquois Pulp and Paper took control of its assets and sold all of the land ranging from McKeever to Woodhull Mountain to the state in 1918. Iroquois's pulp mill and land holdings were sold to the Gould Paper Company in 1923. The mill passed through several hands over the following decades before finally closing in 1961.

Bloodsucker Pond

Waypoints along Wolf Lake Landing Road

Miles

0.0   Wolf Lake Landing Road forks right from McKeever Road, 0.2 mile from NY 28, next to former train station. *No winter maintenance beyond this point*

0.2   Tracks of the Adirondack Railroad

0.5   Road bears right through parking area, where gate is closed in spring. Left leads to second parking area, **section 48**

1.8   Intersection, foot trail to Bear Lake, **section 49**

3.6   Remsen Falls parking area, **sections 50-51**

5.0   Trail to Woodhull Lake Lean-to, **sections 53-54**

5.1   Gate at end of road near Wolf Lake Landing, **section 52**

Today there are numerous landmarks in McKeever remaining from this era. The tracks of the Adirondack Railroad are still in use, and the station survives as a private residence. All of the secondary tracks are gone, but the bed of the Moose River Lumber Company's logging railroad survives as a modern ski trail. Most impressive to motorists, perhaps, is the shell of the pulp mill that still stands beside the Moose River, in full view of the NY 28 highway bridge.

This chapter describes the state lands once owned by Dix's companies, which are now accessed by the DEC-maintained Wolf Lake Landing Road. To find it, turn onto McKeever Road from NY 28 south of the Moose River bridge. It leads into the hamlet area, now a quiet residential neighborhood, where it loops left and dead-ends. Wolf Lake Landing Road veers right near the old train station 0.2 mile from the highway. This gravel lane crosses the train tracks and reaches a parking area at 0.5 mile. It then extends for 4.6 more miles to an interior parking area 400 feet from Woodhull Lake, a total of 5.1 miles from McKeever.

Depending on the season, however, automobile access may be blocked at one of two locations. None of Wolf Lake Landing Road is plowed in the winter, for instance, meaning you will have to park on the side of McKeever Road and walk or ski across the tracks to reach state land. In the spring you can drive an additional 0.5 mile to the first parking area past the railroad tracks, where the road is usually gated during "mud season." It is only from about mid-May through the fall hunting season that you can drive to all of the interior trailheads described below.

Wolf Lake Landing Road is narrow, remote, and rough, but with care ordinary cars can drive to its end. The deep access this road provides makes this a great area for day hiking—as well as for some of the shortest overnight hiking anywhere in the Adirondacks.

48 Remsen Falls from the West

Cross-country skiing, mountain biking, hiking
3.1 miles, 1¼ hours, relatively level (spring and summer)
3.8 miles, 1½ hours, relatively level (winter)

The first route branching left from Wolf Lake Landing Road is the bed of the Moose River Lumber Company's railroad spur, which was later converted by the state into a truck trail to provide administrative access to the fire tower on Woodhull Mountain. Since the opening of Wolf Lake Landing Road as an automobile route in 2004 the railroad grade has primarily become a foot trail, favored by cross-country skiers in the winter and useful in the spring for access to Bear Lake. In the summer, however, this section is bypassed by most people in favor of the road.

In the winter, park on the side of McKeever Road near the start of Wolf Lake Landing Road. Walk or ski along the access road, which is a well-used snowmobile trail. Follow it across the tracks and into the woods to the first parking area at 0.5 mile, bearing left to a second parking area at 0.7 mile. Here there is a yellow gate, beyond which the railroad bed becomes a trail. Outside of winter, the road is easy to drive to this point.

Beyond the gate, the trail needs little description. It is a wide and obvious skier's highway through a park-like forest with a ferny understory. At a point 0.9 mile past the gate, the blue-marked foot trail to Bear Lake, section 49, turns right. The railroad grade passes two small clearings on the right that are full of bottled gentian in late August. Wetlands lie beside the roadway, which was raised to keep it level and dry. Roughly thirty minutes past the Bear Lake intersection there is a large meadow on the left with an intriguing old foundation. At 2.7 miles (3.4 miles from McKeever) you reach a four-way intersection.

From this intersection you can continue straight toward Woodhull Mountain (section 51) or right toward a trailhead on Wolf Lake Landing Road. Both of these are viable routes for skiers, but the route to the left is something that skiers in particular might not want to miss. It leads in 0.4 mile to a site on the South Branch Moose River called Remsen Falls. The wide trail descends about 100 vertical feet in a series of gentle runs that ends at a campsite next to a bend in the river. The falls are little more than a set of rapids, but the joy is in the act of getting here, not in the drama of the scenery. If the snow conditions are favorable, this can be one of the best half-day ski outings covered by this guide.

The campsite is 3.1 miles past the gate, and 3.8 miles from McKeever. There is a lean-to at Remsen Falls, but it is on the north side of the river and inaccessible from this trail in the winter.

For summer visitors, section 50 describes a route to Remsen Falls that is so much shorter that few hikers (other than railroad buffs, perhaps) will be tempted to follow this trail. It is, however, very well suited for mountain biking.

49 Bear Lake

Hiking, camping, snowshoeing
1.4 miles, 45 minutes, 435-foot elevation change (summer)
2.5 miles, 1¼ hours, 495-foot elevation change (spring)
3.2 miles, 1½ hours, 495-foot elevation change (winter)

Bear Lake is one of the star attractions for hikers in the McKeever area. Not only is this 52-acre pond a scenic destination with a good brook trout fishery and a lean-to, but it is relatively isolated from the motorized trails that loop through the rest of the region. Three trails lead to its shores—all of them groomed for foot access only—and this one from the northwest is by far the shortest and most popular.

For summer access, follow Wolf Lake Landing Road for 1.8 miles to a small clearing where brown signs indicate the crossing of a blue-marked foot trail. There is room for two cars to park on the right. The trail to Bear Lake also starts on the right, and from this trailhead it is a mere 1.4 miles to the lean-to.

However, since this trailhead is inaccessible in winter and spring, the alternate approach is to follow the ski trail described in section 48 for 0.9 mile past the last gate, and then turn right (south) on the blue-marked link trail that leads in another 0.2 mile to the summer trailhead. The total extra distance from McKeever is 1.8 miles, but this is still well within reason for snowshoe hiking.

Bear Lake Lean-to

Starting at the summer trailhead, the foot trail leads through a wet area and bears left at 0.2 mile to begin a moderate climb. One interesting feature about this region is that despite the proximity of the Moose River to the north, all of the ponds and lakes send their waters south. In the case of Bear Lake, a range of hills cradle the north shore to form the watershed divide. It is a 185-foot ascent to a height-of-land 0.6 mile from the road, followed by a 250-foot descent toward the pond. Along the way, the trail passes some impressive rock outcrops where intermittent rivulets emerge to form a sizeable inlet.

At 1.1 miles you reach a campsite on the north shore of Bear Lake, where there is a tiny "beach" suitable for swimming and launching ultralight pack canoes. The trail turns sharply left, crosses the inlet, and heads out along the east edge of the lake. Here a side trail leads left, inland, to the lean-to constructed in 2010. It faces away from the lake, but it is otherwise an attractive campsite.

The main trail continues south for 300 feet to cross a second inlet, reaching a junction at 1.4 miles. Left is the yellow-marked foot trail coming from Bloodsucker Pond, section 54. The blue-marked trail continues south to Neejer Hill and Mill Brook, section 41.

50 Remsen Falls

Short hike, camping
0.6 mile, 15 minutes, 160-foot vertical descent

Remsen Falls is a set of rapids on the South Branch Moose River—pretty, yes, but not the dramatic cascade its name suggests. This needs to be understood beforehand to avoid your disappointment upon arrival. What Remsen Falls offers is an attractive short walk along a road-like trail to a scenic bend on the river, where two tent sites await. People with mobility impairments can obtain special permits to drive vehicles on this trail, and the first campsite has been adapted for wheelchair use.

South Branch Moose River near Remsen Falls

Follow Wolf Lake Landing Road for 3.6 miles to a pull-off on the left where signs mark the start of the trail. Heading north, it begins a gentle descent to a four-way junction at 0.2 mile. The cross trail is the bed of the Moose River Lumber Company logging railroad. Left leads back toward McKeever (section 48) and right leads to Woodhull Mountain (section 51). Continuing straight, the trail continues to descend through a forest of black cherry to the modified campsite with its view of the river, 0.6 mile from Wolf Lake Landing Road. A short path leads down to a spot on the bank where boats are commonly launched.

Another path continues north alongside the river, heading downstream to a second campsite at 0.1 mile beside the rock ledge that creates Remsen Falls. This path is more rugged than the main trail, but it appears to be used frequently enough that its tread is clearly established.

The path continues downstream, leading another 0.2 mile to the next bend on the river where it resumes flowing west, opposite the mouth of Nicks Creek and the lean-to on the north shore. The only way to get across the river is by fording, and that is no small task. Indeed, even in the summer the water can be deep above and below Remsen Falls. If you are intent on getting to the shelter—and you have the means to carry a boat or canoe down from the trailhead—then the surest method is to float across.

51 Woodhull Mountain

Hiking, cross-country skiing, mountain biking
4.7 miles, 2½ hours, 750-foot vertical rise

If you travel across the width of the Black River Wild Forest east from McKeever, almost to the point where state land ends and the Adirondack League Club begins, you will find Woodhull Mountain and its fire tower. This is one of the lesser-known towers in the Adirondack Park, partly because of the length of the hike to reach it, and partly because the radio repeater installed in the cab prevents public access to the top. The summit is wooded so there are few good views without the tower.

When Wolf Lake Landing Road was opened to automobiles in 2004, the Remsen Falls trailhead became the closest public access point to the mountain. You will find it 3.6 miles from McKeever at a pull-off on the left with signs marking the start of the trail. Heading north, it begins a gentle descent to a four-way junction at 0.2 mile. The cross trail is the bed of the Moose River Lumber Company logging railroad. Left leads back toward McKeever (section 48) and straight leads to Remsen Falls (section 50).

Bear right onto the railroad grade. Just 0.4 mile past the junction you see a lumber clearing and a pond visible through the trees to the left. The 1912 USGS McKeever Quadrangle showed six buildings immediately west of the pond and the tracks ending at the north shore. Many items remain from the logging days, and some spots are suitable for camping. An earthen levee forms the north bank of the pond. It has been breached, but beavers sometime fill the gaps to maintain the water level.

The modern trail—still on the old truck trail but no longer following the railroad grade—passes south of the pond. For the next 2 miles it passes smoothly through the predominantly hardwood forest. You see small clearings and faint old roads. Then the trail enters the narrow valley of the Moose River's South Branch. After 2.7 miles of hiking, you reach the end of the truck trail in a large clearing. In dry weather you may wish to consider bicycling to this point. In the winter, skiers do venture this far all the way from McKeever.

The trail, now maintained for foot travel, crosses a stream on the east side of the clearing and passes through an area of spruce, balsam, and hemlock where many old logging roads converge. Pay close attention to the markings. The trail turns right, heading back into open hardwoods, and as it begins to ascend it turns left. If it is winter and you have skied in, you may want to change over to snowshoes here. After a gradual climb up a hill, a short descent takes you to two stream crossings and a beaver meadow visible in the woods to the south. The trail now begins a steady, moderate climb in an easterly direction to the summit, where it levels off in mixed hardwoods and spruce, 4.7 miles from Wolf Lake Landing Road or 7.9 miles if you have traveled all the way from McKeever.

After such a long journey, it is sad to behold the lonely tower, since you can no longer enjoy the vista from the top. This is unfortunate since the best views of the surrounding forest—in many cases, the only views—are from the tower. To the north, the ridges cradling the Fulton Chain Lakes trail off into the hills of the lower Moose River region. The Tug Hill Plateau with the Snow Ridge ski slopes near Turin is visible far to the northwest. The South Branch of the Moose River winds west past Remsen Falls, and to the southwest you can see an extension of Woodhull Lake. To the east, the rolling terrain surrounding the Moose River Plains leads your eye to the distant ranges of the West Canada Lake Wilderness, a view encompassing some of the wildest lands in the state. Without the tower, views are severely limited to a few rock outcrops.

Note that there is a footpath to the east. This is a private trail originating on Bisby Road, a major thoroughfare in the Adirondack League Club's preserve. For club members it is a mere 0.5-mile climb to the summit from their side of the mountain.

Woodhull Mountain overlooks a section of the Moose River that was the scene of one of the most significant Adirondack conservation battles of the past century. If you backtrack to the northeast side of the clearing at the end of the old truck trail, you can, by careful searching and by staying on the west side of Raven Run, find the remains of the old access road that runs north 0.2 mile to the river. At this point the Moose is a delightful, winding river, but it was also the proposed site of an 1800-foot-long dam that would have flooded 600 acres of Forest Preserve as well as a portion of the neighboring Adirondack League Club.

Although a similar proposal for a dam near Higley Mountain had been rejected, the Panther Mountain Dam, backed by the Black River Regulating District, seemed a near certainty in 1945. Opponents of the project included myriad conservation and sportsmen's groups, who came together as the Moose River Committee. They unapologetically lobbied state lawmakers and courted public opinion in an effort to kill the proposal and maintain the legal sanctity of the Forest Preserve. Their achievement was to convince the legislature to repeal the regulating district's authority to flood state lands by means of a constitutional amendment. The voters of the state approved this amendment in 1953, and when the U.S. Supreme Court refused to hear an appeal filed by the regulating district in 1956 the proposal was finally laid to rest.

52 Woodhull Lake

Canoeing, camping

At 5.1 miles, Wolf Lake Landing Road ends at a gate about 400 feet from Woodhull Lake, which is by far the largest body of water in the area. The clearing where the road meets the shore is called Wolf Lake Landing, and while the name seems incongruous with the setting, it actually offers two clues to the history of the area.

Wolf Lake was one of two natural water bodies that once existed side-by-side in this remote V-shaped valley. It shared a common outlet with the larger Woodhull Lake to the east, which canal engineers first surveyed in 1849 in a quest to secure water sources for a section of the Erie Canal near Rome. The first dam—a temporary structure that raised the water only 5 feet—was completed on November 9 of that year, apparently to test the rate at which the water would rise. With 4 to 5 feet of snow in the surrounding woods that winter, the dam was first observed to be overflowing on March 1. For the canal engineers, this was a favorable result.

Funding issues delayed completion of a permanent dam until 1860, when the structure was raised to a total of 18 feet. Wolf Lake was permanently engulfed by the larger Woodhull Lake, but its name was not forgotten. When a steamboat route was established on the lake in later years, its western terminus was called Wolf Lake Landing.

The landing remains the best place to launch a canoe or kayak in the summer. If the final gate on the road is open, you can drive the remaining 400 feet to the water. From there it is just a 0.2-mile paddle south to the large lean-to described in section 53. This is the only established public camping area on the lake.

Woodhull's water is relatively clear, and as you tour along the shorelines this clarity reveals a forest of downed logs from the pre-reservoir days scattered across the bottom. The builders of the Canal Lakes were generally good about clearing their flowed lands of stumps and logs, so it is interesting to speculate what the difference might have been here. Woodhull Lake was one of several reservoirs under construction in 1856 where work was suddenly halted due to a shortage of funds. Canal Commissioner Cornelius Gardinier reported that the "clearing of the flow ground" was one of only a handful of unfinished tasks at Woodhull, and suggested that if this step was skipped the cost of completion would be a "trifling expenditure." An engineer confirmed in 1858 "that the entire cost to bring this important reservoir into use, exclusive of chopping and clearing the flow ground, is $1,200." However, when the project to complete the reservoir was finally contracted out in 1859, the cost to the state was $10,818.44. Did this include the cost to clear the land? Perhaps after the passage of three years some of the timber felled in the original effort had rotted and could not be removed, and was therefore left on the ground when the reservoir was flooded.

You can of course paddle anywhere across the surface of Woodhull Lake, but state land encompasses only the west end. Most of the eastern arm is owned by the Adirondack League Club, with an array of independent properties on the north shore. This leaves boaters with no legal place to land east of Remsen Point and Brooktrout Point. Woodhull's lake trout population, however, will likely draw some fishermen to some of the deep holes found along the eastern arm.

It is interesting to go at least as far as the outlet bay where the earthen dam is located. The League Club has a small community of camps clustered at the dam's west end. According to club policy, members can paint their camps

Woodhull Lake

any color they want so long as it's either green or brown. The one exception is the State House, which is white like the similar structure at North Lake.

Note that even though the dam is a state-owned property within the Adirondack Park, there is no public access. A state attorney general ruled in 1919 that canal properties acquired before 1885 are not part of the Forest Preserve, and are therefore exempt from the "forever wild" clause of the constitution.

53 Woodhull Lake Lean-to

Snowmobile trail, hiking, camping
0.5 mile, 15 minutes, rolling terrain

The lean-to at the northwest end of Woodhull Lake, near Wolf Lake Landing, is twice as long as most Adirondack lean-tos. Conversely, the trail leading to it from the end of Wolf Lake Landing Road is only a fraction of the length of most Adirondack hikes. Therefore this is a popular destination among people who would not normally consider a longer hike, as well as families with young children. The trail is well suited for both groups.

At a point 5 miles from McKeever, or just 0.1 mile shy of the gate at the end of the road, a marked snowmobile trail veers right, south. It follows the bed of an old road on a gradual descent to a trail junction and a bridge at 0.3 mile. The yellow-marked trail right leads to Bloodsucker Pond and Bear

Lake, section 54. Immediately across the bridge, another side trail turns left. This is the route to the lean-to. The snowmobile trail continues south and southwest toward Mill Brook as described in section 40.

The last 0.2 mile on the side trail hooks southeast to approach the lean-to from behind. The shelter stands very close to the water, with rock ledges from which to swim, fish, or take in the view. The DEC inventory lists it as "organizational size," and it could easily accommodate a dozen campers and their gear.

54 Bear Lake via Bloodsucker Pond

Hiking, camping
2.2 miles, 1 hour, rolling terrain

This trail links the lean-tos at Bear and Woodhull lakes, and it is therefore probably most commonly used by campers at either end wishing to see what the other side looks like. It also factors into some of the region's loop hike possibilities. Overall, it is not used very often and the tread can be faint as a result. By the same token, it provides a good sense of seclusion for the brief hour it takes to traverse it from one end to the other.

The east end is located 0.3 mile south of Wolf Lake Landing Road along the trail to the Woodhull Lake Lean-to, section 53. It leads west immediately north of the bridge over Bloodsucker Pond's outlet, bringing you to the pond itself in just 0.1 mile. You have to step off the trail and bushwhack about 200 feet to find the best view, which can be enjoyed from the tip of a small promontory on the north shore. It is easy to imagine this boggy place living up to its name during the spring black fly season.

The west end of the trail begins near the east shore of Bear Lake, south of the lean-to and beside a prominent inlet stream. Either one of the trails described in sections 41 and 49 will bring you to this junction. The prettiest section from this side might be the first 0.6 mile, which pass alongside the stream.

The middle portions of the trail pass pleasantly but uneventfully. At one point it is routed to within 350 feet of Wolf Lake Landing Road, but the remainder is satisfyingly remote. Since Woodhull Lake is higher in elevation than Bear, there is a slight advantage in hiking it east to west—but the grades encountered in the opposite direction are hardly imposing.

Minnehaha

FOR MANY YEARS, the primary route into the Moose River headwater region was Brown's Tract Road. Originally constructed in 1817, it began at Boonville and led northeast through the lower portions of John Brown's Tract for which it was named, to the settlements that eventually became Thendara and Old Forge. Despite its prominence, the northern half quickly fell into disrepair and apparently remained that way for most of the nineteenth century. The road was impassable to carriages, and for many years travelers needed to ford the Moose River. By all accounts, traversing the route was not an easy task. It was traveled frequently by foot, by horse, and by buckboard wagon, but the experience was never regarded fondly.

The road was so rough that it inspired several commentators to malign it in prose. In 1855 it was traveled by a party that included Lady Amelia M. Murray, maid of honor to Queen Victoria, and Horatio Seymour, who had just concluded his first term as New York's governor. Brown's Tract Road was their exit route from the woods after a traverse of the Adirondacks from Elizabethtown. In Murray's written account of the trip, the road clearly made an impression:

> The path we had to follow was a road cut through the forest fifty years ago; planks had been laid down and corduroy bridges made; but, as no settlement followed, left to entire neglect, the rotten timbers only made bad worse; and I imagine that it would be impossible to find anywhere a tract so difficult to get over as that through which we patiently laboured for ten consecutive hours. Mr. Seymour's patience and good humour never gave way. Putting off the packages on his back, he now extricated one companion, now another, from a boggy 'fix.'

George Washington Sears, writing under the pen name Nessmuk for *Forest and Stream* magazine in 1883, described the road as "thirteen and one half miles of muddy, rock trail," or more bluntly, "a muddy ditch." He likened it to a purgatory that one must pass through to reach the paradise of the Fulton Chain.

His preferred route bypassed as much of the road as possible. In 1880 he described a trail that branched off Brown's Tract Road toward Jones' Camp, a "comfortable log camp (or house)" located at the foot of a stillwater on the Middle Branch of the Moose River. The owner, Albert Jones, kept half a dozen boats on site and took in boarders "at most reasonable rates." From Jones' Camp, Nessmuk could paddle his canoe up the river to the Forge House, thus eliminating the need to be jostled along the northern half of Brown's Tract Road.

Other interests sought to replace the road altogether. In 1889—several years after Albert Jones' death and Nessmuk's last visit to the Adirondacks—Jones' Camp found itself at the eastern end of a new railroad. Officially known as the Fulton Chain Railroad, its wooden rails and trestles earned it the nickname "Peg Leg." The line was built by Dr. Alexander Crosby and Samuel Garmon, who had just purchased the Forge House, and Gordias Henry P. Gould, the founder of the Gould Paper Company and the owner of the southern half of Township 1, where the line was to be primarily located.

Passengers boarded the railroad at Moose River and disembarked about 6 or 7 miles later at Jones' Camp. To complete the journey to the Forge House, riders then transferred to a small steamboat called the *Fawn* operated by the deCamp family. Local blacksmith Leonard Ingersoll served as its inaugural engineer. Perhaps for the sake of the tourists, the name of the landing was changed to Minnehaha, a reference to Longfellow's popular 1855 poem *The Song of Hiawatha*. Small dams helped deepen the river, and a lock carried the Fawn over the river's one major rise.

But the Peg Leg was only in service for three seasons before its usefulness was permanently eclipsed by the much larger Adirondack Railroad in 1892, which followed the river through Minnehaha. The *Fawn* continued to operate for a few years more by offering pleasure cruises on the Moose River, but now that tourists could ride in modern comfort from any point along the New York Central system all the way to the Fulton Chain train station, interest in the steamboat quickly waned.

Today, state lands and conservation easements surround Minnehaha on the north, south, and west. These include parcels once owned by Gould and the deCamps, as well as portions of the Peg Leg and Brown's Tract Road. The exact route of the wooden railroad is a matter of conjecture since the line did not survive long enough to appear on detailed topographic maps. But portions of Brown's Tract Road remain clearly defined. Its reversion to a foot trail has only improved its condition, and as you hike it today you may wonder what all the fuss was about in the nineteenth century.

All of the excursions described in this chapter begin at two easy-to-find

View of Bare Mountain from Six Mile Hill

trailheads on NY 28, located diagonally across the road from each other. But despite their prominence, you will find they are not heavily used.

Nelson Lake Trailhead: A sign on the east side of NY 28 marks a driveway leading into state land 2.9 miles north of McKeever and 6.8 miles south of Thendara. You can drive it for 350 feet to a parking area near a gate. The continuing road, closed to public motor vehicles, leads to a private inholding but can be used for foot access to Nelson Falls and Nelson Lake, sections 55 and 56. The parking area is not plowed in winter.

John Brown Tract Easement Trailheads: Just 0.1 mile north of the Nelson Lake trailhead, a brown DEC sign on the west side of NY 28 marks the start of an access road. The trail to Gull Lake, section 57, begins at the very first parking area on the left. Follow the access road right and continue for 0.5 mile to a parking area on the right. The second trailhead begins as a side road 100 feet further on the left. This is the access trail to the Ha-de-ron-dah Wilderness, sections 58 through 60. Note that this access road (which is an older segment of NY 28) is not plowed in winter, and is in fact a major snowmobile corridor. To access the foot trails on skis or snowshoes, you would need to park on the highway and follow the snowmobile tracks.

55 Nelson Falls

Path

The Middle Branch of the Moose River passes through a turbulent series of rapids and rocky steps at a bend 2.8 miles north of its confluence with the South Branch. Although it is not a falls in the true sense of the word, Nelson Falls commands the respect of the whitewater enthusiasts who run this section—and those who choose to portage around it. During the summer months it is an attractive spot with rocky slabs that invite picnicking, and pools that beckon bathers and anglers. Giant cedars shelter the banks near the falls.

Beginning at the Nelson Lake trailhead, follow the continuing road past the gate. Bear left at 0.1 mile, and at 0.3 mile cross the tracks of the Adirondack Railroad. The route forks immediately past the tracks, with the more obvious roadbed bearing left to the site of a long-gone bridge across the river. Look for the herd path that continues upstream between the tracks and the rapids, becoming vague where large rocks fill the woods.

In 0.4 mile the path returns you to the railroad tracks next to a bridge over

Nelson Lake

the river. Except that the resumption of regular rail service has made walking across the bridge dangerous, this would be the best way across the river. On the far side there is a good herd path leading along the falls downstream, right, with numerous opportunities to view the rapids. It can be followed for 0.4 mile from the bridge to the snowmobile trail from Bisby Road, section 81. A right turn here will bring you in less than a mile to Nelson Lake.

56 Nelson Lake via the Moose River

Canoe route accessible by short hike, camping, fishing

Below Nelson Falls, the Middle Branch Moose River briefly changes its tempo and flows calmly for about three-quarters of a mile. Nelson Lake lies a half mile to the east and its wide outlet converges with the river in this section. By carrying a canoe down the old road from the Nelson Lake trailhead, you can easily launch into this waterway and enjoy either a three-hour trip or a weekend outing.

Beginning at the Nelson Lake trailhead, follow the continuing road past the gate. At 0.3 mile cross the tracks of the Adirondack Railroad and bear right on the short trail that leads down to a side channel of the river below the foot of the rapids, 0.4 mile and 10 minutes from the parking area. You can launch a canoe here, although you may find obstacles such as beaver dams blocking the passage into the main channel of the river.

Nelson Lake

A lazy current carries you along the river, where there could be signs of beaver and muskrat. Herd paths approach the water's edge and a variety of tracks can be discovered. Ducks and great blue herons frequently rise up from along the grassy banks, and belted kingfishers and cedar waxwings swoop through the air overhead.

About 0.6 mile downstream the river bends right, and by 0.7 mile it drops to a series of rapids that continue all the way to the confluence with the South Branch near McKeever. Turn left at the bend and you will be pointed into the Nelson Lake outlet. As you paddle into this quarter-mile-long channel, you may notice blue trail markers off in the woods to the right. This is a seldom-used route to Remsen Falls, as described in section 82.

You paddle to the right of a marshy backwater area, and then the channel narrows. In midsummer it is filled with pickerelweed. You can easily negotiate around the few rocks and logs at the outlet, which soon opens up onto the lake itself. Your eye is drawn up the length of the lake to the northeast where the wooded dome of Little Roundtop rises in the distance. Red-tailed hawks patrol the skies above and you may see a playful otter bobbing in the water near a swampy bay to the right. The southeastern shore becomes rugged, with large rocks extending out into the water. The northwest shore is brushy in places and blue flag irises are found there in early summer. A few stands of conifers lie in the lower areas where the ground tends to be wetter, but the forest cover is otherwise dominated by maturing hardwoods.

There are two campsites at Nelson. One is located on the west shore about 0.2 mile north of the outlet, where you will find a lean-to set several hundred feet back from the water. The second campsite is at the northeastern end, a choice spot for swimming, picnicking, and relaxing in the sun. Here you will find a sandy beach and a rocky point, with herd paths leading inland to the trail system from Bisby Road and Nicks Lake, sections 80 and 81.

57 Gull Lake

Snowmobile trail, hiking, snowshoeing
0.5 mile, 15 minutes, 100-foot vertical rise

Nessmuk referred to this pond as Little Gull Lake, and that is perhaps a fair description. Not to be confused with the larger Gull Lake near Woodgate, this one lies just a short distance above NY 28 on the John Brown Tract Easement and makes for a pleasant diversion. The trail is short and entails few difficulties, other than the occasional fallen log perhaps.

As you pull off the highway onto the John Brown Tract Easement access road described in the chapter introduction, the Gull Lake trailhead is immediately on the left. Following red markers, the hiking trail follows the route of a wide snowmobile trail, from which most of the rocks have been removed to allow better grooming in the winter. These rocks now line both sides of the trail.

After climbing 0.2 mile and less than 100 feet, the foot trail turns right off the snowmobile trail, which continues south toward the pond's outlet without offering any views. The foot trail is now a narrow woodland path leading northwest across a hilltop, eventually hooking left to end at a cove on the north shore.

Though its easternmost point is barely a quarter mile from the highway, Gull has the appearance of a wild and secluded place deep in the backcountry. With a pack canoe, you could extend your visit with an exploration of its islands and hidden coves.

58 Middle Settlement Lake from the South

Hiking, camping, snowshoeing
3.6 miles, 1¾ hours, rolling terrain (summer)
4.1 miles, 2 hours, rolling terrain (winter)

Middle Settlement Lake is an enchanting little body of water that is popularly regarded as the heart of the Ha-de-ron-dah Wilderness, even though geographically it lies well south of center. Of the two routes that lead to it from NY 28, this one is used the least—perhaps because it is less visible from the highway. It is 0.5 mile longer than the better-known route described in section 62, but it lacks the steep climb that marks the beginning of that trail. Otherwise, the scenic qualities of both routes are similar.

To find the trail, follow the John Brown Tract Easement access road for 0.5 mile from the south to a small parking area. The trail starts 100 feet further north as an old logging road on the left (west) side. As mentioned earlier, this access road is not plowed in the winter, and snowshoeing or skiing it adds half a mile to the one-way journey.

Beginning at the summer trailhead, hike up the logging road past an enormous white rock to a trail register on the left, at the start of the yellow-marked foot trail. After a short rise, the trail levels and crosses multiple logging roads. Pay very close attention to the markers as you pass through these easement lands, because some of the intersecting roads could be misleading.

You cross into state land, and at 0.9 mile the first leg of the footpath ends at a junction with the primitive Copper Lake Road, an ATV trail that crosses the Forest Preserve to reach a private inholding. The route to Middle Settlement turns left and follows this road for 0.4 mile, a distance that for most people will be long enough. Signs clearly mark where the foot trail bears right off the road and into wilder terrain. The ATV trail continues west for another 1.4 miles before entering private land around Copper Lake.

First, though, pause before leaving the intersection. The diverging foot trail is actually the bed of the old Brown's Tract Road, the northern half of which has been incorporated into the Ha-de-ron-dah trail system. Turning the other way, however, you will see there has been no maintenance to the southwest in many years. This ancient wagon road—once the main overland route to the Fulton Chain region—is now little more than a linear depression in the forest floor. This is what natural growth will do to even the most prominent of thoroughfares if given the opportunity!

Turning northeast off the ATV trail, you enter Ha-de-ron-dah and follow the Brown's Tract Trail for 0.2 mile, dropping to cross a small stream in a rocky glen. The trail climbs to another junction at 1.5 miles where the trail to Middle Settlement Lake forks left. The old wagon road continues right, as described in section 60.

Still following yellow DEC markers, you are now once again on a true foot trail. It steadily ascends away from the junction through a scenic hardwood forest with large rocks lying about. Wet areas and occasional blowdown slow your pace, but fifteen minutes from the junction you reach an attractive little vly. The trail turns right to follow its edge, crosses a small inlet at 2.1 miles, and then climbs away on the other side.

Rolling terrain takes you to a stream crossing at 2.5 miles. Rounding the shoulder of a hill, you begin a steady descent to the edge of Middle Settlement Lake's southwestern end. From here, the trail works its way clockwise around the bay to a junction with the blue-marked trail to Lost Lake, section 59. This point is 3.1 miles from the trailhead.

The yellow trail bears right to follow along the north shore of Middle Settlement. The woods are so open that there is little to obstruct the view. At 3.4 miles you reach a log bridge over the outlet, not far below the massive beaver dam that enlarges the lake. The 1958 USGS McKeever Quadrangle shows the lake as two smaller ponds surrounded by open wetlands, a configuration that would surely return if the beavers were to ever abandon this structure. Across the bridge, the trail crosses a knoll and descends toward the Middle Settlement Lake Lean-to at 3.6 miles.

Located on a rock ledge that commands an excellent view of the pond, this is the most highly prized campsite in the vicinity. The fishing and swimming opportunities are good, and you will likely have a pair of loons for company. It is a rare weekend that passes without someone visiting this spot, if only to stop for lunch. Like many such favorite campsites, firewood can be scarce.

There is a small island across from the lean-to with a low hill above the far shore. One of the more unusual aspects of Middle Settlement Lake (and a few other neighboring lakes too) is the fact that the surrounding woods are so open. With only a handful of red spruce and white pine trees at the water's edge, the maple forest across the lake may seem bare and exposed compared to other Adirondack lakes and ponds.

Section 62 describes the continuing trail around the north end of the lake, which originates at the Scusa Trailhead on NY 28.

59 Lost Lake to Pine Lake

Hiking, camping, snowshoeing
3.6 miles, 1¾ hours, rolling terrain

The trail to Pine Lake via Lost Lake has a very wild character. It is one of the remoter trails in the Ha-de-ron-dah Wilderness, and since it does not receive as much use it will seem a bit fainter. It passes through varying terrain as it connects the popular destinations at both ends, with a few wet areas, several short-but-steep hills, and park-like stands of black cherry along the way. Lost Lake, Middle Branch Creek, and East Pine Pond all make scenic waypoints.

From the junction at the west end of Middle Settlement Lake, 3.1 miles from the conservation easement trailhead and 0.5 mile west of the lean-to as described in section 58, the blue-marked trail leads west through a rocky landscape. You may see or hear ravens near the jagged rock outcroppings to the north. The mixed forest becomes denser as you drop to step across a small brook at 0.6 mile. The twin beaver flows to the north and south will appear either dismal or attractive, depending on the condition of the dams. You circle around the foot of the northern pond and enter a swampy area, which you must cautiously cross on fallen logs.

Back on dry ground, you reach a sign marking the Herkimer-Lewis county line at 0.8 mile. (Comparing its location to USGS maps, the sign may be about 450 feet too far to the west.) The trail continues west until it draws near Lost Lake at 1.2 miles, where it angles north. A rocky hump hidden in the woods to the left of this bend provides decent views for people willing to make the short bushwhack.

View from the Middle Settlement Lake Lean-to

For the next 0.2 mile the trail loops around the northeast end of the lake, with several opportunities to stop and enjoy the views. The pond is flanked by large rock bluffs, and if the beaver dam is intact then this could be a beautiful place. As of 2012, however, the dam has been out for several years and Lost Lake is quite shallow as a result.

At 1.4 miles the trail crosses the outlet atop a rocky cascade. It makes a long U-turn through a narrow valley with an old beaver dam on the left at 1.5 miles, and then it traverses the foot of a broad hillside. You will notice the hardwoods getting thinner as the forest floor becomes grassy. The basin of Middle Branch Creek becomes visible through the trees to the right, and then the trail climbs a bank overlooking its extensive wetlands. A very steep drop brings you to an elaborate wood-and-steel bridge spanning the creek at 2.3 miles, with the water flowing lazily below.

Black cherry trees dominate the landscape, with a park-like growth of ferns underneath. This persists for about 15 minutes, and then the forest character abruptly changes. Dense spruce and balsam (with a few pines intermixed) lead you to a small wet area crossed by the remains of an old boardwalk. Tunneling through the evergreens, the trail pitches up onto an esker revealing East Pine Pond on the other side at 3 miles. Its low, shrubby shoreline and floating plants would seem to be ideal moose habitat.

Dropping off the esker, the trail crosses the outlet on a second wood-and-steel bridge at 3.2 miles. This one spans the sluggish outlet of East Pine Pond. Scotch pines grow in the sandy soil beyond the bridge, and as you enter the tall woods again, take time to notice the large poplars. All of these tree varieties—the cherries, the Scotch pines, the poplars—are considered "pioneer" species, meaning that they are among the first to inhabit an area that has been burned. In this case, the disturbance was the large forest fire that swept through the Ha-de-ron-dah region in 1903. East Pine Pond reappears briefly on your right, with a small tent site located on a bank above its marshy shore.

Pine Lake is visible to the left. A faint path leads along its eastern edge through pines and gray birches to an open view of the water. The blue-marked trail ends just ahead at a junction 3.6 miles from Middle Settlement Lake. The cross route is the snowmobile trail from Partridgeville Road to Big Otter Lake described in sections 91 and 92. If you turn left, it is just 0.2 mile around the north end of Pine Lake, past a tent site, to a side trail leading inland to the Pine Lake Lean-to.

60 South End of the Brown's Tract Trail

Hiking, snowshoeing, cross-country skiing
1.9 miles, 1 hour, rolling terrain

Because this section of Brown's Tract Trail does not lead directly to any

Middle Settlement Creek

specific destination or create any shortcuts, its value is largely limited to its historical significance. It does, however, link the two main routes to Middle Settlement Lake into a potential 8.6-mile loop beginning and ending at the John Brown Tract Easement. It also provides access to the scenic bushwhack

(Continued on page 132)

A Note About
Middle Settlement Clearing

THE SITE LABELED by DEC as "Middle Settlement Clearing" on the Brown's Tract Trail next to Middle Settlement Creek warrants further mention. Two explanations exist for its origin, both of them potentially tied to the naming of nearby Middle Settlement Creek and Middle Settlement Lake. While they do sound plausible on the surface, neither is supported by the rich historical record surrounding Brown's Tract Road.

The location of the clearing roughly corresponds with the description of John Brown's "Middle Settlement" provided by historian Charles E. Snyder, who wrote in 1896, "The remains of three houses are said to be still discernible in the woods, about six miles west of the Fulton chain" in Township 1. At the time of Brown's death in 1803, the Middle Settlement consisted of two cabins, a barn, and some cleared land as itemized in his will. But Snyder cautioned that few other records existed of the Middle Settlement, and that some

of the information he was citing was "a mere tradition among a few old people." He had not seen any of the ruins himself.

David Beetle, a columnist for the Utica *Observer-Dispatch* who hiked Brown's Tract Road in 1947, wrote that the clearing was the site of a "Middle Settlement House" that "briefly competed with Arnold's," a boarding house located at the north end of the road from 1837 until about 1873. No further information on this establishment, including the author's source, is offered.

During its heyday from 1817 through 1889 many travelers wrote about their travels along Brown's Tract Road, some in great detail. A correspondent of Jeptha Simms named W. S. Benchley insisted in 1848 that there were no clearings or habitations between Moose River Settlement and Arnold's, and that the intervening distance was "very well covered with timber, such as spruce, balsam, beech, birch, some maple and hemlock."

Simms assumed the name "Middle Settlement" referred to the Herreshoff residence in Township 7, which later became Arnold's.

In an 1859 edition of *Harper's New Monthly Magazine*, T. B. Thorpe described in detail the rustic mile markers that he passed along Brown's Tract Road and how the "continued shade of the trees" made him feel stressed and tired. His mood did not lift again until his party finally reached the "neglected clearings" near the far end of the road, at Arnold's. If he had encountered the remains of the Middle Settlement or a boarding house erected in its place, it certainly would've warranted a paragraph or two in this descriptive writer's article.

Likewise, had Lady Amelia Murray (1855) or Nessmuk (1883) encountered an establishment of any kind offering shelter or provisions, they would surely have availed themselves of its services.

Therefore this utter lack of firsthand commentary from four observant writers makes it seem doubtful that this was the true location of the Middle Settlement, and even less likely that there was ever a commercial establishment of any kind along this part of the road.

As for the small clearing that does obviously exist today next to Middle Settlement Creek, it should be remembered that this entire part of the forest was swept by fire in 1903. If the old forest was burned away, then a clearing that existed prior to that date would not be recreated by the returning growth. Therefore it seems more likely that this clearing was a product of human activities in the twentieth century, perhaps even after state acquisition in 1909.

Two last wrinkles in this story come from Edwin R. Wallace, who for many years published an annual guidebook to the Adirondacks beginning in 1872. He claimed that Middle Settlement Lake "takes its name from a clearing once made near it mid-way, on the Deacon Abbey road," referring to a route that led to Copper Lake from the west. Preceding this passage, however, is an allusion "to the famous Middle Clearing Spring Hole," located on the Middle Branch Moose River and reached from Brown's Tract Road by turning onto a side trail "60 rods beyond the '6 mile tree.'" This raises the distinct possibility that the real Middle Settlement was not on the road but on the river, near the mouth of Middle Settlement Creek, where people were indeed living at the time. Today this area is known as Minnehaha.

(Continued from page 129)

up Six Mile Hill described in section 61. Its one distinguishing feature is the crossing of Middle Settlement Creek, which is the one location that does live up to the nineteenth century hyperbole quoted in this chapter's introduction. The remainder of this 1.9-mile segment passes without much fanfare.

Beginning at the junction 1.5 miles from the easement trailhead along the southern approach to Middle Settlement Lake, section 58, the old roadbed bears right, northeast, and begins a 100-foot climb. Note the parallel tracks indicating the road had been slightly rerouted on this slope. It then levels off in an open forest of black cherries that lasts for less than a mile but still seems monotonous. The metal components of one old buckboard lie to the side of the trail, partly covered by leaves.

The trail approaches a large beaver flow on Middle Settlement Creek on the right with the slopes of Six Mile Hill on the left. From the base of the hill there is no indication of the open ledges above. Pieces of ancient corduroy are exposed in the trail. The foot trail detours uphill briefly where the old roadbed disappears into the wetland, but the two routes are soon reunited. At 1.5 miles the trail bears right toward the wetland, with the site known as Middle Settlement Clearing to the left. See the historical note on pages 130-131 regarding this site.

Now angling southeast, the trail ventures out into the wide beaver flow. This crossing looks disastrous at first, and indeed a dry crossing is often not possible. There are parts of an old beaver dam, hummocks of grass, and the occasional log that can be used as stepping points, but the gaps in this network may require a change in footwear. Overall, this rugged crossing is adequate for the small number of hikers that are likely to come this way, but it is easy to see why someone traveling by buckboard would have been less appreciative.

Once past the vly, it is a quick 0.3-mile walk to the next trail junction at 1.9 miles. The Brown's Tract Trail continues right, east, toward the Okara Lakes and the Scusa Trailhead, 1.5 miles away. Left leads to the north end of Middle Settlement Lake and its lean-to, which is 1.6 miles distant. Both directions are described in section 62.

61 Six Mile Hill

Bushwhack

Waypoints along Brown's Tract Road were marked by "mile trees," on which the remaining distances to the next settlement were inscribed on patches of exposed heartwood. An illustration of the "seven mile tree" accompanied an article by T. B. Thorpe in the July 1859 issue of *Harper's New Monthly Magazine*. Not only was he amused by the crude writing, but he also doubted their accuracy. "Honestly registered miles they were," he quipped, "with many rods and roods thrown in no doubt for Christian measure."

None of these "mile trees" have survived, of course, and their precise locations are unknown. The "six mile tree" was roughly the halfway point between Moose River Settlement and Arnold's. Nearby was a side trail to the Moose River, a spring, and a landmark called Six Mile Hill. Modern measurements of the road suggest that it was probably near the beaver flow on Middle Settlement Creek described in section 60. If so, then the hill looming 230 feet above the flow immediately west of Middle Settlement Clearing could very well be Six Mile Hill.

Although not visible from below, the summit ridge is a bald knob of lichen-covered rock that extends for several hundred feet, probably the result of the 1903 forest fire that swept through much of Ha-de-ron-dah. The hillside is so gentle that you can approach it from any point along Brown's Tract Trail where it parallels the flow, although the northeastern and southwestern flanks are the most advisable ascent routes. The off-trail hiking distance is a minimum of 0.1 mile.

The views are best from the southwest end of the bald, suffering only from a lack of foreground interest (treetops completely hide all views of the beaver flow at the foot of the hill). The most recognizable landmarks are Tamarack Lake to the south, Bare Mountain to the east (which as you can see is not bare at all), and the radio tower on Flatrock Mountain to the southeast. Only one short stretch of NY 28 is visible amidst this sea of trees.

There is a second bald knob a short distance to the north, at the far side of a swampy vale. It is fun to climb but offers no views. In both cases, it is imperative that hikers do their best to avoid stepping on the fragile lichens.

Ha-de-ron-dah Wilderness: Scusa Trailhead

THE SPRING OF 1903 had been alarmingly dry. From April 17 to June 7 only trace amounts of rain fell in the North Country, making conditions ripe for fires. Indeed, from April 20 until June 8 over 600,000 acres of forest were burned in what was undoubtedly the worst fire season in the Adirondacks. A report published by the federal Bureau of Forestry in 1904 claimed there had been thousands of fires burning in the Adirondacks that spring, many of them relatively small but with several exceeding 10,000 acres in size.

A variety of causes were suspected, including arson in certain instances, as well as smudge fires built by fishermen seeking protection from black flies. The most common culprits, however, were sparks emitted from locomotives. The report charged that the railroad operators had not only been indifferent to the danger, they had flaunted it by running heavy loads of freight that resulted in greater amounts of exhaust. The author considered this an "inexcusable negligence," since existing state laws required locomotives to be equipped with spark arresters.

The Adirondack Railroad alone triggered several fires in the western woods, including one west of Old Forge that burned parts of Townships 1, 2, and 7 of John Brown's Tract. It likely started in the vicinity of Minnehaha and Onekio, and then fanned northeast and northwest in two separate thrusts. The narrower northeastern arm extended to the hills near East Pond before eventually dying, but the northwestern arm laid bare a wide swath of forest. Judging by the 1912 USGS McKeever Quadrangle, the expansion of this fire was not hindered until it reached the natural obstacles of Otter Lake, Otter Creek, and South Inlet. The Bureau of Forestry estimated the extent of the entire fire to be 10,000 acres; later estimates placed it at 25,000 acres.

Much of this land had until recently been owned by Julia Lyon deCamp, who in 1886 inherited it from her father, Lyman Lyon. Her holdings extended from Middle Settlement Lake in the west to First Lake in the east, and it included Nicks Lake and several miles of the Moose River. In 1893 she had designated the tract a private preserve, partitioned into four regions called Wilderness Park, North Park, South Park, and East Park. A report

View of Lake Easka from Cross Hill

by the state's Forest Commission that same year, a decade before the fire, described the property favorably, stating that the "greater part of the land is well timbered with an almost primeval forest containing various species of hard and soft timber."

Wilderness Park and North Park were the sections most impacted by the fire. Roughly a third of North Park was burned, and only a few patches of Wilderness Park escaped unscathed. In 1909 Julia deCamp's son and heir, Lyon deCamp, sold these burned areas to the state. This acreage included Middle Settlement Lake, Grass Pond, Blackfoot Pond, and several miles of Brown's Tract Road.

Today this area is known as the Ha-de-ron-dah Wilderness, and it is perhaps the most popular hiking destination in the Thendara region. Though it was pieced together from properties "discarded" soon after the 1903 fire, few modern visitors have cause for complaint. Only indirect evidence remains of the burn, mostly in the consistency of certain forest stands. There are pockets throughout Ha-de-ron-dah where the only trees are black cherries, which you will recognize by their scaly bark and graceful forms. These are one of several "pioneer" tree species that flourished when the land was cleared. The cherry stands are frequently accompanied by grassy or fern-filled understories, in contrast with the woody brush usually found in unburned stands. Many of the trees have reached impressive heights.

The name Ha-de-ron-dah is popularly believed to be the native word that European settlers corrupted into "Adirondack." The usual translation is "bark eater," and it refers to the story of an Algonquin attack on the Iroquois. According to the version told by Alfred Billings Street in 1869, the attackers were repelled and driven north through the eastern Adirondacks where they sued for peace. This was granted by the Iroquois, "who taunted them by saying that they had become so weak and powerless they could not kill game but had been forced to eat trees." The Iroquois in this story were most likely Mohawks, who were also known to eat bark during severe winters. It should be noted that the Mohawk spelling of "bark eater" is *ron de ron deh*, pronounced "lon-de-loon-deh."

The Ha-de-ron-dah trail system is groomed exclusively for foot travel and connects all of the area's major ponds. Two of those ponds feature lean-tos, and they are by far the most popular destinations. This chapter describes the trails accessible from Ha-de-ron-dah's most prominent trailhead, located near the Okara Lakes on NY 28. Called the Scusa Trailhead after the previous landowner, Paul Scusa, it is located opposite a large DOT parking area 5.7 miles north of McKeever and 2.8 miles south of the Thendara train station. The parking area is maintained all year long.

62 Middle Settlement Lake

Hiking, camping, snowshoeing, cross-country skiing
3.1 miles, 1½ hours, 110-foot initial climb, rolling terrain thereafter

The most popular hike in the Ha-de-ron-dah Wilderness is this route to Middle Settlement Lake. The attraction is a handsome pond with a scenic lean-to perched atop a rock ledge, deep enough into the woods to offer a sense of seclusion but near enough to be within the comfort limits of many hikers. Loons return to its waters every year, and beavers do their part to keep the pond enlarged for the enjoyment of all.

The route to the lake is not a single trail, but a sequence of trails with three key turns. Beginning at the Scusa Trailhead, the first trail quickly reaches a steep hillside. The 110-foot climb to its nearly bald summit is perhaps the steepest ascent of any trail in Ha-de-ron-dah, and because it occurs so early in the hike—before you have had a chance to warm up—it never fails to feel tiring. It is unavoidable, however, since private land to the right and left leaves few other routing options.

Soon after crossing the rocky summit, the trail hooks right past a yellow post, which marks a corner in the state land boundary. At 0.6 mile this first section ends at a junction with a yellow-marked trail; bear left for Middle Settlement. The route to the right leads to Cedar and Grass ponds as described in section 66.

Heading generally west, you are now following one of the more obvious sections of Brown's Tract Road, now called the Brown's Tract Trail. This 0.9-mile section provides a good sense of what the road was like: a narrow trail through unbroken woods; rough for wheeled vehicles perhaps, but perfectly fine for foot traffic. This was once the most direct link between Old Forge and the outside world, and from 1886 to 1888 it even featured a telephone wire strung through the trees. Only a few wet areas are encountered, none of which are causes for alarm.

Signs mark the second trail junction at 1.5 miles. Here, the Brown's Tract Trail continues straight toward Middle Settlement Creek, section 60. Bear right for Middle Settlement Lake onto a trail with blue markers. At 1.8 miles it dips through a low area near the head of a beaver meadow that lies to your right. As the trail ascends the next hillside there are views of the meadow through the trees; the meadow is sometimes a pond depending on the status of the dams.

A very gradual climb of 120 feet leads to a height-of-land in a forest of maple and birch, followed by a descent to the third trail junction at 2.6

Campsite at Middle Settlement Lake

miles. This is one of the most visually interesting parts of the hike. The junction is located at the foot of a rocky ridge with massive boulders at its foot, all of which are fragments that have broken off the steep rock wall behind them. The yellow trail bearing right leads to Cedar Pond, section 64, but you may want to walk the first 100 feet to a "cave." This is actually a crawlspace under one of the wayward boulders that is just big enough to serve as an ad hoc shelter.

Bearing left at the junction, the trail reaches the muddy northeastern tip of Middle Settlement Lake. It veers right past the last of the boulders to circle around the lake's north shore, generally staying within sight of the water. You may not notice the poorly marked trail to the overlook, section 63, but the side trails leading left to two prominent tent sites are hard to miss.

At 3.1 miles the trail reaches the lean-to. Located on a rock ledge that commands an excellent view of the pond, this is the most highly prized campsite in the vicinity. The fishing and swimming opportunities are good, and you will likely have a pair of loons for company. It is a rare weekend that passes without someone visiting this spot, if only to stop for lunch. Like many such favorite campsites, firewood can be scarce.

There is a small island across from the lean-to with a low hill above the far shore. One of the more unusual aspects of Middle Settlement Lake (and a few other neighboring lakes too) is the fact that the surrounding woods are so open. With only a handful of red spruce and white pine trees at the water's edge, the maple forest across the lake may seem bare and exposed compared to other Adirondack lakes and ponds.

Section 58 describes the continuing trail around the southeast end of the lake, which originates at the John Brown Tract Easement trailhead on NY 28 near Minnehaha.

63 Middle Settlement Overlook

Hiking, snowshoeing
0.1 mile, 5 minutes, 100-foot vertical rise

A ledge northeast of Middle Settlement Lake once offered a view over its waters, and it was reached by a short side trail just 0.4 mile east of the lean-to. The ledge is still perfectly bare, but the surrounding trees have grown tall enough to block all views of the lake. Interest in the trail has therefore waned, and maintenance has become infrequent. The start of the trail near the northeast end of the lake may not be easy to spot, but it follows old red markers northeast, looping around to approach the ledge from behind. Only the nearby hilltops are now visible above the trees.

64 Middle Settlement Lake to Cedar Pond Junction

Hiking, snowshoeing
1 mile, 30 minutes, rolling terrain

This trail section leads from the junction at the northeast end of Middle Settlement Lake, section 62, to a junction near Cedar Pond with the trails described in sections 65 and 66. This connectivity among the various trails is what makes Ha-de-ron-dah so fun to explore, since it is easy to plan loops and through hikes. The link described here factors into several such trip-planning possibilities.

Beginning near the foot of the cliff at Middle Settlement Lake, it follows yellow markers past the "cave"—really just a crawlspace underneath an enormous rock—and leads northeast out of the valley. Once clear of the hill it angles north. At 0.6 mile, just 15 minutes into the hike, the trail reaches the side of a small creek that can be aflame with cardinal flowers in late July and August. Though easy to step across in the summer, it is wide enough and deep enough to require a change of footwear at other times of the year. Winter hikers should approach this crossing skeptically, because it is impassable if not sufficiently frozen.

Once on the far side, the trail turns right and parallels the north bank for a brief time. There are imperfect views of Cedar Pond a quarter-mile away in the midst of a small wetland complex, and at 1 mile you reach the junction where a lean-to once stood. The red-marked trail to the right leads back toward the Okara Lakes, section 66, and the yellow-marked trail left leads to the lean-to at Middle Branch Lake, which is 1.1 miles away as described in section 65.

65 Cedar Pond Junction to Middle Branch Lake

Hiking, snowshoeing, camping
1.1 miles, 30 minutes, rolling terrain

Middle Branch Lake is second only to Middle Settlement in terms of popularity among Ha-de-ron-dah's various landmarks, and of the two it is perhaps the quieter alternative. Because there are two ways you can reach this lake and its lean-to from the Scusa Trailhead, this section only describes the final section from Cedar Pond Junction. If you follow the western side of the loop described in sections 62 and 64, the overall hiking distance to Middle Branch Lake is 4.7 miles. If you take the eastern trail described in section 66 the distance is only 4 miles.

Whichever trail you take to reach the junction, the trail to Middle Branch Lake is the yellow-marked route leading northwest. It is very wet for about the first 150 feet, but it soon improves as it ascends away from the junction. This trail is noteworthy for traversing several rises. None are very long, but they add up to a hilly experience before you are done. It is just a 120-foot climb to the first height-of-land at 0.2 mile, followed by 160-foot descent to a stream crossing at 0.4 mile. The trail continues in this manner—both up and down—until reaching the next junction at 0.9 mile, located on a hill above Middle Branch Lake. The route to the right leads to the Big Otter Trail as described in section 76.

Turn left and follow red markers for the final leg. The trail keeps to a high rib of land with the lake visible through the trees to your right. It descends from a bit of high ground to approach the lean-to from behind, 1.1 miles from Cedar Pond Junction. Constructed in 1988, this shelter is situated so as to take in the view of the lake's south end. The shoreline features more white pines and fewer rock ledges than Middle Settlement, but otherwise the two lakes have many similarities—including their size. At 42 acres, Middle Branch is only 3 acres larger than its neighbor to the south.

Edwin R. Wallace was one of the earliest writers to describe these lakes in detail. In his *Descriptive Guide to the Adirondacks*, which went through numerous editions in the 1870s and 1880s, he referred to Middle Branch as "the pearl of this entire group." More enticing, however, is his description of a 5-acre pond that he claimed was 1.25 miles to the southwest. He called it Mount Cascade Pond because it was "perched squarely on the summit of a bold acclivity several hundred feet in height.... The outlet of this little tarn forms a most picturesque cascade; being precipitated down the perpendicular side of the parent height with one sheer fall of 60 ft. With the wild surroundings, it offers a spectacle quite impressive."

Indeed, such a landmark would be an unusual addition to an already attractive landscape. But alas, modern topographic maps and aerial photography make it hard to identify any such site, or even a candidate hilltop where such a pond *could* have been.

Middle Branch Lake

66 Cedar Pond

Hiking, snowshoeing
2.9 miles, 1½ hours, 110-foot initial climb, rolling terrain thereafter

Cedar Pond is not a destination, but a landmark that you pass on the way to other places. It *was* once the site of a lean-to, and perhaps for that reason three trails converged on this spot about a quarter-mile north of the pond. The lean-to is gone but the junction remains. This trail looping to the east of Cedar Pond is part of the shortest route to Middle Branch Lake when combined with the trail described in section 65, but it also factors into several potential loops and point-to-point hikes.

This hike follows a sequence of trails with three key turns. Beginning at the Scusa Trailhead on NY 28, the first trail quickly reaches a steep hillside. The 110-foot climb to its nearly bald summit is perhaps the steepest ascent of any trail in Ha-de-ron-dah, and because it occurs so early in the hike—before you have had a chance to warm up—it never fails to feel tiring. It is unavoidable, however, since private land to the right and left leaves few other routing options.

Soon after crossing the rocky summit, the trail hooks right past a yellow post, which marks a corner in the state land boundary. At 0.6 mile this first section ends at a junction with a yellow-marked trail; bear right for Cedar Pond. The route to the left leads to Middle Settlement Lake as described in section 62.

Heading northeast, you are briefly on a section of Brown's Tract Road until signs direct you to turn left in just 400 feet. The bed of the old wagon road can still clearly be seen straight ahead, but it leads into the private lands surrounding Lake Easka. Its modern successor, the Brown's Tract Trail, turns northwest across a set of boardwalks to the second junction at 0.8 mile. The trail to Cedar Pond turns left, while the Brown's Tract Trail turns right as described in section 69.

Now heading west and following red markers, the trail begins an easy climb around the foot of Cross Hill. Any point between the last junction and the next would be a good place to start the bushwhack to its summit, as suggested in section 68. At 1.1 miles you reach the third junction, where a yellow-marked side trail leads right to Grass Pond. See section 67 for details.

A gradual descent brings you to Grass Pond Outlet at 1.6 miles, a wide stream that you can easily step across in the summer, but which needs time to freeze before attempting in the winter. You cross several small streams and can then see Cedar Pond basin through the trees to the left at around

2.3 miles. Dropping into a low area, the fragrances of balsam and spruce fill the air. This is a beautiful section in a forest filled with conifers as the trail hooks from north to west, and then southwest for the final push to the lean-to site.

An old spring hole lies to the right of the trail, just before the junction where the red markers end at 2.9 miles. Yellow-marked trails branch off in two directions. The one to the left leads to Middle Settlement, section 64, and the one to the right leads to Middle Branch, section 65.

67 Grass Pond

Hiking, snowshoeing, cross-country skiing
0.5 mile, 15 minutes, relatively level

Edwin R. Wallace called this pond Spring Lake, claiming that it furnished "fine deering and trouting." Located at the foot of Moose River Mountain and cradled by hills on three sides, Grass Pond is a handsome place to explore in the winter, but it is harder to appreciate in the summer. Its 13 acres of water are surrounded by a wide, marshy shore that is more favorable to snowshoes and skis than to hiking boots. Nevertheless, the fact that it lies a mere 1.6 miles from the Scusa Trailhead makes it easy to reach, and Grass Pond is certainly worth a visit.

From the junction 1.1 miles along the trail to Cedar Pond, section 66, the yellow-marked trail leads northwest over a rise. It then steadily descends to a poorly located campsite on the edge of the pond's brushy outlet. The markers extend a few yards further to the northeast, ending where solid ground gives way to the marshy shore. As you walk through the leatherleaf and sheep laurel toward the pond, you will see signs of past and present beaver activity, tracks of raccoons and otters, and waterlilies in abundance. In late summer, bottle gentian speckles the meadow with its brilliant blue flowers.

68 Cross Hill

Bushwhack

The 1903 fire left other telltale signs on the landscape beside the stands of black cherries: a series of bald knobs and knolls scattered throughout the southeastern part of the Ha-de-ron-dah Wilderness. These are places where the thin soil was burned away, and where the returning forest has yet to make inroads on the exposed bedrock. Of these, Cross Hill is perhaps the most photogenic since it directly overlooks Lake Easka. Its name is a matter of local usage and derives from the fact that someone has placed a birch-log cross on its summit, visible from the lake below.

Cross Hill is the very first knob north of Lake Easka when looking at a map. It is most easily approached from the trail to Cedar Pond, section 66, at any point between the Brown's Tract and Grass Pond trail junctions. The maximum ascent to the 2070-foot summit is only 250 vertical feet, and the distance from the trail ranges from 0.4 to 0.5 mile, depending on your starting point. The hardwood forest offers little resistance, and the view from the bald knob is a more-than-adequate reward for the effort expended to reach it.

This hilltop was probably even more exposed in 1920 when Lyon deCamp first began developing the Okara Lakes into the residential community that it is now. It almost certainly inspired the cover of the marketing brochure that he printed to woo prospective buyers, which featured a man with an elaborate feathered headdress shouting through cupped hands from a ledge over a wild pond below. While it is far from a literal depiction of Cross Hill, no other summit looms as close to the Okara Lakes.

In addition to Indian imagery, deCamp exhibited a clear preference for Indian place names in his real estate dealings, as well. The modern toponyms Thendara, Okara, Easka, and Tekeni can all be traced to him. (Quite possibly the name Ha-de-ron-dah also reflects his influence, even though it was not officially applied until many years after his death.) He kicked off his Okara Lakes project with an elaborate public pageant that invoked Iroquois ceremonies and traditions. Haudenosaunee representatives feigned the process of ceding title to the land, which no one doubted deCamp already owned; they inspected the boundaries and erected stone cairns at each of the corners, and sent smoke signals from Cross Hill for the entertainment of those below. Also on the agenda that June night were a Feast of Welcome and a Fire Dance.

Cross Hill is just the southernmost knob on a long ridge that extends northeast toward Moose River Mountain. There are a few other exposed ledges further up the ridge, and they allow unrestricted views that range from the hills to the south to the distant mountains in the east—all within a span of 1.5 miles. It is easy to spend an afternoon traversing the ridge and enjoying the various lookouts. You can return the same way or drop down to Rock Pond and follow the wetlands along its outlet back to the Brown's Tract Trail.

Ha-de-ron-dah Wilderness: Thendara Trailheads

FOR MANY YEARS, the site of the modern hamlet of Thendara was known as Arnold's. This was a reference to Otis and Amy Arnold, who moved their family in 1837 from an unproductive farm in Boonville to an abandoned house near the north end of Brown's Tract Road, deep in the Adirondack wilderness. The old house stood on the edge of a large clearing that was surrounded by tenantless cabins, where three previous attempts at settlement had failed. For most people it would have been a foreboding environment in which to take up residence, but the Arnolds arrived with their six children intent on starting a new life.

Their new home had been built circa 1817 by Charles Frederick Herreshoff, son-in-law to the late John Brown of Providence, Rhode Island. The house was to be the seat of a new farming colony on the banks of the Moose River, but the land had refused to bend to Herreshoff's will. The agricultural endeavors failed, an iron mine produced no usable ore, and his acquaintances in New England had refused to back his continued unprofitable enterprises. Alone and despairing—and perhaps too prideful to return to Rhode Island in defeat—he committed suicide in 1819.

But where others had failed, the Arnold family prospered and thrived. Their story is movingly told in Joseph F. Grady's *The Story of a Wilderness*. The land furnished a sufficient amount of vegetables, the streams provided ample amounts of fish, and the woods provided game. The house had been built facing the road so that anyone traveling to and from the Fulton Chain was bound to arrive at the Arnolds' front door. With no other sources of hospitality for miles around, passersby would stop and inquire on the possibility of food and lodging. The family was happy to accommodate, and the paying guests left satisfied. Word quickly spread of the services to be found at Arnold's Clearing.

As more people undertook outings to John Brown's Tract, an addition was built across the rear of the house to accommodate the increasing patronage. For over thirty years the former Herreshoff Manor served as the commercial center of the Fulton Chain universe. Six more Arnold children followed the original six born in Boonville, bringing the final count to ten girls and two boys. The Arnold girls generally tended to avoid social interactions with their guests, but were apparently quite happy to show off their skills at horsemanship.

The idyll that Otis Arnold established for himself at Brown's Tract unraveled in a single morning in September 1868, however, when a quarrel over a dog collar escalated into tragedy. It was an unpremeditated event that neither party could have predicted. An Essex County guide named James Short was placing the collar onto a hunting dog he had just purchased as he prepared for departure. Arnold recognized the strap as an object belonging to the household, and he assumed (incorrectly) that it had been stolen. He challenged Short to return it. Short reacted defensively to the accusatory tone. Tempers quickly flared, and misunderstanding built upon misunderstanding. Contact was made between the two men, and a gun was fired. Short fell to the floor of the kitchen, mortally wounded.

Arnold, 64 years old, was immediately remorseful. He begged Short's forgiveness, whispered a few worried instructions to one of his daughters, and hiked over Humphrey Hill to Nicks Lake where he drowned himself in shame for his actions. Short died at the house five hours after the altercation.

The oldest son, Ed Arnold, half-heartedly ran the family business for a few more years but abandoned it in 1873. With the mother passed away and the children grown and dispersed, the house remained vacant for the next 20 years. By the time the new Adirondack Railroad opened in 1892, Arnold's had become a dilapidated ruin. Residents of the new hamlet of Fulton Chain deemed it an eyesore and a safety hazard, so they razed it in the mid-nineties, leaving only the cellar hole on the sandy knoll upon which the house had stood for eighty years.

Today the site has been modified beyond recognition. The sand from the knoll had been hauled away to create the beach at Old Forge by the first half of the twentieth century, leaving an open pit located diagonally across the new state highway from the Thendara train station. In 2006 the realignment of NY 28 placed the highway where the sandpit had been. This makes the approximate location of Arnold's, in terms of modern landmarks, the intersection of NY 28 and Watson Road.

This chapter describes the hiking trails to the west of Thendara, which penetrate the central and northern regions of the Ha-de-ron-dah Wilderness. Like the southern region described in the previous two chapters, this part of the wilderness is known for its gentle contours and secluded ponds. The 1903 fire swept through these parts, too, leaving a few additional bald knobs and stands of black cherries. Some of the trail miles tend to be a little longer, so this section appeals to hikers who enjoy exploring remoter areas. By con-

McKeever to Thendara	**Waypoints along NY 28 McKeever to Thendara**	Thendara to McKeever
0.0	Bridge over the Moose River in McKeever	9.7
2.9	Nelson Lake Trailhead, **sections 55 & 56**	6.8
3.0	Brown's Tract Easement access road, **sections 57-61**	6.7
5.7	Scusa Trailhead, **sections 62-68**	4.0
6.8	Intersection with Okara Road East, **section 69**	2.9
8.2	Intersection with Quarry & Browns Tract Roads, **sections 69-71**	1.5
8.5	Thendara train station	1.2
8.7	Intersection with Herreshoff Road, **sections 72-77**	1.0
8.8	Intersection with Beech Street in Thendara, **section 79**	0.9
9.7	Bridge over the Moose River between Thendara & Old Forge	0.0

trast, the bald summits of Coal Hill and Quarry Mountain can be very easy to reach if one is willing to engage in short bushwhacking exercises.

Three trailheads service this area: one near Lake Tekeni in the Okara Lakes development, one on Browns Tract Road west of Thendara, and one at the end of Herreshoff Road beside the railroad tracks.

69 North End of the Brown's Tract Trail

Hiking, snowshoeing, cross-country skiing
1.2 miles, 40 minutes, rolling terrain (section north of Okara Lakes)
1.4 miles, 45 minutes, rolling terrain (Okara Lakes to Thendara)

These two sections of the Brown's Tract Trail do not provide direct access to any destination, and therefore they are probably used by local residents more than anyone else. The section between Thendara and the Okara Lakes follows the route of the historic Brown's Tract Road, and its wide turns and gentle grades make it suitable for cross-country skiing. The section north of the Okara Lakes is a more rugged foot trail that was cut as a detour around the development, since the original wagon road passed through what is now private land. Both are accessed by two small trailheads in residential areas with limited parking.

Okara Lakes Trailhead: From a point 6.8 miles north of the Moose River bridge in McKeever, or 1.7 miles south of the Thendara train station, turn west onto Okara Road East from NY 28. Bear right at 0.2 mile (staying on Okara Road East) to reach the marked trailhead at 0.4 mile, where the road bends left. The parking area is little more than a wide spot on the shoulder on the right, but it is plowed in winter.

Brown's Tract Road Trailhead: One short section of town highway still uses the name Brown's Tract Road. It shares a common beginning on NY 28 with Quarry Road 0.3 mile south of the train station, and you can follow it for 0.3 mile west to the last camp. Here the improved town road ends and the unimproved trail continues. However, there is no designated parking area, nor is there much of a shoulder. In the summer it might be possible to park single-file in the trail itself. Parking at this trailhead should be avoided in snowy weather to keep the road clear for plows.

OKARA LAKES SECTION

Heading west from the Okara Road East trailhead, the trail passes behind several camps to reach a creek (the outlet of Rock Pond) at 0.4 mile. Despite its lack of remoteness, this valley has a rugged appearance. It is easy to step across the stream in summer, but in the winter you may need to detour upstream to find a beaver pond with better ice.

The trail continues west toward the foot of Cross Hill, and at one point the well-marked state land boundary presses the path part way up the rocky slope of the ridge. The level terrain to your left is on private land. At 1.2 miles you reach a junction with the trail to Cedar Pond, section 66. Left leads to the Scusa Trailhead in 0.8 mile, and right leads to Cedar Pond Junction in 2.1 miles.

OKARA TO THENDARA

Heading east from the Okara Road East trailhead, the trail is awkwardly

Stream on the Brown's Tract Trail north of the Okara Lakes

placed on the side of a slope for the first 500 feet before it angles right to intercept the route of Brown's Tract Road, which exits a private parcel at this point. Expect the first 0.3 mile to be rough and wet—one of the sections that would have vexed buckboard drivers in the nineteenth century—but things improve as you gain some higher ground and traverse a hardwood forest. In this case the trail doubles as the state land boundary; the Ha-de-ron-dah Wilderness encompasses everything to your north, and all of the land between the trail and NY 28 is private. At one point as you jog around the southern slopes of Coal Hill the trail passes within 400 feet of the highway. Brown's Tract Road was widened in this vicinity to accommodate motorized logging equipment; the old ruts that you see are not from oversized wagons, but from skidders. The surface is firm and dry, however; and if you are skiing, the final 0.2 mile to the Brown's Tract Road trailhead is an exciting downhill run. The distance between trailheads is 1.4 miles.

70 Coal Hill

Bushwhack

As travelers on Brown's Tract Road neared Arnold's, the first clearing that they reached was at Coal Hill. The trees at this location had been felled to manufacture charcoal for Herreshoff's iron works during the years 1817 to 1819, leaving the entire hillside denuded. The forest had apparently recovered by the end of the century, but the hill was scorched again in 1903 when a forest fire swept through the Ha-de-ron-dah region. The result of these two events is a sprawling bald spot on a hill where normally such features shouldn't be found. Coal Hill in fact bears the most open summit of any in Ha-de-ron-dah. The only thing missing is a trail.

Since this is a hill, not a mountain, the slopes are relatively gentle on most sides. Therefore there is no reason to become attached to one preferred bushwhack route to the summit, because any approach is viable. The closest access point is the Brown's Tract Road trailhead described in section 69. From there it is an easy matter to follow the long northeastern ridge that parallels the trail on a gentle ascent for 0.5 mile. Or if you prefer a somewhat steeper scramble you can follow the Brown's Tract Trail southwest for that same distance and climb directly up the southeastern face. Either way, the elevation differential between trailhead and summit is about 340 vertical feet.

The bald area covers roughly 3.5 acres of the summit, with arms extending northeast and southeast. On a more peaked mountain this would be more

Summit of Coal Hill

than sufficient exposure to create a full 360° view. Because Coal Hill's slopes are so gentle, however, some of the peripheral trees still manage to block certain angles. You can clearly see Moose River Mountain and the long, rocky ridge connecting it with Cross Hill to the west; you can see the summit knob of Quarry Mountain with the various small mountains flanking the North Branch Moose River to the northeast; and you can easily identify McCauley Mountain to the east by virtue of its ski slopes. The Okara Lakes are obscured by trees, as are most of Thendara and Old Forge.

Any quibbles with the views, however, are beside the point. This distinctive little peak is highly unusual for the southwestern Adirondacks, and it should not be missed. Note that the exposed bedrock is carpeted with thick patches of lichens, which hikers should be careful not to trample.

71 Quarry Mountain

Bushwhack

Quarry Mountain is a local name for small ridge west of Thendara. It is a hump of rock that provides a slightly more rugged bushwhack experience than its close neighbor Coal Hill, although the view from the summit bears some similarity. Like Coal Hill, it can be reached from the same Brown's Tract Road trailhead described in section 69. Park as best you can past the last camp and venture northwest into the woods. The summit knob is due north of the road, but it is best approached if you swing out west a bit and tackle the climb from its southwestern side. When the leaves are down you can see the mountain's silhouette through the treetops, and this may be all the navigational aid you will need.

The southwestern slope is forested with open hardwoods and relatively little brush. Several small ledges provide some modest climbing excitement near the top, but when you reach the 2083-foot summit you will be disappointed. There is a bald patch here, but no views. It is interesting to note that this "mountain" is about 30 feet lower than the summit of Coal Hill.

Continue northeast over the summit and along the ridge, arriving at a second opening where the views are better. Standing up, you can see over the trees east toward Thendara and McCauley Mountain. A better view lies on the west side of the ridge, although you may have to poke through a barrier of spruce trees to find the best ledge. A rocky slope with pockets of ferns, moss, and grass angles steeply down, but from its top you can enjoy a 180° view that extends from Cross Hill on the extreme left, to the wilderness region north of Moose River Mountain ahead and to the right. Depending on your bushwhack route, this spot is about 0.4 mile from the road.

There is an even larger bald area further northeast along the ridge, although a corner of it falls on private land. The size of this patch of rock does not necessarily enhance the quality of its views. Like all of the Ha-de-ron-dah hills, be careful not to trample the beautiful lichens that carpet much of the ridgeline.

72 Big Otter Trail

Hiking, camping, cross-country skiing
7.8 miles, 3¾ hours, rolling terrain

This trunk trail is the key to unlocking the northern and central regions of the Ha-de-ron-dah Wilderness. Before it was a wilderness trail, it was a "truck trail" built in the 1930s by the Civilian Conservation Corps for emergency fire-prevention access to the backcountry. It has been closed to motorized and mechanized vehicles since 1972, so now its wide surface and gentle grades form a hikers' highway. The trail is also a designated horse and ski trail, although instead of horses you are more likely to see people pushing handcarts filled with camping gear, especially in the fall.

The trailhead parking area is located at the end of Herreshoff Road, which turns north off NY 28 immediately south of the railroad underpass in Thendara. Follow this gravel road 0.4 mile to a barrier beside the tracks of the Adirondack Railroad, where there is ample room to park to the left. Herreshoff Road is plowed in the winter, but it is sometimes barricaded for a few weeks in early spring.

HERRESHOFF ROAD TO EAST POND JUNCTION
1.5 miles, 35 minutes

Follow the continuing road beyond the gate for 250 feet, where the Big Otter Trail makes the first left turn. It curves uphill through land owned by the Town of Webb to the state land boundary at 0.4 mile, where you will find a gate and a register.

The trail follows a hilly, winding course for the next 0.6 mile. In the spring, marsh marigolds add some color to the nearby glens. At 1 mile you reach the open wetlands surrounding Indian Brook, with a small pine-covered esker exposed to your right. As you reenter the woods, the trail turns northeast through a cherry-filled forest to reach the first trail junction at 1.5 miles. The narrow foot trail to East Pond, section 73, bears right.

EAST POND JUNCTION TO MIDDLE BRANCH JUNCTION
3.3 miles, 1¼ hours

Beyond the side trail to East Pond, the Big Otter Trail begins a long, easy ascent up the shoulder of Moose River Mountain. You reach the junction with the trail to the summit, section 75, at 2.2 miles. The Big Otter Trail then works its way around and down the mountain in a series of descents

Marsh marigolds near the Big Otter Trail

broken by occasional even sections. The appearance of spruce and balsam stands tells you that you have reached the foot of the mountain and entered the lowlands surrounding South Inlet. At 3.9 miles, soon after crossing a small stream called Mink Run, an unmarked footpath leads left for 200 feet to a secluded campsite favored by sportsmen.

For the next twenty minutes there is little elevation change until a short drop brings you to the junction of the yellow-marked trail to Middle Branch Lake, section 76, at a point 4.8 miles from the trailhead. The lean-to is 0.9 mile away.

MIDDLE BRANCH JUNCTION TO SOUTH INLET JUNCTION
1.6 miles, 45 minutes

Beyond the turnoff to Middle Branch Lake, the Big Otter Trail veers north across a small hill. It then reenters the spruce-dominated lowlands, and at 5.9 miles (1.1 miles from the last junction) you reach the trail's one major impediment to overland travel. A large wetland fed by several streams extends to the south, with the water moving sluggishly toward South Inlet. The problem is that 400 feet or so of the old roadbed is apt to be flooded.

Don't waste your time looking for a dry way across; just put on a change of footwear and let your feet get wet. The water is only shin deep, and the base is firm. Woodpeckers, cedar waxwings, jays, and chickadees are just some of the birds you may see in this wetland.

Beyond the open area, the trail rises into a forest of black cherries. Before going any further, you may want to consider a brief bushwhack of 0.1 mile north to a beautiful waterfall on South Inlet. The water cascades over ledges and boulders for a total drop of about seven feet into a wide, deep pool. You can take pictures and have lunch from the nearby rocks.

Back on the trail, at a junction 0.5 mile past the wetland, or 6.4 miles overall, a fourth side trail turns right. This one can be used to access the east shore of Big Otter Lake, Lost Creek, and East Pond as described in section 77.

SOUTH INLET JUNCTION TO OTTER CREEK
1.4 miles, 30 minutes

The old roadbed remains essentially flat as it pulls near Big Otter Lake. At 7.2 miles (0.8 mile past the last junction) you will pass an old beaver dam on the left with dead standing timber behind it. Just ahead on the right, a path leads 200 feet to a prominent campsite on the narrow southwestern arm of Big Otter Lake. The wilderness area ends at the shoreline, and you will likely hear ATVs on the far side of the channel.

The Big Otter Trail soon narrows and reaches an intersection with the snowmobile trail to Pine Lake, which leads left as described in section 92. Turning right, you cross a large trail bridge over the lake's outlet, where Otter Creek begins. At 7.8 miles you reach the motorized trail that follows the creek, section 93. It is a 3.4-mile hike along that trail to the trailhead parking area on Partridgeville Road.

73 East Pond

Hiking, camping, snowshoeing
2.8 miles, 1½ hours, rolling terrain (from Big Otter Trail)
4.3 miles, 2¼ hours, rolling terrain (from Herreshoff Road)

Big Otter Lake is fed by three appropriately named ponds to its west, north, and east. Of these, East Pond is the largest. It lies just beyond the northeasternmost extent of the 1903 forest fire and is surrounded by a handsome mixed forest as a result. But while it is about the same size as Middle Settlement Lake, it is visited far less frequently, perhaps because of its lack of a lean-to and its more out-of-the-way location. The foot trail to East Pond is a pleasantly rugged route that by design does not receive as much maintenance as other Ha-de-ron-dah trails to the south—part of an effort to manage the northern half of the wilderness in a more primitive state.

The trail begins on the Big Otter Trail at a marked intersection 1.5 miles from Herreshoff Road. After winding through an open hardwood section, you come to a broad wetland along a branch of South Inlet at 0.3 mile. You push through a brushy area at the edge of the vly to a wet stream crossing, where an old puncheon-style bridge has been deteriorating for years. Enough of it remains to get you over the deepest water, but a muddy section awaits you at the far end. This crossing could be impassable in early spring. Several species of birds, from hummingbirds to great blue herons, can be found in this diverse area.

The trail rises away from the wetland and passes through a hardwood forest with a wide-open understory. The trail is often little more than a simple track through the ferns, grass, and lycopodium club mosses that cover the ground. It goes over the shoulder of a small hill and then drops to a second branch of South Inlet at 0.8 mile. A log bridge spans this stream.

At 1.7 miles the trail approaches a vly on the right where blueberries abound in July. After stepping across its small outlet, you soon enter an area of old blowdown near Little Simon Pond caused by high winds in November 1988. The trail has been cleared, but thick brush flanks its corridor. A favorite camping area on the south side of the pond was buried by the downed trees and was never reclaimed. You reach the pond's pretty outlet 2 miles from the Big Otter Trail, 3.5 miles from Herreshoff Road. The stream, which is yet another South Inlet tributary, flows through a narrow rock flume. It routinely washes away the improvised log bridges that are sometimes thrown across it, and the rocks do get quite icy during the colder months.

The best views of Little Simon Pond come as you ascend a knoll near its southern end. Then the trail veers inland toward the foot of a hill, with an unnamed beaver pond almost visible through the trees to the west. This was where the 1903 fire reached its limit and where a more natural-appearing forest begins. Larger beeches and yellow birches are the most notable additions, as well as the occasional hemlock. The ensuing climb is not steep, but it is the longest on the trail. You climb 140 feet to a height-of-land, followed by a 120-foot descent to a junction at 2.5 miles (4 miles from Herreshoff Road). The trail to Big Otter Lake, section 77, bears left.

Continuing straight ahead, the trail passes the southeastern bay of East Pond. The trail to Blackfoot Pond, section 74, turns right at 2.7 miles just

Blackfoot Pond

before the trail dips to cross a small stream. There is a good campsite on the right, and then the trail reaches the site of an old lean-to in a spruce-filled stand. This shelter was destroyed by accidental fire in the late 1970s and was never replaced. The spot makes a poor campsite now, but if you follow the remaining footpath it ends at 2.8 miles at a small shoreline ledge with a big view. This is the best spot for relaxing and possibly even swimming, although the bottom is mucky. Most of the pond's remaining shoreline is brushy, and the dead standing timber adds a deep-woods beauty to the scene.

74 Blackfoot Pond

Hiking
1 mile, 25 minutes, 120-foot vertical rise

Blackfoot Pond is sometimes a pair of ponds when water levels are down, each one occupying its own half of an inverted V-shaped wetland northeast of East Pond. Although few people visit Blackfoot Pond today, it was in the past the site of several human endeavors, including a logging camp at the outlet and a small mica mine near its western arm. The two equal-sized lobes once reminded someone of a pair of feet, hence the name.

From the last junction on the trail described in section 73, just before the East Pond campsite, this red-marked trail climbs northeast through a small valley. It parallels a stream on your left, and in some sections it is clearly piggybacking on the route of an old logging road. After reaching a height-of-land, the trail dips to cross a muddy inlet within sight of the western pond at 0.7 mile. A wet, grassy shoreline makes exploration of Blackfoot difficult, but it does enhance its wild character.

The trail is only briefly near the pond, though. It goes beyond the inlet, following a very faint tread across some wet ground to a series of rock outcrops on the left. The markers come to an end 1 mile from East Pond near one particular rock wall with deposits of mica, a translucent mineral that was once used in stoves and lanterns. Overgrown piles of fractured rock trailing away from the wall indicate this was the site of an excavation, but not a very big one. How much mica this small site produced is hard to speculate.

In addition to the mica mine, you can search the nearby woods for scattered pieces of rusted hardware—the remains of an old camp.

Waterfall on South Inlet

75 Moose River Mountain

Hiking, cross-country skiing
0.7 mile, 20 minutes, 200-foot vertical rise (from Big Otter Trail)
2.9 miles, 1½ hours, 430-foot vertical rise (from Herreshoff Road)

No one climbs Moose River Mountain for its view, because there isn't one—not even a teasing glimpse. The 2205-foot summit was once the site of a fire tower, but it was removed in May 1977 when its services were no longer needed. Skiers like this trail because it offers an enjoyable, uninterrupted downhill run that extends from the summit to the East Pond trail junction, a distance of 1.4 miles. Curious hikers passing through on the Big Otter Trail are also apt to make the short climb, if only to see the small clearing where the tower stood.

The trail begins 2.2 miles along the Big Otter Trail, section 72, leading southwest on a gentle ascent. It passes to the south side of the summit and bends right, north, climbing only slightly steeper on the final ascent. The faint tread attests to the fact that few people come here.

The tower stood on the rock at the far north end of the clearing, 0.7 mile and 200 vertical feet above the Big Otter Trail. It was a steel structure built in 1919 to replace a wooden one erected seven years prior in Lewis County. That first tower had been called the Moose River Observation Station because of its location between McKeever and Port Leyden, but its low elevation afforded an inferior view. When the station was moved to this higher location, the name was transferred with it—and thus this previously unnamed hill became Moose River Mountain.

Note that although the summit is the highest in its immediate vicinity, it is not the highest point in the Ha-de-ron-dah Wilderness. That distinction belongs to an unnamed mountain northeast of Blackfoot Pond.

76 Middle Branch Lake

Hiking, camping, cross-country skiing, snowshoeing
0.9 mile, 20 minutes, relatively level (from Big Otter Trail)
5.7 miles, 2¼ hours, rolling terrain (from Herreshoff Road)

At a point 4.8 miles along the Big Otter Trail from Herreshoff Road, section 72, a short connector leads southwest for 0.9 mile to the lean-to on Middle Branch Lake, one of the key features of the Ha-de-ron-dah Wilderness. Its popularity as a camping and fishing destination is probably second only to Middle Settlement Lake, which lies less than a mile to the south. There are several ways to get to Middle Branch, and while the overall distance from Herreshoff Road is 1.7 miles longer than the shortest route from the Scusa Trailhead, some hikers still prefer this route's faster pace and easier grades.

The trail is a narrow footpath with no hills of note. It reaches a junction at 0.7 mile with the trail from Cedar Pond Junction, section 65. It then keeps to a high rib of land with the lake visible through the trees to your right, descending from a bit of high ground to approach the Middle Branch Lake Lean-to from behind. Constructed in 1988, this shelter is situated so as to take in the view of the lake's south end. The shoreline features more white pines and fewer rock ledges than Middle Settlement, but otherwise the two lakes have many similarities—including their size. At 42 acres, Middle Branch is only 3 acres larger than its neighbor to the south.

77 Big Otter Lake to East Pond

Hiking, camping
3.9 miles, 2 hours, rolling terrain

This remote and lightly used foot trail loops past the east shore of Big Otter Lake to East Pond, passing through some of the remotest terrain in the Thendara region. It is 3.9 miles between its western and eastern ends, but when you add to this the long approach along the Big Otter Trail and the side trips to Big Otter Lake and Lost Creek, the miles add up quickly. This is a trail for people who enjoy the challenge of a long hike through the deepest woods.

Beginning on the Big Otter Trail 6.4 miles from Herreshoff Road, section 72, the faint trail leads northeast for 300 feet to a bridge over South Inlet, one of the larger streams in the area. The trail hooks left on the far side and follows the bank for another 300 feet before veering inland.

The topography is flat and nearly featureless as you pass through cherry forests and pockets of blowdown from a July 1995 windstorm. At 0.8 mile an unmarked path leads left. Although it can be easy to miss, it leads to an attractive camping area on Big Otter Lake, located on a point on its eastern shore about 0.2 mile off the official trail. Since the state trail never approaches the lake itself, this side path is your best opportunity to get to the water.

For the next 1.1 miles the trail parallels the course of Lost Creek, eventually reaching a junction 1.9 miles from the Big Otter Trail. East Pond is to the right, but the marked trail to the left continues for another 0.5 mile to a secluded spot on the edge of Lost Creek. You can follow the route of the quickly fading old road 0.2 mile farther to a large clearing upstream that was the site of an old logging camp.

Turning east at the junction, the trail now follows the outlet of East Pond on a gradual 275-foot climb stretched over a 2-mile distance. Most of the forest in this section escaped the 1903 forest fire, so it is distinguished by an attractive mixture of hardwoods and softwoods—including hemlocks, which are common throughout the Adirondacks but rare in the burned lands to the south. You have some enticing views of East Pond as you first approach its long western finger, but then the trail veers inland and uphill. It ends at a junction at 3.9 miles with the trail described in section 73. Left leads in 0.3 mile to the campsite on East Pond, and right leads in 4 miles to Herreshoff Road.

This trail is most commonly used as part of a loop linking Middle Branch Lake, Big Otter Lake, and East Pond. Beginning and ending at Herreshoff Road, this tour of the northern Ha-de-ron-dah Wilderness is 17.1 miles long—a figure that includes the mandatory detours to each pond. Strong hikers can (and have) covered this distance in a single day, but it is especially well suited for 2-day or 3-day camping trips. This is southwestern Adirondack backpacking at its best!

Nicks Lake and Beyond

THE NORTH END of the Black River Wild Forest is anchored by DEC's Nicks Lake Campground, a 112-site facility that features a playground, picnic area and beach—not to mention its own 205-acre lake where no motors are allowed. All of this makes Nicks Lake one of the more popular Adirondack campgrounds, but it is the surrounding trail system that is the focus of this chapter.

If you ask for whom Nicks Lake is named, you will almost certainly be told the story of Nicholas Stoner. A native of Fulton County, "Nick" Stoner is celebrated in Adirondack lore as an expert marksman, a veteran of the American Revolution and the War of 1812, a legendary Indian fighter, a tavern celebrity, and a dedicated husband three times over. The vast wilderness to the north beckoned him and he ranged countless miles through the forest harvesting its bounty of furs, fish, and game. On one of his backwoods rambles he is said to have discovered a heretofore-unknown lake. Nick boasted of his lake's beauty and bountiful game, but kept its location secret. Eventually, other woodsmen found it and Nick's Lake became public knowledge.

This is the popular story, which has nearly eclipsed the more plausible explanation offered by Charles E. Snyder, a Herkimer-based lawyer who had professional cause to research the history of John Brown's Tract. In the 1890s Snyder represented such clients as Lemon Thomson and John Alden Dix, as well as William Seward Webb, in legal matters concerning the Moose River and the Adirondack Railroad right of way. In 1896 he published a paper on the history of John Brown's Tract that has been cited by historians ever since.

According to Snyder, the naming of Nicks Lake is linked to Charles Frederick Herreshoff's attempt to settle Township 7 in the late 1810s. One of the settlers that he attracted northward was named Nicholas Vincent, a nail fabricator from the Town of Russia who married Elizabeth Joy, the daughter of one of the other settlers. Snyder believed their union "was the first wedding upon the Tract, save perhaps the red man's nuptials." He went on to say, "Vincent is said to have been a great hunter and fisherman, and a beautiful lake where he used to fish, now known as Nick's Lake a few miles southwest of the Joy clearing was named in honor of Nicholas Vincent, the first bridegroom of John Brown's Tract."

Trail between Nicks and Nelson lakes

Even though the settlement soon folded after Herreshoff's suicide in 1819, the Vincents and Joys remained. Snyder interviewed their descendants, who remembered "many stories of the difficulties going back and forth from Russia to Brown's Tract." The shortest route to Russia for these families would have still been the Remsen Road, which was built in 1799 as the original route to John Brown's settlement. It passed straight through the lands described in this chapter, leading south along Nicks Creek to Remsen Falls—so named because of its location along the road—and onward to the Remsenburgh Patent. It was never a road in the modern sense, and the construction crew may have simply modified an old Indian trail.

The Remsen Road had been replaced by Brown's Tract Road in 1817, but in his paper Snyder provided a brief sketch of the trek to and from Russia that suggests the Vincents and Joys were still using the Remsen Road:

> An ox team was generally used. The journey took them thirty miles through the woods. Snow three or four feet deep had to be shoveled away to make camp for the night, and stakes and poles cut to build temporary shelter which was covered with hemlock boughs. Camp fires were built with flint, steel and punk wood, with which to frighten off the wolves and to keep themselves from freezing. Their bed was hemlock boughs. Can it be wondered at when the journey in and out was attended with such hardships, that the settlement was not a success[?]

Because it was probably never more than a rudimentary track through the wilderness, it did not take long for nature to reclaim the Remsen Road once it had been abandoned. Edwin R. Wallace wrote in the 1880s that it was "now mostly overgrown with trees and only a hunters' trail indicates its course." One unaltered portion does still exist near Nicks Creek, so you can see for yourself just how primitive this route was.

The state lands described in this chapter extend from Nicks Lake to the South Branch of the Moose River, with an extensive trail system based upon the wide logging roads built in the twentieth century. The area was pieced together in three acquisitions, beginning in 1918 when former governor John Alden Dix sold his vast holdings in Township 1 of the Moose River Tract to the state. The 3747 acres surrounding Nicks Lake were acquired in 1962 from A. Richard Cohen and two business partners, and the 2400 acres surrounding Nelson Lake were acquired from the Gould Paper Company the same year. This acquisition pattern explains why the northern lands feature so many old roads that are still obvious, while the southern lands (which

Waypoints en route to Nicks Lake Campground

Miles

0.0	Intersection of Beech Street with NY 28, immediately east of railroad underpass in Thendara
0.5	Bridge over Moose River. Road bears left, trailhead on right, **sections 78 & 79**
0.9	Intersection with Moose River Trail. *BEAR RIGHT*
1.2	Intersection with Bisby Road. *BEAR RIGHT*
1.25	Trail to Humphrey Hill, **section 78**
1.3	Bisby Road trailhead, **sections 80-82**
1.8	Intersection with McCauley Road
1.9	Nicks Lake Campground entrance, **sections 83-84**

were acquired much longer ago) do not.

The most popular trail by far is the loop around Nicks Lake, but other destinations include Nelson Lake and Remsen Falls. Many of the northern trails are designated for snowmobiles, but as you range southward they become groomed exclusively for foot travel. Skiers will find some attractive terrain between Nicks and Nelson lakes, as will mountain bikers.

The area is accessed from side streets on the outskirts of Thendara and Old Forge. There are numerous signs to direct travelers to the Nicks Lake Campground and the nearby McCauley Mountain ski center from downtown Old Forge, but for the purposes of this guide (and for those less familiar with these streets) a somewhat different route is suggested in the accompanying waypoint chart, beginning near the railroad tracks in Thendara. It links all three trailheads and is actually a substantial shortcut if you are coming from the south. Pay close attention to the street signs, since road names change with little warning from intersection to intersection.

78 Moose River Lock and Dam

Snowmobile trail, hiking, mountain biking, cross-country skiing
1 mile, 20 minutes, minimal grades

This short trail is part of a larger snowmobile trail system at the northernmost end of the Black River Wild Forest. It leads to the site of the lock and dam on the Middle Branch Moose River first built in 1889 to accommodate the steamboat *Fawn* on its passage between Old Forge and Minnehaha. The lock is long gone, but a dam still raises the river for the benefit of boaters in Thendara.

The trailhead is easy to find on the outskirts of Thendara. From NY 28, turn south onto Beech Street at the very first intersection immediately east of the railroad underpass. The street makes a sharp S turn and becomes Green Bridge Road, leading to a bridge over the river at 0.5 mile. The road swings left at the far end, with the trailhead parking area on the right. This spot is plowed in winter.

Two trails depart from the trailhead: one leading south and uphill (see the notes on Humphrey Hill below), and one leading west on the level. Take that western route, pulling away from the river and climbing no more than 45 feet through wide-open hardwoods. At 0.7 mile you reach a junction. The trail to the left loops back to Humphrey Hill.

Bearing right, you descend the same 45 feet in a single grade to reach the dam at 1 mile. There is a large clearing beside the structure with plenty of room to picnic.

The trail is very well suited to skiing, although you might want to arrive early after a fresh snowfall to beat the moderate snowmobile traffic. You can also reach this spot by canoe, as described in section 79.

HUMPHREY HILL

The trail leading south from the Green Bridge Road trailhead was once a key hiking trail to Nicks Lake, and it was likely the final route that Otis Arnold took after shooting James Short in 1868. It leads in 0.4 mile to a four-way intersection near the top of Humphrey Hill. The level trail to the left leads in 0.6 mile to Bisby Road, and the trail to the right leads in 1.2 hilly miles to the dam described above.

Continuing straight, the trail descends 115 feet in 0.3 mile to a junction with the main trail from Bisby Road described in section 80. With the right snow conditions, this can be an exhilarating run for skiers. The final 0.2-mile section of the original trail leading directly to the north side of Nicks Lake is no longer maintained, but it can still be found. Otherwise, turning right at this junction will take you to the modern foot trail loop around the lake described in section 83.

The initial ascent from the trailhead to the four-way junction near the summit is the roughest section in winter, so this is recommended as the ascent route. If you arrive ahead of the weekend snowmobile traffic, all of these trails are very well suited to skiing. Snowmobile traffic is light by Town of Webb standards, but it is just high enough to spoil some of the fun of the downhill runs if you arrive too late.

79 Middle Branch Moose River

Canoeing

You will seldom find a canoe trip so close to a developed area that offers such a wilderness-quality experience as the Moose River does south of NY 28. From the hamlets of Thendara and Old Forge, the river follows a sinuous course southwest and you will find at least 6 river miles of flatwater paddling. Extensive, grassy wetlands border much of the way and most creatures indigenous to the Adirondack forest can be seen here. The rewards are great if you paddle slowly and silently, starting, perhaps, at dawn when animal activity is high and continuing through the day.

The best access point is found by turning onto Beech Street in Thendara. It is the first street branching south from NY 28 on the east side of the railroad underpass. Follow it for 0.5 mile and cross a bridge over the river. Turn sharp right and park at the trailhead for the snowmobile trails described in section 78. There is room for several cars here and you may put your canoe in from the banks near the bridge.

Heading down river, you immediately enter a widened section with a beaver lodge. Great blue herons frequently feed here among the patches of pickerelweed and marsh grass. Some homes stand along the north shore and old large buildings tell of a more prosperous past. The river narrows and closely parallels the railroad tracks to the right. Twenty minutes into your trip, at about 1.1 miles, you reach the wooden dam and spillway that once made steamer traffic between McKeever and Thendara possible. The lock, however, is no longer there. It is easy to carry around the dam, but you must do so on the left bank since the land on the right bank is private. There is a clearing with campsites on the left side and a snowmobile trail leads from here to the trail network near Nicks Lake, section 78.

Below the dam, the river wanders for about 4 miles, interrupted only by two or three shallow riffles. Let the current guide you and paddle only to steer or avoid obstacles. As you round each bend, have your binoculars and camera ready.

Finally, near the base of Flatrock Mountain, shallow rapids form and it is time to turn back. There is no legal exit point for the general public above these rapids in Minnehaha. However, the Adirondack Scenic Railroad does offer a shuttle service back to Thendara from a designated landing area. See their website, *www.adirondackrr.com*, for current details.

80 Nelson Lake from Bisby Road

Snowmobile trail, hiking, camping, mountain biking, cross-country skiing
6.2 miles, 2½ hours, rolling terrain

There are certainly much shorter ways to reach Nelson Lake, but this route is the central trail with which all of the other Nicks Lake trails intersect. It is a wide old logging road for its entire length, with several small hills and a few small wetlands to provide some scenic variety. The first 2.4 miles closest to Nicks Lake enjoy some popularity, but usage levels fall off precipitously for the next 3 miles. The snowmobile trail does not lead directly to Nelson Lake, so to see water you will need to be curious and explore the unmarked paths leading to the shoreline campsites.

The trail begins at a prominent trailhead on Bisby Road that is easy to find as you drive to the Nicks Lake Campground. If you follow the signs from downtown Old Forge, the driving distance is 1.1 miles from NY 28. Following our recommended route, turn south in Thendara onto Beech Street at the very first intersection immediately east of the railroad underpass. The street makes a sharp S turn and becomes Green Bridge Road, leading to a bridge over the river at 0.5 mile. Turn right onto Moose River Trail at 0.9 mile, and right onto Bisby Road at 1.2 miles. The trailhead is on the right at 1.3 miles, just 0.6 mile shy of the campground entrance.

BISBY ROAD TO NICKS LAKE LOOP
1.7 miles, 45 minutes

From the Bisby Road trailhead, the wide trail leads southwest and descends gently to a trail junction at 0.7 mile, where the old trail from Humphrey Hill (section 78) comes in on the right. A short distance further, at 0.9 mile, signs mark where the north end of the Nicks Lake Loop (section 83) comes in on the left.

For the next 0.8 mile, the Nicks Lake Loop piggybacks on the snowmobile trail—with trios of red, yellow and blue trail markers to denote the various designations. You pass within 0.1 mile of Nicks Lake's northwest bay without ever seeing it. The trail remains essentially level all the way to the next trail

Nelson Lake

junction at 1.7 miles, where the loop trail veers left on its way to the beach and picnic area.

NICKS LAKE TO NELSON LAKE
3.9 miles, 1¾ hours

The snowmobile trail continues southwest, gaining only 76 feet in elevation in the 0.7-mile distance to the next junction, 2.4 miles from Bisby Road. The trail to the right is the little-used route to the Middle Branch Moose River described in section 81.

At 2.8 miles (0.4 mile past the junction) you begin to pass a long, open wetland on your left. Given the consistency of the woods up to this point, even this unremarkable vly seems noteworthy. It may have been a beaver meadow in the past, but it has been abandoned long enough that it is beginning to fill in with trees again.

There is little to say about the rest of the trail, other than that it winds in numerous directions and passes between two hills at 4.3 miles. Maintenance is spotty, and even snowmobile use is inconsistent. There are two more small wetlands to see, and then a trail junction at 5.3 miles. The blue-marked foot trail to the left leads to Remsen Falls, section 82.

The snowmobile trail begins a gentle descent of 100 feet, reaching a tiny clearing at the foot of the hill at 5.6 miles. This is a subtle-but-key landmark, because it is here that an unmarked path leads left to a choice campsite on the shore of Nelson Lake. The beginning of this path can be especially faint. It leads southwest on a route that parallels some rock bluffs on a hillside to your left. The path is 0.2 mile long and leads to a well-used (and oft-littered) campsite on the northeast shore of the lake. It features a scenic rock ledge, as well as a small sand beach when water levels are low.

AROUND THE NORTH END OF NELSON LAKE
0.6 mile, 15 minutes

The snowmobile trail loops around the north end of Nelson Lake without ever approaching it. An intervening wetland is partly at fault, but so is the road's origin: because this was once a logging road, the builders were more interested in accessing the inland forest than creating a scenic recreational trail. The route is relatively level during this section, and it makes for a speedy hiking experience.

Watch for a prominent bend to the right 0.6 mile from the unmarked path, 6.2 miles from Bisby Road. This is where a side trail leads left to the Nelson Lake Lean-to, which was placed here in 2012. The logs came from a shelter that once stood in the High Peaks; when that lean-to was decommissioned, its walls were reconstructed here. The site is several hundred feet from the shore, with a path leading from the lean-to to an older campsite beside the water. Overall, the lean-to site is less distinctive than the northeastern campsite, but it is no less attractive.

The continuing snowmobile trail is the route described in section 81.

81 Middle Branch Loop

Snowmobile trail, hiking, camping, cross-country skiing
4.4 miles, 1¾ hours, relatively level

This trail will be of interest to only the most thorough of hikers and skiers— those determined to visit even the most out-of-the-way places. Officially, it is the continuation of the snowmobile trail beginning at Bisby Road described in section 80. It branches off near Nicks Lake and rejoins it at Nelson Lake to create a "lollipop loop" that is 13 miles in length if you begin and end at Bisby Road. Every trail through the deep woods has some intrinsic value, and that is no less true in this case; but the long miles, flat terrain, and lack of distinctive scenery will likely deter the majority of casual hikers from considering this route.

The northeast end begins at a fork 2.4 miles from Bisby Road along the main snowmobile trail to Nelson Lake, section 80. There is a beaver meadow crossing at 0.4 mile, and then a gradual descent of about 80 feet into the valley of the Middle Branch Moose River. It passes along the feet of Little Roundtop and Jones Mountain as it inches nearer to the river. You are parallel to the Moose for about a mile, although it is only briefly within view. The final glimpse comes at 2.9 miles, at which point you are directly across the river from Minnehaha.

Turning south, you begin to ascend through a draw between Jones Mountain on the east and an unnamed hill to the west. The trail becomes excessively wet and is very difficult to walk. Finally, a gradual descent leads to a clearing on the Moose River, just below Nelson Falls, 3.8 miles from the fork. You may find the faint herd path to Nelson Falls to the right, as described in section 55.

The trail veers east away from the river, and at 4.4 miles it makes a right-angle turn to the left, northeast. Here a side trail to the right leads to the lean-to near the west side of Nelson Lake. From this point forward, refer to section 80 for notes on the continuing trail.

82 Nelson Lake to Remsen Falls

Hiking, camping
5.8 miles, 3 hours, rolling terrain

This long trail receives far less use than it deserves. Much of it is a narrow footpath with attractive views of the Middle and South branches of the Moose River, making it one of the more scenic routes in the region. But its faint tread attests to the fact that few people come here—perhaps because of the long distances required to reach either end from the Nicks Lake area, or the two river fords if you intend to cut the trail off at Nelson Lake and Remsen Falls. As with any lightly used trail, maintenance is also light. Expect some measure of blowdown, as well as some poorly marked sections where

Middle Branch Moose River

the route may not be obvious.

The Nelson Lake end of the trail begins at a junction with the snowmobile trail described in section 80, located 5.3 miles from Bisby Road. Like all of the trails described so far, it begins on a wide and level logging road. At 0.7 mile it crosses a small stream on a wide bridge, and then turns to follow that stream southwest. At 1.5 miles, near the south end of Nelson Lake, the foot trail parts company with the logging road and veers right, closer to the river. At 1.7 miles there is a large rock on the bank of the Middle Branch Moose River that makes an excellent place to stop. It overlooks the place where the outlet of Nelson Lake flows in.

This is the start of a long, scenic section with frequent views of the nearly continuous rapids from Nelson Lake to the confluence with the South Branch. The trail is not always beside the river, but it is never far away, either. There are plenty of views as the river and the trail turn together from southwest to east to south. At 3.2 miles you dip to cross the outlet of a beaver pond that is hidden just upstream, and at 3.5 miles you have one last glimpse of the Middle Branch just before it reaches the confluence with the South Branch, seen off in the distance after the last rapid.

Observant hikers may have noticed the presence of Norway spruce trees throughout this last section. This European species was often planted in the Adirondacks by foresters during the early years of that profession. Sometimes called "weeping spruces," they can be identified by their drooping twigs and long cones. Their presence at this location might be explained by understanding the tract's history. They appear soon after you leave the former Gould lands and enter those once owned by John Alden Dix and the Moose River Lumber Company. Several biographies on Dix point out that forest conservation was one of his priorities, and that he "made it a rule that for every tree which was cut down another should be planted." These Norway spruces, which obviously did not sprout here on their own, may be the evidence of that rule.

Unfortunately, the hiking trail bypasses the confluence of the two rivers. Instead it turns inland, keeping to the foot of a hill as it swings east. The forest of black cherries has almost no understory other than ferns and herbs, and with so little foot traffic the tread can be unreliable and faint. You need to look carefully for the blue trail markers.

The next time you see the Moose River at 4.1 miles, it is the South Branch instead of the Middle Branch. This begins the second phase of the hike as you follow this arm of the river upstream toward Remsen Falls. Whereas the Middle Branch was a nearly continuous stretch of whitewater, the South Branch is a much gentler stream characterized by riffles and the occasional small island. The wide banks are free of trees, suggesting that they are scoured by blocks of ice during the larger spring floods. This is a process common on larger Adirondack rivers and it prevents the growth of any woody vegetation.

At 4.4 miles you cross a small stream with a noisy cascade to the left. Then at 4.6 miles, just a few minutes later, the trail makes an unexpected turn left, uphill. It spends much of the next half-mile on a ridge above the river to avoid the steeper terrain below. Pinxter bushes announce their presence with bright pink azalea blossoms in early June. The river splits, with the smaller channel flowing around the north side of an island. Then, at 5.8 miles, you arrive at the small clearing where the Remsen Falls Lean-to stands watch over the mouth of Nicks Creek.

It is somewhat disappointing to note after the long hike to get here that the lean-to is much more frequently reached from the shorter trail from Wolf Lake Landing Road described in section 50. Although one must somehow cross the river to access the lean-to from that direction, the amount of litter at this site suggests plenty of people have overcome that obstacle. The view from the lean-to is perfectly aligned with the upstream bend in the South

Branch, with Remsen Falls about 0.2 mile away. The alders and wetland surrounding Nicks Creek make it difficult to access the falls from here, and fording the river is not an undertaking that should be approached lightly.

The blue-marked foot trail continues northeast through the clearing and back into the woods towards Nicks Lake, as described in section 84.

83 Nicks Lake Loop

Hiking, snowshoeing
4.5 miles, 2¼ hours, rolling terrain

This is perhaps the premier hiking trail in the Nicks Lake region. It completely encircles the lake, and while it is groomed for guests of the campground it can also be accessed from the surrounding wild forest. It links all five campground loops with the beach and picnic area, and only 0.5 mile of the loop follows the park roads. Not all of it is located close to water, but overall the loop provides an enjoyable experience with elements of a backwoods adventure.

If you follow the signs from downtown Old Forge to Nicks Lake and Mc-Cauley Mountain, the driving distance to the campground entrance is 1.7 miles from NY 28. Following our recommended route, turn south in Thendara onto Beech Street at the very first intersection immediately east of the railroad underpass. The street makes a sharp S turn and becomes Green Bridge Road, leading to a bridge over the river at 0.5 mile. Turn right onto Moose River Trail at 0.9 mile, and right onto Bisby Road at 1.2 miles. The entrance to the Nicks Lake Campground will be on the right at 1.9 miles, just past the ski center entrance.

Within the campground, there are several potential starting points. Of course if you are a camper you can access the trail from any of the five loops. For non-campers there is a small parking area on the A Loop (the first right turn after the entrance station) that is also available in the spring and fall off-seasons. Alternately, you can park near the beach at the far south end of the park when the gate is open. You may be charged an entrance fee from May to October when the facility is operating. In the winter the park roads are often unplowed, and they are never cleared further than the entrance booth.

Alternately, you can access the loop from the Bisby Road trailhead described in section 80. From this direction there is a 0.9-mile approach to the northwest corner of the loop.

One thing to bear in mind is that dogs are not allowed on the beach, which the trail crosses on its way to the south end of the lake.

FROM THE "A LOOP" TO THE BEACH
1.3 miles, 45 minutes

The hike along the east shore of Nicks Lake is the least remote portion of the loop, but it is also closest to the water. If you drive into the A Loop past the entrance station, you will find a small parking area on the right next to the start of the trail. A 450-foot connector leads from the trailhead to the loop, which you intersect on an esker (a glacial ridge created by a river-like channel of meltwater millennia ago) high above the lake. The loop goes in both directions, but for a clockwise circuit turn left.

The yellow-marked trail briefly dips off the esker but quickly climbs back to the top. At 0.2 mile you reach a confusing turn. The marked trail veers left to drop down the side of the esker, but a well-worn herd path continues straight along the crest, which extends out into the lake as a crooked point. It would be a scenic detour except that thick brush all along the peninsula leaves little standing room.

The trail leaves the esker and passes quite close to the water, more or less hugging the shore past C Loop and D Loop. Several campsites on D Loop are actually quite close to the trail. There is a long gap between D and E loops where you feel you are briefly in deep woods, and then at 0.8 mile the foot trail ends at E Loop.

Follow the paved road to the right, walking through the loop to the main campground road at 1.1 miles. Turn right past the boat launch and continue toward the picnic area and the beach, which you reach at 1.3 miles from the A Loop trailhead.

FROM THE BEACH TO NICKS CREEK
0.8 mile, 20 minutes

Continue past the bathhouse to the woods on the far side of the beach, and follow the edge of the beach (where no pets are allowed) to where signs clearly mark the resumption of the loop trail. It briefly reenters the woods before coming to a large footbridge over an inlet. On the far side is a long boardwalk that leads through a boggy area back to dry land, where the loop goes back to behaving like a trail again, 0.1 mile from the beach.

The traverse around the south shore is one of the prettiest sections of the entire loop. You are in a mixed forest with a substantial cover of spruce and hemlock, with several choice views of the south end of the lake. Look for a small stream crossing at 0.2 mile.

It is interesting to note that this section of Nicks Lake was briefly owned by the Adirondack League Club. The boundary between John Brown's Tract and the Moose River Tract passes through the lake's southern lobe, and at one time Lyon deCamp owned everything to the north of the line (including the majority of the lake) and the club owned everything to the southeast. The club apparently had little need for the sliver of Nicks Lake on their side of the line, but they *were* interested in a small piece of deCamp's land near First Lake. Therefore in 1906 the two parties entered into a land swap in which deCamp completed his ownership of Nicks Lake, and the League Club gained a permanent access corridor to Little Moose Lake. In 1957 the Nicks Lake property passed from the deCamp estate to three local business-men, who sold it to the state in 1962.

At 0.6 mile, a red-marked side trail leads left for 0.2 mile to an aging fish barrier dam on Nicks Creek, designed to keep non-native species out of the lake. Just past the side trail, at 0.7 mile, the loop trail comes to a bridge over the creek just below the foot of the lake. On the other side, it climbs very steeply to a junction 80 vertical feet above the lake, 0.8 mile from the beach. The blue-marked trail to Remsen Falls described in section 84 bears left.

AROUND THE WEST SHORE
1.7 miles, 50 minutes

Now on high ground with views of the lake ranging from little to none, you bear right at the junction and follow an old logging road northwest. There is little to say about this section other than that it is wider than the previous sections and contains fewer surprises. The road was originally constructed to bypass the lake rather than show off its scenic charms, and it accom-plishes that goal rather well. At 0.9 mile you reach a second junction, this one with the snowmobile trail to Nelson Lake, section 80. The loop trail bears right onto this former logging road and follows it wide around the west shore (again with no views) for another 0.8 mile. The total walking distance around this far side of the lake is 1.7 miles. At this point you reach a third junction. The snowmobile trail continues straight to Bisby Road, but the loop trail bears right to approach the north shore.

AROUND THE NORTH SHORE
0.7 mile, 20 minutes

The loop trail begins to redeem itself on the north shore after pulling away from the snowmobile trail. At 0.2 mile you reach a prominent side trail on

Skiing over Nicks Creek

the right that leads to a gravelly landing on the lake, where people sometimes camp. (This site is located outside of the designated campground, so it is subject to the standard rules for camping in the Forest Preserve.) At 0.5 mile you cross a small stream, and soon afterwards the trail scrambles back to the top of an esker. This is the same esker on which you began, and after a few more glimpses of the lake you reach the sign marking the spur leading back to the A Loop trailhead. The 450-foot spur will guide you off the esker and back to the starting point, after a satisfactory half-day excursion around this beautiful lake.

84 Remsen Falls from Nicks Lake

Hiking, camping, cross-country skiing
4.2 miles, 2 hours, rolling terrain

This remote trail is a fine wilderness footpath, though not a very exciting one. It follows the course of Nicks Creek southwest to the lean-to at Remsen Falls on the South Branch Moose River, generally keeping too far back from the creek to offer any views. Additionally, the scenic qualities of Remsen Falls are best described as "subtle," and some people may not consider them motivation enough to hike such a long distance (especially when they can be reached much more easily from McKeever as described in section 50).

The appeal of this trail is not in its scenery, but rather in its history, for the middle 3.5 miles appear to be an original, unaltered section of the Remsen Road. This was the route commissioned in 1799 by John Brown to provide access to his new settlement from the south. Perhaps twenty families were enticed to follow this trail north to where Brown had built a gristmill and a dam on the outlet of the "Moose River Lakes," as the Fulton Chain was then known. A few years later those same twenty families retreated along this road, finding the agricultural conditions too marginal compared to greener prospects elsewhere.

When Charles Frederick Herreshoff attempted the second settlement he commissioned a shorter road from Boonville, and the Remsen Road apparently fell into neglect. A few segments were improved and incorporated into later road networks, but the route as a whole was effectively abandoned. The section described here is probably the only unmodified portion still in existence, and therefore the oldest trail in the southwestern Adirondacks.

It begins near the south end of the Nicks Lake loop trail described in section 83, at a junction 0.8 mile from the beach and 2.1 miles from the A

Loop trailhead. Alternately you can start at the Bisby Road trailhead, follow the snowmobile trail described in section 80, and then follow the loop trail to Nicks Creek. This approach is 2.6 miles long.

The trail leads south from the junction, following a wide old road on a gentle descent—but, notably, *not* the Remsen Road in this case. You seem to be edging closer to Nicks Creek, but at 0.4 mile a corner of the Adirondack League Club's posted property comes in on the left and nudges the trail to the right. This corner was created in 1906 after the club completed a land swap with Lyon deCamp, trading their corner of Nicks Lake for an access corridor between First and Little Moose lakes.

It is actually just 300 feet after passing the corner that a sign directs you to turn left off the logging road in a rock-studded area. If what you see next does not look like a road in the modern sense, remember that a wagon road cut through the wilderness in 1799 would not have been a two-lane highway. In fact, the Remsen Road was rumored to be a modified Indian trail. As it continues southwest, dipping through small glens and winding through the open mixed-wood forest, note its consistent width, the faint signs of a grade on certain slopes, and the deliberate way it makes each turn. All of these indicate that it was indeed once a road, even if few of these clues are obvious. The subtlety merely tells us that this is an *old* road. If it were not being marked and maintained as a trail today, it would be almost impossible to discern.

The trail crosses small tributaries at 1 and 1.3 miles. The route corresponds roughly with a depiction of the Remsen Road on a map appearing in *Asher & Adams New Topographical Atlas and Gazetteer of New York* published in 1871, including an odd east-leaning bend in the trail as it parallels a similar bend in the creek. At 3 miles it pulls near—and then crosses—a wider tributary that cascades off the hill to your right. This is the outlet of Bloodsucker Pond, which lies only 0.2 mile to the northwest. A snowmobile trail once led past it, but that route has been abandoned for decades. The foot trail continues southwest with the outlet stream now on your left.

Eventually the woods open up into park-like stands of black cherries that reveal a variety of rock outcrops on the hillside to your right. This area was last logged by the Moose River Lumber Company prior to 1915, and it appears that the road was widened and smoothed at that time, although it is still a soft path through the woods. At 4.2 miles you enter the small clearing where the Remsen Falls Lean-to stands watch over the mouth of Nicks Creek.

It is somewhat disappointing to note after the long hike to get here that the lean-to is much more frequently reached from the shorter trail from Wolf

Paddling the Middle Branch near Mudhole Pond

Lake Landing Road described in section 50. Although one must somehow cross the river to access the lean-to from that direction, the amount of litter at this site suggests plenty of people have overcome that obstacle. The view from the lean-to is perfectly aligned with the upstream bend in the South Branch, with Remsen Falls about 0.2 mile away. The alders and wetland surrounding Nicks Creek make it difficult to access the falls from here, and fording the river is not an undertaking that should be approached lightly.

Looking at this scene, it is not immediately clear where the Remsen Road could have crossed the river. The Asher & Adams map suggests that it might have been just around the upstream bend, and Snyder mentions a short-lived bridge that washed away before the last of the original settlers were able to vacate the woods.

The blue-marked trail extending west from the lean-to is the foot trail to Nelson Lake, section 82.

Brantingham Lake South: Steam Mill Road

THE WESTERN BOUNDARY of the Ha-de-ron-dah Wilderness is accessed by several trails originating near Brantingham Lake, in an adjoining tract of state land known as the Independence River Wild Forest. Unlike the eastern boundary described in the previous chapters (parts of which are abutted by a major state highway) the western boundary is much more remote. The trailheads can only be reached by exploring the back roads of Lewis County, which often begin as paved byways but end as gravel lanes. Two such roads branch north and south around Brantingham Lake, and this chapter focuses on the southern route, Steam Mill Road.

Although somewhat isolated from other Adirondack communities, Brantingham Lake (named for Thomas Brantingham, who once owned a 74,400-acre tract in the region) was well known by nineteenth-century sportsmen. Hamilton Child's 1872 *Gazetteer of Lewis County* reported, "Brantingham Lake is a beautiful sheet of water irregular in shape and is entirely surrounded by forest which is full of game. The lake is well stocked with fish, pike, pickerel, and bass, pickerel being caught weighing three pounds."

Guidebook writer Edwin R. Wallace noted: "Brantingham, though a sheet of rare beauty, makes no pretension to the grandeur of the *mountain* scenery witnessed from many of the Adirondack lakes, but its various *other* attractions bring thither numerous sportsmen, invalids and picnic parties, who are never disappointed with the visit." The fact that the lake was only seven miles from a major railroad made it easy for many to access.

A landmark of the area was the Brantingham Lake Hotel, which catered to hunters and fishermen. In the early 1870s, the hotel was almost destroyed by fire. What remained was sold to George Graves, rebuilt, and later called the Brantingham Inn.

With the coming of the automobile, the resort business in the Brantingham Lake area declined. In 1966, the inn was torn down and the land was turned into thirty-one cottage lots. In 1984 a new inn, the Brantingham Inn Motel, was constructed to serve a new breed of recreationists—snowmobilers, cross-country skiers, and hikers—as well as those who still come back to hunt and fish. The hamlet of Brantingham Lake remains the place to seek food

Waypoints along Steam Mill Road

Miles	
0.0	Steam Mill Road begins as a right fork from Brantingham Road near the golf course, 1 mile from Brantingham
0.2	Road forks, pavement ends. *CONTINUE STRAIGHT* on Steam Mill Road
1.1	State land boundary, end of winter plowing
1.4	Southern trailhead for the Centennial Ski Trail, **section 90**
2.2	Poison Creek, view of wetlands near Fish Creek
4.7	Drunkard Creek Trailhead, end of road, **sections 85-87**

and accommodations.

Nearly all of the state land immediately east and north of Brantingham Lake was acquired during the years 1954 through 1965, creating a continuous band of wild forest from Thendara to the Adirondack Park's boundary near Greig. Most of this area is covered by young stands, but the forest immediately east of Brantingham Lake is thick and tall. You need take only a few steps in that direction to plunge into what has all the trappings of a remote, unpopulated wilderness. You can most easily experience this kind of environment if you take Steam Mill Road to its end within the Independence River Wild Forest.

You can reach the Brantingham Lake area from NY 12, which runs north-south between Boonville and Lowville. Turn east from NY 12 at Burdick Crossing Road, between Lyons Falls and Glenfield. Cross the Black River to the intersection with Lyons Falls Road. Turn left and drive 0.7 mile north through the hamlet of Greig to the intersection with Brantingham Road. Turn right and follow it uphill for 3.6 miles to the hamlet of Brantingham, located at the intersection with Partridgeville and Middle roads.

Continue to follow Brantingham Road past the golf course. Steam Mill Road continues straight at a fork 1 mile past Brantingham, and it narrows to become a single-lane gravel road with turnouts. Plowing ends after the last residence at the state land boundary at 1.1 miles, but in the summer you can drive into the Forest Preserve for 3.6 miles to an interior parking area called the Drunkard Creek Trailhead. You could ski to this point, but the relatively high volume of snowmobiles may be discouraging.

85 Pine Lake via Spring Hill Junction

Hiking, camping
4 miles, 2 hours, rolling terrain

This hike is not only the most appealing of the available options at the Drunkard Creek Trailhead, it is one of the best hikes in the entire south-western Adirondacks. It begins as one of Brantingham Lake's ubiquitous snowmobile trails, but after the first junction it becomes a dedicated foot trail leading through the post-glacial topography to beautiful Pine Lake, on the edge of the Ha-de-ron-dah Wilderness. The water views are enchanting, and in spite of the fact it winds through so many wetlands the tread remains dry as a bone. The reason for this is twofold: good bridges span the wettest areas, and the trail is so seldom used that there is very little erosion.

Beginning at the Drunkard Creek Trailhead (see the chapter introduction for driving directions) the snowmobile trail follows an old woods road through brushy woods. The forest opens into taller hardwoods as the trail swings from southeast to northeast, climbing over 100 feet at an imperceptible grade. At 1.6 miles you reach a four-way intersection known as Spring Hill Junction, located between two small hills known locally as Big Pico and Little Pico mountains, to the northwest and southeast respectively. In a region with no topographic eminences of any kind, the term "mountain" was certainly applied to these landmarks with tongue in cheek.

At Spring Hill Junction, the yellow-marked foot trail to Mudhole Pond (section 86) turns hard right, southeast. The continuing trail to Pine Lake is the second right turn off the snowmobile trail, which swings left, northwest, as described in section 87.

Following red markers, the foot trail passes along the lower slopes of Little Pico Mountain for the next 0.9 mile, with Eight-foot Swamp visible through the trees down to your left. The trail then dips to cross Eight-foot Creek on a sturdy bridge, where the Ha-de-ron-dah Wilderness boundary comes in on the right. Once on the other side of the bridge you scramble up the side of a small esker, and as you follow along its top you have clear views of the wetlands and bogs on either side of you. The trail then leaves the esker and keeps well to the east of Pine Creek for a while, but at 3.2 miles you catch your first glimpse of Pine Lake. For the remainder of your hike you are never very far from the shore.

The most scenic parts of this trail come at 3.6 miles and 3.7 miles, where a pair of long footbridges carries you across a large wetland adjacent to the lake. The view is unimpeded. The trail reenters the woods and passes good

Trail beside Pine Lake

viewing areas on the right. There is a campsite to the left (perhaps a little too close to the trail for comfort) just before you reach an intersection at 3.9 miles, or 2.3 miles from Spring Hill.

The yellow-marked trail to the left leads to Partridgeville Road, section 91, while the red trail turns right. Once again you are on a snowmobile trail, which in this case defines the technical boundary of the Ha-de-ron-dah Wilderness. It is just a 0.1-mile walk around the north end of Pine Lake to the side trail that leads left to the Pine Lake Lean-to, which stands inland with no views of the water. This is a relatively new shelter built in 2004, and it is 4 miles from Drunkard Creek.

If you are looking for a campsite with views of the lake, there is a better option about 450 feet east along the snowmobile trail, in a wooded setting between the trail and the shore.

The continuing route to Big Otter Lake is described in section 92.

86 Mudhole Pond and Little Pine Lake

Hiking trail to canoe route
1.2 miles, 30 minutes, relatively level (from Spring Hill Junction)
2.8 miles, 70 minutes, relatively level (from Steam Mill Road)

Land-bound explorers will find this trail of minimal interest, since it ends on a wide section of Pine Creek with limited views. People with ultralight canoes will be very intrigued, however, since the end of the trail is the beginning of a navigable section of the creek and three of its tributaries.

Beginning at Springhill Junction, 1.6 miles from the Drunkard Creek Trailhead along the trail described in section 85, the trail to the Mudhole bears southeast over the broad, flat "summit" of Little Pico Mountain—which is so unlike a mountain that you must use your imagination to perceive any significant elevation change. The walking is fairly easy, although there is some evidence of illegal ATV usage. The upland beech and maple forest gives way to crooked cherry trees in the lowlands as you near the creek, and after a quick 1.2 miles (or 2.8 miles from Drunkard Creek) the trail ends on the grassy bank of Pine Creek.

This spot is adequate for the launching and landing of canoes. You can only paddle downstream for about 550 feet before running out of navigable water, so head north, upstream. The outlet of Pine Lake is at 0.2 mile, and Mudhole Pond itself at 0.4 mile. This spot is more "mud hole" than "pond," being little more than a wide and shallow backwater filled with pickerelweed. Your presence will almost certainly startle the resident ducks.

Navigable waters extend in three directions. The outlet of Pine Lake—let's call it "North Branch Pine Creek"—is the largest tributary, and while rapids will prevent you from paddling straight into the lake, a sequence of beaver dams will help you get tantalizingly close.

From the northeast corner of the Mudhole, the Middle Branch (of Middle Branch Lake fame) can be paddled for about 0.7 mile before a rocky section brings you to a stop. Whether it is worthwhile to carry around these rocks and continue paddling upstream really depends on the status of the beaver dams, because without their assistance the Middle Branch becomes unnavigable for a much longer distance beyond this point.

Finally, there is the "South Branch Pine Creek," which leads to Little Pine Lake. This small stream extends south from the Mudhole, but it quickly disperses its waters through a set of diminishing channels. Only by trial and error can you find the best way upstream. Although the distance to Little Pine Lake is only 0.3 mile, several beaver dams and a rocky riffle will stand in

Catspaw Lake

your way. There is a campsite to the north of the outlet and 34 acres of open water to explore once you reach the lake. Bullheads, suckers, pumpkinseeds, and even brook trout have been found here.

87 Pico Mountain Trail

Snowmobile trail, hiking
2.4 miles, 1 hour, rolling terrain

This section of the snowmobile trail north of Spring Hill Junction—extending over the hill known as Big Pico Mountain—is useful to hikers only if you are trying to make a loop. It is wide, wet, and monotonous. Snowmobile traffic is moderate to high in winter. It bears northwest away from Spring Hill Junction but leads generally north. It ends at an intersection with the snowmobile trail to Pine Lake from Partridgeville Road, section 91. Left leads to the trailhead in 0.9 mile, and right leads to Pine Lake in 1.9 miles.

Brantingham Lake North: Partridgeville Road

THE OTHER ROAD beginning at Brantingham Lake and extending into the Independence River Wild Forest is called Partridgeville Road. It begins at the four corners in the hamlet of Brantingham and passes in an out of state land before ending at a small inholding near Otter Creek. Numerous trails branch off into the woods from both sides of the road, including hiking trails, snowmobile trails, ski trails, and horse trails. While not all of these routes are well suited for hiking and skiing, this is nevertheless a key area for anyone wishing to explore the westernmost fringe of the Adirondack Park.

Older maps label this as Dolgeville Road rather than Partridgeville, but both names refer to the area's industrial past. Alfred Dolge had a large piano factory in Dolgeville on the Mohawk River, and while his primary source of lumber was the Jerseyfield Tract in the southern Adirondacks he also logged this area for cherry and other hardwoods. He erected a mill on Otter Creek to convert the lumber into piano sounding boards and broom handles, and this site, too, was called Dolgeville. The mill made an impression on guidebook writer Edwin R. Wallace, who wrote, "The machinery is so perfect that a log fresh from the stream or woods is converted into broom-handles in 15 minutes."

Nearby was the hamlet of Partridgeville, where Charles Partridge owned a sawmill and a dam on Otter Creek. And in 1867 the brothers H.J. and G.M. Botchford established a tannery that consumed 4000 cords of hemlock bark annually and employed fifty men. This operation folded in 1889 after exhausting all of the closest supplies of bark, but for a while all three of these operations were in existence at the same time.

One of the oddest stories occurred during the twentieth century. In 1927 a Pennsylvania-based company established a wood distillation mill in Glenfield (on the Black River south of Lowville) under the name Keystone Chemical Wood & Lumber Company. They had logging operations on Tug Hill that were connected to their mill by railroad, but they soon became interested in the larger Adirondack forests to the east. In 1928 they secured an agreement to log lands owned by Fisher Forestry and built a second railroad to support the operation. It led past the north end of Brantingham Lake to a place called Lower Balsam Flats on Crooked and Yellow creeks. The track was completed in the winter of 1929, but by that summer the company began to encounter financial issues. Their Adirondack operations limped into the winter of 1930 before coming to an end, just months after the stock market crash. As a result, the Glenfield and Eastern line was shut down within its first year.

Today, the area along Partridgeville Road remains in mixed ownership, with several restaurants, numerous homes, a few large forestry tracts, and generous amounts of state land found all along its 8-mile length. As you drive along the road you will find frequent opportunities to stop and explore the woods, from short and easy trails to longer hikes suitable for weekend backpacking trips.

This chapter describes the best of the trails that you will pass. There are additional snowmobile and horse trails available, but these are less interesting and are therefore not described. The Otter Creek Horse Trail System due north of Brantingham Lake offers many miles of looping, interconnected trails that lead sometimes to tiny ponds and scenic streams, and sometimes to nowhere in particular. This network is half trail and half road in nature. There are so many junctions, segments, turns, and potential access points that all you really need to navigate the area is a good map. Therefore the majority of these trails are omitted from this guide.

You can reach the Brantingham Lake area from NY 12, which runs north-south between Boonville and Lowville. Turn east from NY 12 at Burdick Crossing Road, between Lyons Falls and Glenfield. Cross the Black River to the intersection with Lyons Falls Road. Turn left and drive 0.7 mile north through the hamlet of Greig to the intersection with Brantingham Road. Turn right and follow it uphill for 3.6 miles to the hamlet of Brantingham, located at the intersection with Partridgeville and Middle roads. Partridgeville Road will be on the left.

88 Catspaw Lake

Snowmobile and horse trail, hiking, camping
1.2 miles, 45 minutes, rolling terrain

The first trailhead encountered along Partridgeville Road is a multi-use trail that forks north 0.9 mile from Brantingham, located where the road swings right, northeast. It is part of the Otter Creek Horse Trail System, but it is also widely used by snowmobiles and ATVs. Catspaw is an irregularly shaped

Waypoints along Partridgeville Road

Miles

0.0   Partridgeville Road begins in Brantingham at intersection with Brantingham Road

0.9   Trail to Catspaw Lake, **section 88**

1.7   Intersection with Long Point Road. *BEAR LEFT* to stay on Partridgeville Road

2.6   Access road to Shingle Mill Falls, **section 89**

4.8   Ten-Mile Crossing, parking for Centennial Ski Trail, **section 90**

7.7   Otter Creek Trailhead immediately before bridge over Otter Creek, **sections 91 & 92**

8.0   End of Partridgeville Road in residential area, site of Dolgeville; primitive road continues as Big Otter Lake Road, **section 93**

pond with numerous coves and peninsulas, and the road-trail that hooks around its eastern and northern ends makes for an easy hike.

There is no formal trailhead parking area, but there is ample room to park on the side of Partridgeville Road. The trail to Catspaw Lake may be designated as a road by DEC, but in reality it is only suitable for ATVs.

The trail heads north across level terrain, but at 0.3 mile it swings northwest and begins to descend in stages toward the lake. The pine and hemlock stands that occupy the lake's basin are attractive. At 0.6 mile you reach the first clear view of the lake—specifically, the northeastern bay where the outlet stream begins its brief journey to Otter Creek. The trail follows this stream for a moment before crossing it at 0.7 mile. A horse trail to the right leads back to Partridgeville Road.

The trail becomes straight and level all the way to the next junction at 1.1 miles. It continues straight ahead toward Van Arnam Road and other connections with the horse trail system, but to complete your hike you should turn left. This is a short spur trail that leads southeast toward a campsite on the north shore overlooking the widest part of Catspaw Lake, 1.2 miles from Partridgeville Road. It is a pretty spot, but the amount of litter suggests that it is by no means a well-kept secret.

89 Shingle Mill Falls

Access road and short trail
0.5 mile, 15 minutes (from Partridgeville Road)
200 feet, 5 minutes (from interior parking area)

Shingle Mills Falls is a set of cascades on Otter Creek that is very easy to reach, especially if you make the short drive down the access road that leads almost to the very top of the falls. But even if you don't drive in it's still a very short walk. This was the site of a matchbox and match factory, and later the site of a sizeable mill in which shingles were manufactured, hence the name.

You will find the access road 2.6 miles along Partridgeville Road, on the left as you head away from Brantingham. There is no sign, so you need to look carefully to find the entrance. There is a place to park on the side of Partridgeville Road for those who would prefer not to drive. The access road is not gated and its surface is firm, but it is very narrow. If you would prefer to walk, the road makes a fine trail.

Halfway to the falls you cross one of the horse trails. Stick to the road, and at 0.4 mile you come to the small interior parking area. From there a foot trail leads down to the bottom of the falls, which is only 200 feet away. Its photographic opportunities make it an impressive destination. The falls are not one distinct cascade, but a sequence of three rocky steps that are quite turbulent in early spring.

90 Centennial Ski Trails

Cross-country skiing
4.9-mile trail network, rolling terrain

This ski trail network spans the wild forest between Partridgeville and Steam Mill roads, creating the possibility of a loop, a through trip, or an out-and-back excursion. The trails lead to no specific destination. Instead, they wander through the woods to a number of different features, including a beaver meadow and an esker. This is a reliably snowy region, and the trails are most enjoyable on a winter day with ample fresh powder. Much of the route is level, but it is punctuated with short-but-steep hills that novice skiers will find vexing.

The trails were constructed from 1985 to 1986 by Adirondack Mountain Club volunteers to mark the centennial of the Forest Preserve. In 1885

Shingle Mill Falls

the state legislature passed a law declaring the state-owned land within the Adirondack counties—most of it acquired for non-payment of taxes—to be "forever wild." This was the first official action taken by New York State toward the eventual creation of the Adirondack Park in 1892. The Forest Preserve was granted constitutional protection in 1894.

There are trailheads at each end of the trail, but the southern one on Steam Mill Road is not plowed in winter. Therefore the recommended starting point is the trailhead on Partridgeville Road located 4.8 miles from

Brantingham. A prominent snowmobile trail crosses the road just before the trailhead, following the route of the short-lived Glenfield and Eastern Railroad. The point where the tracks crossed the road was exactly 10 miles from Glenfield, and this site is still called Ten-Mile Crossing.

PARTRIDGEVILLE ROAD APPROACH
0.5 mile, several small hills

This segment connects the trailhead at Ten-Mile Crossing with the main ski trail loop. It is only 0.5 mile long, but it features several small hills. The first (a quick downhill scoot) is only about 400 feet from the parking area, and the second (an uphill scramble) is at 0.3 mile. You then pass an old beaver flow on Brantingham Creek and climb a longer-but-gentler grade as you head due south. At 0.5 mile you reach the start of the loop, where the trail splits. Left is the Bear Ridge Trail, right is the Centennial Scoot.

BEAR RIDGE TRAIL
1.7 miles, relatively level with 2 steep hills

This route is the eastern half of the ski trail loop. It is notable for traversing a short esker through the coniferous woods. It is a beautiful winter route, although the hills leading on and off the esker are quite steep. Curiously, the esker does not appear on topographic maps at all, even though it is clearly large enough.

From the junction 0.5 mile from Ten-Mile Crossing, the trail leads southeast over some lesser grades to the initial ascent of the esker. From a skier's perspective the trail is rather steep and narrow here, but once on top it becomes a beautiful route that follows the crest with lowland spruce-balsam swamps on both sides. This section lasts all too briefly, though, because at 0.7 mile it drops steeply off the esker just before reaching an old trail junction.

The ski trail now bears right on what used to be the old foot trail to Pine Lake, which dates to a time when Steam Mill Road was impassable to most cars. This trail bypassed what was then a rutted road and led straight to Spring Hill Junction. Now, the section to the east of the esker has been abandoned, but as you head west along the modern ski trail you will still see old red trail markers, many of them metal ones from the 1960s.

This last mile of the trail features no notable hills. It passes in and out of areas of thick blowdown and brush, with pockets of deep woods in between. At 1.7 miles you return to the Centennial Scoot Trail. Left leads to Steam Mill Road, right leads back to Partridgeville Road.

CENTENNIAL SCOOT
1.2 miles, relatively level

This segment forms the western half of the loop, and the one best suited for novice skiers. Much of it passes along the edge of a ravine enclosing Brantingham Creek, and nearly all of it is level and ideal for skiing. You will reach it by turning right at the junction 0.5 mile from Ten-Mile Crossing.

STEAM MILL ROAD APPROACH
1.5 miles, rolling terrain

This section is also relatively level as it follows various old roads and even a portion of an old railroad grade (one of several spurs that branched off the Glenfield and Eastern Railroad). It is not entirely level, though. A few short grades spaced at long intervals provide a bit of skiing interest.

You can reach this segment from either half of the loop described above. Or if you prefer to approach it from the south, you can ski the 0.3-mile unplowed section of Steam Mill Road to the southern trailhead. From there, it leads 1.5 miles northeast to the junction where the Centennial Scoot bears left and the Bear Ridge Trail leads right.

91 Pine Lake

Snowmobile trail, hiking, camping, cross-country skiing, snowshoeing, mountain biking
3 miles, 1½ hours, rolling terrain

This is the shortest and most popular trail to Pine Lake, a 60-acre body of water with a lean-to and a beautiful pine-rimmed shoreline. The trail is an old one, mentioned in Edwin R. Wallace's guidebooks from the 1880s as a road that offered "3 m. of rough traveling." Botchford's Tannery, "a mammoth concern, managed by a popular and energetic man," was located near the trailhead at the time. The list of significant changes since then is remarkably short: the tannery shut down in 1889; a portion of the woods burned in 1903; the state acquired the land in 1955; the trailhead was relocated in the 1960s; and the lean-to was replaced in 2004. Otherwise today's trail seems to be essentially the same.

The trail begins near the end of Partridgeville Road, just before the bridge over Otter Creek, 7.7 miles from Brantingham. The parking area is maintained year-round for the benefit of skiers and snowshoers.

Pine Lake

Heading south from the road, the initial portion of the trail is used mostly for foot travel. This is the one and only deviation from the original route, and it was created to bypass private land. Snowmobilers still use the original road, which begins a short distance to the west near the site of the tannery. The foot trail joins that route at 0.5 mile, after a gentle ascent of 100 feet. Turn left to reach Pine Lake.

The snowmobile trail is wide and easy to follow, and it leads consistently southeast for the remaining distance to the lake. At 0.9 mile you reach a fork. The trail to the right leads to Big Pico Mountain and Spring Hill Junction, section 87. Bearing left, you begin to encounter several minor hills, most of them downhill. There are several wet areas, although most are contained and easy to sidestep. The most vexing may be at 2.1 miles, where a small stream

flows across the trail with swampy areas on both sides. In early spring there may be no dry way across.

Spruce and balsam fir fills the basin between Pine Lake and West Pine Pond, and the trail happily leads straight through this attractive forest. At 2.5 miles you cross a bridge over an unnamed stream, turning right at the far end. Soon after, at 2.7 miles, you reach a junction with the foot trail to Steam Mill Road on the right. The Drunkard Creek Trailhead is 3.9 miles away as described in section 85.

Turning left, the snowmobile trail crosses another stream and within 300 feet offers your first glimpse of Pine Lake. A moment later, 2.8 miles from the trailhead, a side trail leads left to the Pine Lake Lean-to. It stands inland with no views of the water, but it nevertheless remains a popular camping area.

If you are looking for a campsite with views of the lake, there is a better option about 450 feet east along the snowmobile trail, in a wooded setting between the trail and the shore. If all you want is an open view where you can sit and relax, then there is an even better spot right on the trail 0.2 mile from the lean-to and 3 miles from Partridgeville Road, just before the junction with the trail to Middle Settlement Lake, section 59. The continuing route to Big Otter Lake is described in section 92.

Note that while the lake falls just within the boundaries of the Ha-de-ron-dah Wilderness where mechanized and motorized access is prohibited, the protected area ends at the side of the trail. Snowmobile use of this route is light to moderate, especially in comparison to other trails closer to Brantingham Lake; and while snowshoers may not mind walking on the packed snow, skiers might find the trail more enjoyable immediately after a fresh snowfall.

92 Pine Lake to Big Otter Lake

Snowmobile trail, hiking, snowshoeing, cross-country skiing
1.7 miles, 45 minutes, rolling terrain

This interior trail connects Pine Lake with Big Otter Lake, and it factors into several loop possibilities for hikers contemplating trips from either the Partridgeville or Thendara sides of the Ha-de-ron-dah Wilderness. Some people also consider it the preferred hiking trail to Big Otter from the west, even though the alternative route (the ATV trail described in section 93) is a full 2 miles shorter.

It begins at the trail junction near the northeast corner of Pine Lake, 3 miles from the Partridgeville Road trailhead, where the snowmobile trail described in section 91 meets the wilderness foot trail described in section 59. About 350 feet to the east you pass the northern tip of East Pine Pond, another body of water just within the boundaries of the Ha-de-ron-dah Wilderness. The trail affords only a brief view of the pond, however, before it continues northeast along the foot of a hill.

The woods open up as the trail angles north, then northwest. At 1.3 miles an unmarked trail branches left. It leads in 500 feet to a ford site on Otter Creek where you will also find a non-DEC footbridge; this side trail is essentially a shortcut to the ATV trail. The snowmobile trail swings right (east) at this point and parallels the creek for its remaining distance.

At 1.6 miles you reach a key junction near the outlet of Big Otter Lake. To the right is the Big Otter Trail, which is the foot trail described in section 72.

It leads across the width of the Ha-de-ron-dah Wilderness towards Thendara, and it can be used to reach two secluded campsites on the lake's southern and eastern shores. To the left, the snowmobile trail crosses the lake's outlet on a large bridge built in 2010 to end at a junction with the so-called Big Otter Lake Road, described in section 93.

Below the bridge, the creek now cascades over rocky ledges to form Otter Creek, but in the past a small dam at this site raised the water by several feet. Only a slender portion of the lake is visible from the bridge; the widest portion of Big Otter is about a mile away. There are two ways you can get there, following either of the routes described in sections 72/77 or 93. The latter option is shorter and easier, but people who are generally averse to following ATV trails will prefer the more primitive charms of the first option.

This trail is an acceptable route for winter hiking and skiing, and the relatively rough terrain results in a low volume of snowmobile traffic. Nevertheless, since DEC replaced the bridge over the outlet in 2010 there has been a noticeable increase in motorized usage compared to the previous decade.

93 Big Otter Lake

Snowmobile & motorized access trail, hiking, camping, snowshoeing, cross-country skiing
4.1 miles, 2 hours, rolling terrain

Big Otter Lake is the largest backcountry pond accessible from Partridgeville Road. It is a beautiful destination, but the shortest way to get there—the route described in this section—does not rank high on anyone's list of favorite hiking trails. Officially called Big Otter Lake Road, it generally follows the course of Otter Creek. It does have the *potential* to be a good trail, in terms of the scenic qualities of the route; but ATV use has long been tolerated here, if not legally sanctioned, at the expense of all other users. This is partly because the trail surface is so poor that ATVs are the only type of vehicle capable of traveling it in the summer.

This trail has been caught in a decades-long game of tug-of-war between competing expectations. Some people would like to see it converted into an automobile road that would allow anyone to drive to Big Otter Lake. This would eliminate much of the ATV rutting, but it would make many destinations in the adjacent Ha-de-ron-dah Wilderness much less remote than they currently are, reducing the chances of solitude. Others would prefer to see the road reclassified as a trail and permanently closed to ATVs. These people

Skiing across the outlet of Big Otter Lake

view Big Otter Lake as a backcountry destination and *expect* it to be remote and hard to reach. Meanwhile no action has been taken on the condition of the road, which has continued to deteriorate.

The controversy dates back to 1955, the year when the land that includes the road was purchased for the Forest Preserve. At the time it was already being used by motor vehicles for access to the lake. However, in 1961 a proposal issued by the Joint Legislative Committee on Natural Resources would have closed it to all motorized use. The committee had introduced a bill that would have designated a dozen wilderness areas across the Adirondacks, including the 28,100 acres of state land from Thendara to Partridgeville Road, which was to be known as the Big Otter Lake Wilderness. The namesake lake was to be at the heart of the area, accessible only by foot.

The bill was never enacted, but it sparked a decade-long debate on the management of the Forest Preserve. A report issued by the Temporary Study Commission on the Future of the Adirondack Park in 1970 once again endorsed the idea of zoning the preserve into wilderness and wild forest areas, but at Big Otter the wilderness proposal had been substantially reduced. Rather than a larger area centered on the lake, the new proposed wilderness—renamed "Ha-de-ron-dah"—encompassed only the 25,000 acres to the east and south. This was done to preserve the established motorized access "by hunters and fishermen with jeeps, doodle-bugs, and farm tractors" in the adjacent town of Greig.

The Ha-de-ron-dah Wilderness was officially born in 1972 with the adoption of the original State Land Master Plan, which incorporated most of the commission's recommendations. The waters of Big Otter Lake and the road from Partridgeville were specifically excluded. But while this route has been classified as a road, it has never been maintained as one. As recently as 2004 DEC proposed to harden it to accommodate passage by automobiles, but this effort too has apparently been shelved. Therefore the route remains in limbo, more than a trail but less than a road, and impossible to enjoy either way.

PARTRIDGEVILLE ROAD TO BIG OTTER LAKE OUTLET
3.1 miles, 1½ hours

The trail begins at the very end of Partridgeville Road, 8 miles from Brantingham. The surrounding land is a private residential community, however, so the best place to park is the trailhead near the Otter Creek bridge at 7.7 miles. It is no real hardship to walk the remaining 0.3 mile of the town road. The clearing where the houses now stand was the site of Dolgeville. Nearby, Otter Creek cascades noisily over rock ledges.

Big Otter Lake Road is the primitive track continuing eastward. The most offensive section comes within the first half-mile, most of which is a soupy mess with few redeeming values. At 0.6 mile you reach Tommy Roaring Creek, where a bridge on the left offers a dry crossing for hikers and skiers. Vehicles routinely ford the creek to the right.

At 1 mile it bends briefly toward Otter Creek before winding inland again. A second stream crossing at 1.5 miles may be more problematic since there is no bridge and the road may be flooded for 20 or more feet. You pass close to Otter Creek several more times over the next mile, reaching a junction at 2.6 miles. The route to the right leads downhill to a ford across the creek, with a non-DEC footbridge to the side. It can be used as a shortcut to the snowmobile trail from Pine Lake described in section 92.

At 3.1 miles Big Otter Lake Road officially ends at a junction near the lake's outlet, where a large trail bridge extends south to connect with the trails to Thendara and Pine Lake (sections 72 and 92 respectively). Below the bridge, the creek now cascades over rocky ledges to form Otter Creek, but in the past a small dam at this site raised the water by several feet. Only a slender portion of the lake is visible from the bridge; the widest portion of Big Otter is about a mile away.

FROM THE OUTLET TO THE WEST SHORE
1 mile, 30 minutes

This next section of the road beyond the dam site was officially closed to motor vehicles in the 1980s, but this hardly seems to be a deterrent to the ATV riders who still ride it. The trail extends into Herkimer County on a parcel of land that was purchased in 1909, and it is very wet and rutted. It leads to a prominent campsite on the west shore of Big Otter Lake 1 mile from the outlet and 4.1 miles from the end of Partridgeville Road.

This location is often referred to as the site of an old hotel. In 1889 (twenty years prior to state acquisition) Edwin R. Wallace noted the presence of "1 or 2 substantial camps where visitors may secure comfortable accommodations." He was ambivalent about the lake itself, though, on the one hand calling it a "romantic sheet" with "handsome bays and points," but on the other hand expressing disappointment over the way past forest fires and the raising of the water had "damaged the scenery."

Portions of the lake were burned again in 1903 as the forest fire that devastated the Ha-de-ron-dah region extended westward. Today, though, Big Otter Lake is considered to be tree-lined and sparkling, and a most attractive body of water. It is a reasonably good fishing lake, containing brook trout along with bullheads and sunfish. It is a good lake for swimming too, with sand and gravel beaches scattered around its edges.

You may also find an unmarked path continuing past the hotel site. It leads around the west shore to a second campsite near the north end of the lake.

Number Four Road

THE FIRST PLANNED settlement in the northern reaches of John Brown's Tract came in 1822, when John Brown Francis established a farming community on Township 4 near the Beaver River. Francis was the grandson of John Brown and the nephew of Charles Frederick Herreshoff, and he was the heir to the vast tract that neither of those men had been able to tame. He offered 100-acre lots to the first ten settlers, but once again the area's poor soils and cold climate thwarted his efforts—John Brown's Tract was simply an unlikely place to start a productive farm. None of the families that Francis attracted to Township 4 were willing to stay for long.

The tiny hamlet of Number Four did not fade into complete obscurity, however, because in 1826 a new arrival named Orrin Fenton discovered that the area presented other opportunities. He moved his family into one of the ten abandoned farms and operated it as a boarding house for sportsmen and tourists until he died in 1870. His son Charles Fenton took over and grew the Fenton House into a small campus that featured a post office, a store, a hall for social events, and several cottages. He also leased much of the surrounding land as a game preserve for the benefit of his guests.

Today, the majority of the state land available for hiking in Number Four lies to the east and south, with the focus of this chapter being the region south of Number Four Road, the primary access route from Lowville. This is an area of low rolling hills and pine-rimmed ponds. Like much of the Independence River Wild Forest, it is crisscrossed by numerous old woods roads, some of which have been designated as hiking trails. But as quiet and peaceful as the forest may be, the story of how portions of it came into public ownership is one of the more colorful stories in the southwestern Adirondacks.

Most of the land surrounding Number Four had been purchased from the Brown estate by Lyman R. Lyon, a member of the mill-owning family for whom the Lewis County communities of Lyons Falls and Lyonsdale were named. When he died in 1869 these same Adirondack landholdings eventually passed to two of his daughters, Julia Lyon deCamp and Mary Lyon Fisher. The latter woman became the steward of the northern townships along the Beaver River, including large portions of Township 4.

The controversy began in 1906 when Mary Fisher sold all of the spruce, hemlock, and balsam timber greater than eight inches in diameter to the

St. Regis Paper Company. One stipulation was that "the land should be cut clear as the work progressed," with the contract being in force over a number of years. In 1908, while the St. Regis logging operation was still in progress, Fisher negotiated the sale of the underlying land. This would have resulted in the cutting of the hardwood trees, as well.

The state's forest purchasing board heard of these plans, and fearing that the clear-cutting of 23,000 acres was in progress it invoked its authority under the Forest, Fish, and Game Law to condemn the land and add it to the Forest Preserve. The state claimed title to Fisher's land simply by passing a resolution in January 1909 and obtaining the oral consent of Governor Charles Evan Hughes. Not surprisingly, Fisher challenged the validity of this action; but she also had the backing of the state's comptroller, who "steadfastly refused to recognize the validity of the appropriation proceedings" and prevented the expenditure of any funds. In fact, the lands remained on the tax lists in Fisher's name.

Mary Fisher died in 1913, but her children Clarence L. Fisher and Florence Fisher Jackson were substituted as defendants in the legal proceedings brought about by the attorney general to resolve the title dispute. They argued that the purchasing board had overstepped its authority when it appropriated their mother's land and that there had been no due process of law. A judgment in November 1916 ruled against the Fishers, stating that the condemnation proceedings had been within the letter and intent of the law. However, the state's appropriation was overturned by the Court of Appeals in 1922 on the grounds of "incompleted procedures," and title to the contested acreage reverted to the Fisher Forestry and Realty Company, the siblings' joint landholding entity.

Clarence Fisher immediately went to work as an active manager of the regained land. He built a fire tower on the property and hosted a summer camp of forestry students at Francis Lake. He advertised the property in local newspapers and sold numerous small parcels to individual buyers. He took leadership roles in various forestry organizations and spoke publicly on the importance of forest fire prevention. He also served in the state legislature where he sponsored a bill to provide tax incentives to landowners with reforested properties. The Fisher Forest Act, as it was known, was perhaps his proudest achievement.

In addition to his forestry associations, he served on the board of governors of the Adirondack Mountain Club and was one of its charter members. He was also a trustee of the Association for the Protection of the Adirondacks—which, ironically, had earlier filed an amicus brief in support of the state's claim against the Fisher family. Both of these organizations strongly

Waypoints along Number Four Road

Bushes Landing to No. Four		No. Four to Bushes Landing
0.0	Number Four Road bears northeast (left) at a prominent fork in Bushes Landing, 4.2 miles east of Lowville	13.5
5.0	Crystal Dale, intersection with Erie Canal Road, sections 103 & 104	8.5
7.9	Adirondack Park boundary	5.6
8.9	Intersection with Halfmoon Road, **section 94**	4.6
12.4	Intersection with Smith Road, **sections 95-99**	1.1
13.5	Number Four, intersection with Stillwater Road, **sections 100-102**	0.0

supported efforts to expand the Forest Preserve, and these affiliations may have influenced his later decisions to sell the larger, undeveloped portions of his lands to the state.

After losing its claim in 1922, the state owned very little land in the Number Four area. However, in 1932 it acquired 21,483 acres around the west end of Stillwater Reservoir and north of the Beaver River. This time Clarence Fisher was a willing seller. In 1956 and 1958 the state purchased several other large tracts in the Independence River watershed, including Panther Pond and Sunday Lake. In essence, the state eventually bought most of the land by mid-century that it had condemned decades earlier. Fisher's name now appears repeatedly throughout the acquisition histories of the Independence River Wild Forest and the wilderness areas to the north.

Today, two gravel access roads branch south from Number Four Road to several interior trailheads, and these are the key to unlocking the recreational potential of these lands. This is an area for three-season hiking, since the DEC roads are not plowed in winter (and one is in fact heavily used by snowmobiles). But during those three seasons, the access roads lead you far from the pavement and into some admirably wild terrain.

The area is most easily reached from downtown Lowville, where Number

Four Road begins as River Street at an intersection with NY 12. Follow it east out of town and across the Black River for 4.2 miles to the hamlet of Bushes Landing. Here, Number Four Road bears left at a fork and continues northeast into the Adirondack Park. The accompanying waypoint chart begins at this point. You will need to watch your odometer carefully to find the two forest access roads described below, because the signage is not always obvious.

94 Halfmoon Lake

Hiking, mountain biking, camping, cross-country skiing
1 mile, 30 minutes, relatively level

This small pond lies to the southeast of Crystal Lake, and in the summer months it can be reached by a very easy hike. Signs and markers may be few in number, but if you can find your way to the secluded trailhead then you should have no problem following the trail.

It begins at the end of Halfmoon Road, a gravel lane that begins 1 mile east of the Adirondack Park boundary on Number Four Road, and 8.9 miles from Bushes Landing. The road may not be marked, but several signs remind you that this is a public easement across private land. Heading south, it enters state land at 0.5 mile and continues to the small interior parking area 1.5 miles from the county highway—well over half the total distance to the pond. The road is not plowed in winter.

The trailhead is located above Burnt Creek, a substantial tributary of the Independence River to the south. The culvert that carried the road across the creek has long since washed away, so the beginning of this hike begins with a ford. In the summer this should not be an issue, but during times of high water you will have to step through knee-deep water or take your chances on slippery rocks.

Beyond the crossing, the trail to Halfmoon Lake follows the continuation of the old road. It leads southwest across level terrain, with evidence that sportsmen have camped in the open woods along the way in the fall. At 0.5 mile it swings left, southeast, and crosses Tuttle Creek. You reach the outlet of the pond at 0.8 mile, where beaver flooding may challenge you to find dry ground on which to step—the trail surface is scarcely higher than the level of the pond. You curve closely around the edge of a cove before arriving at the site of two long-gone camps, located on a point at the northeast corner of

the pond. This spot is 1 mile from the parking area, and a total of 2.5 miles from Number Four Road.

Halfmoon Lake has long been a popular hunting and fishing destination for residents of the Lowville area, although due to its warmth and acidity it is not stocked today. The state acquired it in 1980 from a retired veterinarian, but in decades past the Lowville Fish and Game Club occasionally held events here. The entire shoreline is rimmed by pine trees, with the only break occurring at the cabin site.

This route, which spends so much of its time in pine forests, would be an attractive ski trail. The biggest concerns for winter travel are the lack of a parking area on Number Four Road, and the lack of a bridge over Burnt Creek.

95 Smith Road

Access road, camping

The second DEC access road leading south from Number Four Road is called Smith Road. This is a fair gravel lane 3.8 miles in length, passable to ordinary vehicles except in the winter when it is primarily used as a snowmobile trail. It is of interest to hikers because several routes begin here: one marked trail, one former trail, and one bushwhack. The state has designated several good drive-in campsites all along its length, including one near the Panther Pond trailhead parking area at the end. It is an attractive area in the summer, but it is probably most heavily used during the fall hunting season.

A brown DEC sign prominently marks its beginning on Number Four Road, 12.4 miles from Bushes Landing and 1.1 miles from Number Four.

	Waypoints along Smith Road
Miles	
0.0	Road begins at junction with Number Four Road, 1.1 miles from Number Four
0.2	Large campsite with driveway on right, access to Number Four Fire Tower site, **section 96**
2.2	Gate at intersection with private road. *BEAR LEFT*
3.8	Trailhead parking area at end of road, **sections 97-99**

When the state acquired the 11,416-acre Panther Pond tract to the south in 1958 (from the Fisher Forestry and Realty Company, of course) it also acquired an easement on Smith Road for public access to its boundary. Smith Road was at that time located on private land and ended where the new state land began. However, when that property was added to the Forest Preserve in 1979 the road was allowed to remain—permitting legal motorized access deep into the woods.

96 Number Four Fire Tower Site

Very short walk
400 feet, 2 minutes, 20-foot vertical rise

Nowhere in the Adirondacks will you find a fire tower summit easier to climb than this! It will take you longer to read this description of the Number Four Fire Tower than it will to reach the site by foot.

The tower was built in 1928 as a joint effort between the Conservation Department and the Fisher Forestry and Realty Company. It was manned by Fisher Forestry until 1945, and operated by the state thereafter until it was dismantled in 1986. (The upper portion was reassembled at DEC's demonstration site in Dadville, on NY 812 outside of Lowville, where the public can still climb it.) There is no view here, but fire tower aficionados will find such an easily accessible site hard to resist.

As you drive south on Smith Road from Number Four, section 95, a driveway on the right at 0.2 mile leads to a large designated campsite. This was the location of the observer's cabin, and if no one is camping here you can use it for parking. A clear path leads southwest into the woods from the rear left corner of the campsite, climbing roughly 20 vertical feet to the spot where the tower stood. All that remains are the concrete footers, one of which is inscribed with the initials of those who constructed it.

The Number Four tower was actually Fisher Forestry's second observation station. It was intended to replace a wooden tower erected in the spring of 1922 southeast of Halfmoon Lake, on an unnamed hill that was described simply as a "rock mountain." That station featured telephone service despite its relatively remote location and primitive construction. There was apparently a high need for these towers, for reports of small-scale fires were common in the Number Four region—including one spotted from "rock mountain" in May 1923 by a watchman named Fayette Fee.

97 Panther Pond

Hiking, camping
1.1 miles, 30 minutes, relatively level

By driving to the end of Smith Road you will find the trailhead parking area for Panther Pond, a remote body of water at the heart of this section of the Independence River Wild Forest. Panther Pond is shallow, warm, acidic and fishless, so the primary reason to pay it a visit is to enjoy the peaceful setting and intrinsic beauty that comes with any wild place. It is an easy hike with a short trail across gentle terrain, and the lean-to at the pond's north end is an inviting setting for a backpacking trip.

From the end of Smith Road, section 95, the trail follows the continuing roadway past a gate to a crossing of Pine Creek 300 feet away. At 0.2 mile there is a fork where a snowmobile trail veers left toward McCarthy Road—a route of minimal interest to hikers. Bearing right, the remaining route to Panther Pond is a much narrower trail. It leads southwest, generally parallel to Pine Creek but at some distance removed.

Watch for a second fork where the marked foot trail bears left; the route to the right is an older woods road too wet and swampy for enjoyable hiking. The foot trail does encounter a few small muddy areas of its own, but nothing like the old route below and to your right. You then enter the coniferous woods and approach the Panther Pond Lean-to from behind at 1.1 miles.

The shelter is surrounded by pine trees and commands an excellent view of the pond—a classic setting for a campsite. If there is one drawback to Panther Pond, it is the fact that it is never more than seven feet deep. This shallowness is especially problematic around the shoreline, where it can be difficult to access the water without stirring up the muck. Certainly, this is no place to go swimming!

The continuing foot trail veers to the left and away from the lean-to, leading to the Independence River as described in section 98.

98 Independence River via Panther Pond

Hiking
3.5 miles, 1¾ hours, rolling terrain

This remote, seldom-traveled trail connects the lean-to at Panther Pond with the Independence River near Mount Tom. It passes through the wild heart

Site of the Number Four Fire Tower

of the area, traversing several small hills and dipping through the intervening glens on its way from one point to the next. Its best use might be as part of a through-hike from Beach Mill Road (section 103) to Smith Road, but if you enjoy exploring solitary routes through little-known areas, then the hike to the river and back along this trail will be hard to beat.

The description begins at the Panther Pond Lean-to, 1.1 miles from Smith Road as outlined in section 97. The trail leads east to curve around the corner of the pond, and at 0.2 mile a faint path veers right to a small lookout perched atop a rock on the east shore, with a view back toward the lean-to. The trail then continues to parallel the east side of the pond, which tapers into a set of beaver meadows at its south end.

At 0.9 mile you make a rock-hop crossing over a tributary of Third Creek. As you continue southward, the trail winds up and over several small ridges, including one with a patch of lichen-covered rock. The trail is lightly used and the markers are sometimes more than just a convenience for finding the way—they are a necessity where the tread is poorly defined. Off-trail map-and-compass navigation in this area would be complicated by the fact that the most recent USGS topographic quadrangles do not accurately portray all of the complexities of the terrain. Where the base map shows a sprawling hillside, there are actually several small ridges—including at least one esker.

At 2 miles the trail dips down from a hilltop to cross another stream, this one called Snake Creek. A moment later, at 2.2 miles, you reach a T intersection with an old woods road. If you are traveling south it is pretty evident that the hiking trail turns right here, but if you are following the trail north it could be easy to miss this left turn and keep on the old road, which used to be a snowmobile trail that looped back toward McCarthy and Smith roads. Situations like this illustrate the need to pay careful attention to your surroundings when following such a lightly used trail!

Turning right, the terrain becomes less hilly but much muddier. You are now parallel to Fourth Creek (one of several numbered tributaries of the Independence River) although you will rarely see it. One sprawling pocket of mud has no foolproof way across, except to hop from one hummock to the next. The trail becomes filled with grasses and ferns—potentially tall enough to obscure the tread—and at 3.2 miles you reach the side of the Independence River.

The last 0.3 mile are very enjoyable and easy to follow, as the trail remains quite close to the river. There is some evidence of ATV trespass here, although the damage has been minimal so far. At 3.5 miles you reach a junction beside a large footbridge over the river. The trail across the bridge is the Fish Trail, which leads in 1.8 miles to Stony Lake Road. The trail that

Bridge over the Independence River near Mount Tom

continues straight along the river leads to Gleasmans Falls, 3.4 miles away. Both directions are part of the exceptional hike described in section 104.

99 Bills Pond

Path & bushwhack

Bills Pond lies to the northeast of the Panther Pond trailhead at the end of Smith Road. It is larger and deeper than Panther Pond, but it is just as fishless. This may explain the lack of a good path to its shore, despite the fact that old logging roads are available to guide you there. It is an attractive place, surrounded by hardwoods that put on a brilliant display in September. Negotiating your way along the old woods roads can be a good test of your navigation skills, but because they are so infrequently traveled this route should be treated more like a bushwhack than as an established path.

Drive to the end of Smith Road, described in section 95, and park at the trailhead for Panther Pond. The marked trail departs from the south end of the parking area, but to reach Bills Pond direct your attention to the northeast end. Beyond the gravel surface, there is a fern-filled clearing of sorts amidst the black cherry trees. There may be no evidence of a path from the parking area, so head across the clearing on a heading of about 40° true. The resumption of the woods at the far end of the fern meadow may help define the edges of a faint woods road; you may also find some subtle evidence that someone has been using it as a path. It continues northeast, climbing at a very gentle rate and slowly turning more east than northeast.

Pay close attention to your compass heading. After 0.7 mile and about 20 minutes of hiking (depending on your pace) the logging road veers just to the south of east. This shift in direction will be the most reliable sign you should expect to find for the next turn you will need to make—the open hardwood forest provides few obvious landmarks. The more obvious road (the one which you have been following) continues southeast, away from the pond. Therefore to reach the pond you need to find the lesser road that heads left, almost due north. You can follow it through a gap between two small hills, and within 0.2 mile (0.9 mile total) you should see Bills Pond ahead through the red maples.

The old road turns to parallel the pond's south shore but becomes less relevant the further you follow it. Feel free to approach the pond wherever you find an advantageous route to the water. There is no rock ledge or other distinguishing feature on the south shore, so any spot is as good as any other.

Stillwater Road

THE ROAD FROM Number Four to Stillwater was once part of the Carthage Road, an east-west route across the heart of the Adirondacks that the state legislature chartered in 1841. With an eastern terminus at Crown Point on Lake Champlain, it passed through the modern-day hamlets of Newcomb and Long Lake, between Raquette and Forked lakes, and then along the Beaver River into Lewis County. The western end of the road became discontinuous when Stillwater Reservoir was enlarged in 1922, flooding more than a mile of the route and isolating the hamlet of Beaver River.

Today, Stillwater Road is a town highway that is primarily used to access the reservoir and all of the wilderness adventures that begin from its shores, as described in *Discover the Northwestern Adirondacks*. However, the road passes through the northern reaches of the Independence River Wild Forest on its way to the reservoir, and for those who are not in a hurry to reach the lake, there are a handful of opportunities to hike and paddle that you may find of interest. These are the focus of this chapter.

Stillwater Road begins in Number Four, 13.5 miles from Bushes Landing and 17.7 miles from Lowville. The westernmost section is paved, but most of it is a bumpy and dusty gravel road. On busy winter weekends, snowmobiles sometime outnumber cars.

100 Francis Lake

Short walk, canoeing

Francis Lake is named for John Brown Francis, the founder of Number Four and later governor of Rhode Island. It was purchased by the state in 1979 from the estate of Clarence Fisher, and at one point there was a proposal to establish a campground on its shores. That project has never materialized, and today Francis Lake is a peaceful setting that is almost within view of Stillwater Road.

With a hidden bog, pine-covered eskers along its northeastern shore, and handsome little rock islands, Francis Lake is certainly one of the most attractive lakes in the region. Although relatively large—120 acres—this body of water is shallow, providing only a warm-water fishery of pickerel and yellow perch.

Waypoints along Stillwater Road

No. Four to Still-water		Stillwater to No. Four
0.0	Intersection with Number Four Road (see previous chapter)	8.2
0.9	Francis Lake, **section 100**	7.3
2.1	Intersection with Moshier Road	6.1
2.3	Herkimer-Lewis county line	5.9
3.6	McCarthy Road, **section 101**	4.6
4.1	Basket Factory Road, vehicular access to state land	4.1
7.8	Intersection with Big Moose Road, **section 102**	0.4
8.2	Stillwater	0.0

As you travel east along Stillwater Road from Number Four, the access for Francis Lake is on the right at 0.9 mile. The parking area closest to the lake is designated for the disabled, but the alternate parking area just up the road—a widening of the shoulder—is hardly an inconvenience.

There are two ways to enjoy Francis Lake. From the disabled parking area, a graded path leads in 250 feet to a fishing platform on the north end of the lake. This is the place to launch a canoe or kayak. With the exception of two private inholdings on the north shore, the lake is entirely state-owned. An esker covered with tall white pine traverses the southeastern part of the lake, almost isolating a large area of marsh and bog. Smooth boulders ring parts of the southern shore. You might see herons and nesting loons as you paddle quietly around the edge of the lake. Its many bays and irregular shape extend its shoreline to allow for a nearly 4-mile paddle.

The other way to catch a glimpse of the lake is by foot. From the alternate parking area along the side of Stillwater Road, a lane leads into the woods along the northeast corner of Francis Lake. It offers fine views of the water without the commitment of a long hike—in just 0.2 mile it enters one of the inholdings, where public access ends. The round-trip walk takes only 10 minutes.

101 Sunday Lake via McCarthy Road

Short hike, camping, canoeing
0.1 mile, 2 minutes, rolling terrain

Like Smith Road and Halfmoon Road described in the previous chapter, DEC maintains two access roads leading south into state lands from Stillwater Road, as well. Called McCarthy Road and Basket Factory Road, both routes make it possible to drive deep into the woods. Drive-in campsites are available, and these are eagerly claimed by sportsmen in the fall.

McCarthy Road offers one short walk of note: the trail to Sunday Lake. You will find McCarthy Road 3.6 miles from Number Four and 4.6 miles from Stillwater. There is a huge parking area at its beginning, but continue through to where the road enters the woods. It is an easy 0.5-mile drive to where the side road to Sunday Lake veers left. This route is narrower and a bit rougher, but you only need to drive it for 0.3 mile to the undeveloped parking area, 0.8 mile total from Stillwater Road. Of course, McCarthy Road and the Sunday Lake spur are not plowed in winter.

By the time you park at the trailhead, you have already traveled most of the distance to the lake. The well-traveled trail (well traveled by ATVs, that is) continues east past a muddy area to the large campsite on the west shore. Sunday Lake is only 19 acres in size, and hardly more than a pond. It is not far enough into the woods to escape the sounds of traffic on Stillwater Road, but its pine-rimmed shoreline is nevertheless quite attractive. The distance to the water is so short that it would be easy to carry a canoe. You can fish for trout, perch, sunfish, and bullheads here.

102 Stillwater Mountain

Proposed trail
0.9 mile, 30 minutes, 550-foot vertical rise
Access available from May 1 to Columbus Day

The fire tower on Stillwater Mountain is the only observation station still standing in this part of the Adirondacks, and it offers the best chance for a far-ranging view in the Stillwater area. It was built in 1919 by the state's Conservation Department, who had no choice but to place it on private land because at the time the state owned almost no land of its own beyond the immediate shoreline of the lake. The parcel to the north of the tower, including the lower half of the trail, was purchased from Clarence Fisher in

1932, but the tower itself remains on private property to this day. In 1988 DEC ceased using it for fire detection, and leaseholders curtailed public access to the summit for several years thereafter. In 2005, however, New York acquired an easement that has permanently restored access to both the trail and the tower. As climbs go, this "mountain" is an easy hill with no truly steep pitches. Fit hikers could get to the top and back and still be on time for breakfast.

Please note that the terms of the easement allow public access only from May 1 to Columbus Day; it is closed through the fall and winter.

The trailhead is located on Big Moose Road, which intersects Stillwater Road 7.8 miles from Number Four and 0.4 mile from the hamlet of Stillwater. Follow this gravel road for 2 miles around the southwest end of the reservoir, which mostly remains out of view. The trailhead parking area is a converted borrow pit on the south side of the road.

Beginning from the back end of the parking area, the trail begins its gentle ascent almost immediately. The first part of the trail is on state land, and it passes through a hardwood forest that provides enough shade to keep the understory relatively open. Within a few minutes, however, you pass into the easement lands where logging has created a more open forest canopy, which in turn allows for a greater amount of brushy growth. The transition from one forest type to the next occurs quite swiftly.

At 0.5 mile you reach a four-way intersection. The left-right route is an ATV trail, while the hiking trail to the summit continues straight. The climbing is never steep, even as patches of bare rock appear in the trail. It should take only half an hour to reach the foot of the tower at 0.9 mile. There is no view from ground level, but from the cab you can see across the reservoir to the distant hills—even as far as the High Peaks on good days.

IMPORTANT! The trail to Stillwater Mountain was not yet completed and ready for use—and the aging tower was not yet rehabilitated—at the time this guidebook went to press. The description above assumes that these tasks will be completed during the lifetime of this edition. In the meantime, the trail is unmarked and unsigned, and the tower may not be safe to climb. If you wish to explore Stillwater Mountain, please contact the Lowville DEC office at (315) 376-3521 to determine the current status.

The Independence River

THE INDEPENDENCE RIVER was named on July 4, 1793 by a surveyor named Pierre Perroux. It begins as the outlet of Little Independence Pond near the hamlet of Big Moose, and before it exits the Adirondack Park 29 miles later it is squeezed between the rugged rock walls of a gorge called Gleasmans Falls. This wild place, where the river descends a total of 60 vertical feet over a series of small cascades, is beyond all doubt one of the scenic highlights of the entire southwestern Adirondack region.

Like many Adirondack rivers, the Independence saw its share of log drives and lumber camps, which in this case continued well into the twentieth century. The adjoining landowners included Fisher Forestry and Taggart Paper. The state, however, owned very little land along the river, only two miles in the vicinity of Hitchcock Pond that it acquired at a tax sale in 1917. This large gap in the Forest Preserve did not go unnoticed by state officials, who in a period from 1954 through 1958 executed a series of targeted acquisitions that brought into public ownership not only Gleasmans Falls, but nearly all of the lands that now comprise the western portion of the Independence River Wild Forest.

It is interesting to note that the seller of the largest parcel—a 12,000-acre tract that sprawled from Crystal Lake to Brantingham Lake—was the power company Niagara Mohawk. The utility's interest in owning such a large, forested property was not in the value of the timber, but rather the river's potential to generate electricity. Not coincidentally, there had been a proposal to dam the Independence River at Sperryville dating back at least to the 1920s when Stillwater Reservoir was last enlarged. At 2500 acres, the Sperryville Reservoir would have been less than half the size of Stillwater, but still plenty large enough to permanently alter Gleasmans Falls and the area around it. However, Niagara Mohawk instead chose to develop a series of hydroelectric facilities on the Beaver River to the north, making the Sperryville project unnecessary.

Today, the trail along the river and its rugged gorge is perhaps the most outstanding hike in Lewis County's portion of the Adirondack Park. Two trailheads serve Gleasmans Falls, and they are both buried deep within the series of back roads near Chase Lake. The Beach Mill Trailhead lies to the west of Gleasmans Falls, and because it offers the shortest hike to the gorge this is by far the more popular starting point. The Fish Trail near Stony Lake

Waypoints along Erie Canal Road

Miles

0.0	Intersection with Number Four Road in Crystal Dale
2.5	Intersection with McPhilmy Road. *LEFT* leads to Beach Mill Road, **section 103**
3.6	Bridge over the Independence River
4.4	Intersection with Stony Lake Road, **section 104**

Beach Mill Road to Beach Mill Trailhead

0.0	Intersection of Erie Canal Road and McPhilmy Road
0.2	Beach Mill Road begins on left. **No winter parking beyond this point**
0.4	State land boundary
1.1	Intersection with Cleveland Lake Road. *BEAR LEFT*
1.7	Intersection with private road. *BEAR RIGHT*
3.2	Beach Mill trailhead at end of road, **section 103**

Stony Lake Road to Fish Trail

0.0	Stony Lake Road begins at intersection with Erie Canal Road
2.0	Chase Upper Lake
3.1	End of winter maintenance
5.5	Beginning of private land surrounding Stony Lake
6.4	State land resumes
6.5	Fish Trail parking area, **section 104**
7.0	End of road

provides the eastern approach, but because it is so far off the beaten path it is much less frequently used. Hikers who appreciate solitude and have more time to spend in the woods will find that this trailhead is worth the extra drive. If you can spot cars at both ends, the 8-mile through-hike is one of the best in the region.

If you are not familiar with this portion of Lewis County, then the least complicated approach is via Erie Canal Road, which intersects Number Four Road at Crystal Dale. Directions to Number Four have been provided in an earlier chapter, but to refresh your memory we have repeated them below.

Begin in downtown Lowville, where Number Four Road begins as River Street at an intersection with NY 12, and drive east out of town and across the Black River. At 4.2 miles the road forks at the hamlet of Bushes Landing. Number Four Road bears left, and 5 miles later it reaches Crystal Dale.

Bearing right (south) onto Erie Canal Road will take you into the woodsy residential area surrounding Chase Lake. Beach Mill Road can be found off McPhilmy Road, a left turn at 2.5 miles. Stony Lake Road turns left at 4.4 miles. Use the accompanying waypoint charts to identify all of the key turns and landmarks along all three of these roads.

103 Gleasmans Falls via Beach Mill Road

Hiking, camping, cross-country skiing, snowshoeing
2.8 miles, 1¼ hours, rolling terrain (summer)
5.8 miles, 3 hours, rolling terrain (winter)

This is the shortest approach to Gleasmans Falls, and therefore the most popular. The easy terrain and clear path make this an attractive route even for less experienced hikers. Even though only the final portion of the hike is located beside the river, that doesn't mean that the remainder lacks interest. This is a fine outing that appeals to a variety of people.

There is no bad time of year to enjoy Gleasmans Falls. The Independence River is a wild force in the spring, of course, when the water levels are at their highest. In the summer it is easier to descend into the gorge and take photographs of the sheer rock walls on both sides. The forest is filled with hardwoods, making the fall foliage quite colorful. In the winter you do have to hike or ski the unplowed access road to reach the start of the trail, but even this extra 3 miles hardly puts Gleasmans Falls out of reach.

The trailhead is located at the end of Beach Mill Road, a DEC access road that can be found by turning east onto McPhilmy Road 2.5 miles south of Crystal Dale. The start of Beach Mill Road is 0.2 mile further on the left. This is a narrow gravel lane that continues for a total of 3 miles into state land, and along the way you pass three trails in the Otter Creek Horse Trail system, all of which loop back to the nearby Cleveland Lake Road. The hiking trail to the falls begins at the last clearing where the road ends. The way is not plowed in the winter, but it is also not barricaded—it can be driven as

Independence River at Gleasmans Falls

soon as it is clear of ice and snow, a fact that spring waterfall seekers will appreciate. (Just remember that snow lingers in woodland areas much longer than it does elsewhere.)

The trailhead was the site of a lumber mill owned by Andrew J. Beach, and a wooden dam on nearby Burnt Creek once created a modest reservoir known as Beach Millpond. That name persists on modern topographic maps, even though the dam washed away many decades ago and the pond no longer exists. This led to a case of bureaucratic chagrin in 1965 when the Conversation Department proposed opening the long-vanished pond to motorboats and floatplanes, apparently not realizing it was now nothing more than a name on a map. Local residents were duly amused, and a tongue-in-cheek notice appeared in a Lowville newspaper a few weeks later announcing honorary memberships in the "Beach Mill Pond Yacht Club, Inc."

Beginning at the far end of the parking area, the trail begins as an extension of the road and descends to a footbridge across Burnt Creek, just below the site of the dam. Beyond the creek, the old road becomes more trail-like as it turns northeast through the mixed woods. At 0.7 mile an unmarked side trail veers left to a campsite near the Beach Millpond wetland. A few small hills are encountered as the trail then veers southeast. At 1.3 miles you pass a sprawling wetland where beaver flooding could force you to improvise a detour. Keep an eye out for wildlife. Who knows? You might find a snapping turtle lurking in the shallows.

The trail approaches the Independence River rather slowly. Your first sighting does not occur until 2.5 miles, after a sharp descent into the valley of Second Creek. Just before you reach the bridge over this tributary, look for a side path leading right to a campsite near the river. Across the creek, the main trail continues another 0.2 mile to a third place where people have camped, this site located right on the trail. A rock ledge extends into the river and offers the best view of the lower end of the gorge.

The next 0.1 mile is what you came to see. Past the last campsite, the trail ascends to the rocky rim of the gorge. Look for a cleft in the rock to your right where the slope angles down at a reasonable pitch; this marks the best place to descend into the gorge when the water is low, although it is still steep enough to require a bit of a scramble. There are open ledges beside the trail further up where it is possible to stand on the edge and see the churning water below. A sign marks your arrival at Gleasmans Falls, in case you had any doubt. You reach this point 2.8 miles from the Beach Mill Trailhead, or 5.8 miles from McPhilmy Road.

If you choose to descend into the gorge through the cleft, you will find a ledge perfectly angled to look up the river to the uppermost cascade—the lower the water, the more this ledge will be exposed. Most of the rest of the gorge is inaccessible, but if you continue along the hiking trail past the Gleasmans Falls sign for another 0.1 mile you will find that it is reasonably easy to bushwhack towards the top of the upper waterfall.

The gorge marks the end of the hike for most people, but it is by no means the end of the trail. For a description of the continuing route along the river, see section 104.

104 Gleasmans Falls via Stony Lake Road

Hiking, camping
5.2 miles, 2½ hours, rolling terrain

This trail to Gleasmans Falls is nearly twice as long as the route from Beach Mill Road. It is also much more circuitous, and parts of it are compromised by ATV usage—but if you appreciate solitude and wild surroundings, then in many ways this route can be much more enjoyable. The Beach Mill Trail is good, but this trail is more engaging, with more landmarks to see along the way, more twists and turns, and more varied terrain. The destination is the same, but in this case Gleasmans Falls will be the cherry on top of the sundae by the time you arrive at the rim of the gorge.

The trailhead is also much more remote. To find it, follow Erie Canal Road 4.4 miles south from Crystal Dale. At this point Stony Lake Road leads left, east, passing the north end of Chase Upper Lake at 2 miles. Winter plowing ends at 3.1 miles, and at 5.5 miles you exit state land to pass through a densely settled area at the south end of Stony Lake. State land resumes at 6.4 miles, and immediately after, at 6.5 miles, you reach the trailhead for the Fish Trail and the starting point for the hike to Gleasmans Falls. The public road dead-ends just 0.5 mile later at the end of state land.

The trail begins as a lightly used footpath that leads in 0.3 mile to a bridge between two beaver meadows. A moment later, at 0.4 mile, it intersects a well-used ATV trail and turns right to follow it. This is the Fish Trail, which originates on private land near Stony Lake and is used to access another private parcel ahead on the river. A very pretty section follows as you parallel the long beaver meadow to your right, the same one that you crossed on the footbridge. Further along, the trail passes through an open hardwood forest near the foot of Mount Tom. This section is marred by large mud wallows, but for the most part they can be easily bypassed.

At 1.5 miles the ATV trail forks left to a ford site on the Independence River. The foot trail bears right, paralleling the river to a large footbridge at 1.8 miles. The river is wide and rocky at this location, with "ordinary" banks that offer no hint of the extraordinary features downstream. At the far end of the bridge you reach a trail junction. The route to the right leads to Panther Pond and Smith Road as described in section 98.

To reach Gleasmans Falls, bear left. At 2.1 miles you reach the north end of the ATV ford, and soon after this point the trail pulls away from the river, reaching another fork at 2.5 miles. The ATV trail continues straight and leads into the private inholding. The foot trail—which here shows evidence of very little use and could be easy to miss—bears right to embark on a long and wild detour around the private property.

The first landmark is Third Creek, one of several numbered tributaries of the Independence River. It would be an unremarkable feature, except that the point where the trail crosses the stream is flanked by two enormous rock bluffs. The hike becomes unexpectedly rugged, with a brief scramble required to ascend the first ledge. You can hear the creek tumbling through the narrow gap between the bluffs, but the view from the open summit is more teasing than it is revealing. Pay careful attention to the markers as the trail crosses the open rock and descends back into the woods, crossing Third Creek at 2.8 miles. This stream might require a good jump to get across without getting your boots wet. Be sure to take a moment to bushwhack downstream no more than 200 feet to where the creek enters the narrow slot between the bluffs.

Bridge over Pine Creek

At Gleasmans Falls

After ascending over the second bluff—the identical twin of the first bluff—the trail angles north and reaches a long footbridge at 3.3 miles. A nearby sign labels this as Pine Creek, and like nearly every other stream in the area this one has been dammed by beavers. Hopefully the beavers will be inclined to stay, because the ponds they have created are quite attractive.

You have already rounded one corner of the square-shaped inholding, but low-lying terrain now forces the trail even further inland. The setting is really quite handsome, with coniferous forests crowning rocky knolls, but at its remotest point the trail is set 0.7 mile back from the river. The route then curves southward, where yet again you pass another large beaver flow nestled amongst the low ridges, this one straddling the west boundary of the private inholding. This marks the end of the detour. Note that the tread can be quite vague as it threads its way through the fern-filled woods.

Having now successfully circumvented the private land, the trail is free to return to the side of the river. It does so at 4.7 miles in a semi-open area with sparse tree cover and lots of brush. For the last 0.5 mile you remain quite close to the river, which follows a gentle course all the way to the top of the first waterfall. At this point the trail veers briefly inland, but your next view of the river will be from the rim of the Gleasmans Falls gorge, 5.2 miles from Stony Lake Road.

The open rock here is a choice location for a rest break, but it is not your only option. If you continue a little further up the trail, you will find a cleft in the gorge's sheer rock wall that allows reasonable off-trail access to the river. By staying on the trail, you only have to travel 0.1 mile further to find views of where the river exits the gorge.

Extended Outings

THE INTERCONNECTED TRAIL networks of the southwestern Adirondacks provide a favorable environment for hikers who enjoy planning loop hikes, through hikes, and multi-day treks. As enjoyable as a straightforward out-and-back hike to a single destination might be, a hike that involves little or no backtracking and strings together numerous destinations takes on the character of an adventure. The previous chapters have already suggested a few possibilities for such extended outings, but this chapter provides some additional ideas intended to spur the hiker's imagination.

Independence River Traverse
1 day, 10.8 miles

This through-trip begins at Beach Millpond and ends at Smith Road, passing Gleasmans Falls and Panther Pond along the way. Heading east through the valley of the Independence River, you will find the falls at 2.8 miles, where the rock ledges will invite you to either explore or relax. You will then be treated to attractive views of the upper part of the river before making a wild detour north around a private inholding. The "slot" through which Third Creek passes is a landmark unlike anything else in the region! You pass the footbridge leading to the Fish Trail at 6.2 miles, and a short distance later your route veers northeast through the seldom-seen country leading up to Panther Pond. The lean-to at the pond's north end is the last landmark before the trail ends at the parking area on Smith Road near Number Four.

Heart of the Ha-de-ron-dah Wilderness
2 days, 17 miles

This loop hike takes you past some of the most popular features of the Ha-de-ron-dah Wilderness, beginning and ending at the Scusa Trailhead on NY 28. Begin by following the well-used trail to Middle Settlement Lake (3.1 miles) and continue across the width of the wilderness to Lost Lake, East Pine Pond, and Pine Lake. Here, a short detour around the north end of Pine Lake will bring you to a lean-to at 7.4 miles. This is one of two camping options near the halfway point of the loop. The other is found by continuing northeast to Big Otter Lake, where there is a tent site on the south shore of the outlet channel, 9.7 miles from the starting point.

From Big Otter Lake, follow the Big Otter Trail southeast through a flooded area to the junction with the trail to Middle Branch Lake. You reach its lean-to at 13 miles, where a stop seems almost mandatory. A hilly trail leads southeast to Cedar Pond Junction. You could return to Middle Settlement Lake from here, although it's shorter (and requires less backtracking) to head east around Cedar Pond. By going this way you will return to the Scusa Trailhead at 17 miles, and only the final 0.6 mile will be duplicated from the start of the hike.

The Great Ha-de-ron-dah Loop
3 days, 24.6 miles

This route describes one of the longest possible loops within the Ha-de-ron-dah Wilderness, beginning and ending at the Herreshoff Road trailhead near Thendara. It connects all of the popular destinations along with a few of the lesser-known places, with attractive campsites at nearly every landmark. The suggested itinerary involves three 8-mile days, but with so many optional stopping points and side trips feel free to adjust the route to suit your hiking style.

Beginning at Herreshoff Road, follow the Big Otter Trail to the first interior junction, where the foot trail to East Pond turns right. East Pond features a small campsite and good views at 4.3 miles. Once you have had your fill, continue west toward Lost Creek, then southwest in the vicinity of Big Otter Lake. It is not always easy to spot, but an unmarked side trail leads to a good campsite on the lake's east shore, 7.9 miles from the beginning. If you are keeping to the 3-day pace, this is where you will want to consider camping for your first night out.

On the second day, return to the Big Otter Trail near South Inlet and proceed westward to the snowmobile bridge over the outlet, then southwest to Pine Lake. A short detour leads to the lean-to at 12 miles. Then turn southeast onto the foot trail leading past Lost Lake to Middle Settlement Lake. You will find its lean-to at 16.3 miles, but if it's already occupied (a frequent occurrence) then you will find alternate tent sites nearby for your second night of camping.

On the third day, follow the trails to Cedar Pond Junction (17.8 miles) and the Middle Branch Lake Lean-to (18.9 miles). From there, return to the Big

Otter Trail for the final time, and then follow it east past the foot of Moose River Mountain. Only the final 1.5 miles will be duplicated from the first day as you retrace your steps back to Herreshoff Road.

Woodhull Creek Loop
2 to 3 days, 25.5 miles

It is possible to enjoy a horseshoe-shaped loop that begins and ends on North Lake Road, passing five ponds, four lean-tos, and one waterfall on a multi-day walk through the Woodhull Creek watershed. The two trailheads (Stone Dam Lake and Little Woodhull Lake) are only 6.7 miles apart, which makes it very easy to spot vehicles at both ends. Depending on how far you like to hike in a single day, the loop can be neatly divided into 2-day or 3-day itineraries.

Beginning at the Stone Dam Lake trailhead, the route heads north to Chub Pond where there are lean-tos near the northern and southern shores. The northern lean-to (located at 7.1 miles) is by far the more attractive campsite, if only because it is located within view of the water. From there, follow the snowmobile trails past Buck Pond to Gull Lake, where you will find another scenic lean-to at 11.9 miles. This spot is just shy of the halfway point of the hike.

Continue to Mill Creek Road and follow it northeast to its end, where the snowmobile trail to Sand Lake Falls veers right. You will reach the fourth and final lean-to at a wooded spot beside the falls at 17.6 miles, in one of the remotest parts of the Black River Wild Forest. This is soon followed by a wet section of trail beside Woodhull Creek, but conditions quickly improve once you cross the outlet of Fourth Bisby Lake. At 20.3 miles you will want to bear right on the lightly used link trail to Little Woodhull Lake. This shallow body of water has no established campsites, but is still worth a visit. From there, it is an easy walk along a good trail back to North Lake Road, which you reach after 25.5 miles of hiking.

For a 2-day trip, the Gull Lake Lean-to at 11.9 miles is the logical stopping point for the night, although this leaves you with 13.6 miles to cover on the second day. If you prefer not to hike such long distances, then consider breaking this same route into a 3-day trek by stopping at Chub Pond's northern lean-to (7.1 miles) and Sand Lake Falls (17.6 miles) for an average of 8.5 miles per day.

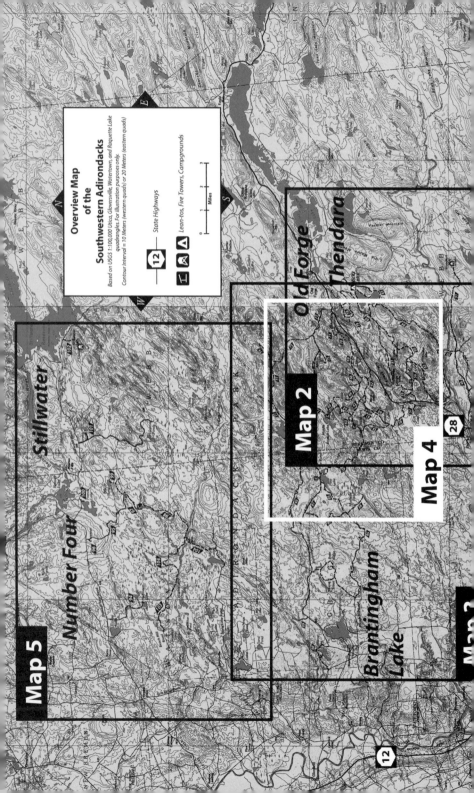

**Overview Map
of the
Southwestern Adirondacks**

Based on USGS 1:100,000 Utica, Gloversville, Watertown, and Raquette Lake
quadrangles. For illustration purposes only.
Contour Interval = 10 Meters (western quads) or 20 Meters (eastern quads)

12 State Highways

🏕 ⛺ 🔺 Lean-tos, Fire Towers, Campgrounds

0   1   2   3
Miles

Stillwater

Number Four

Old Forge

Thendara

Map 5

Map 2

Map 4

Brantingham
Lake

ADIRONDACK PARK

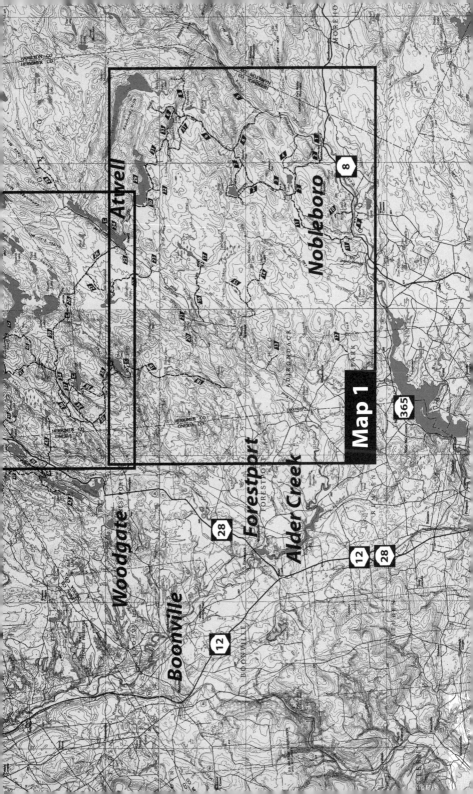

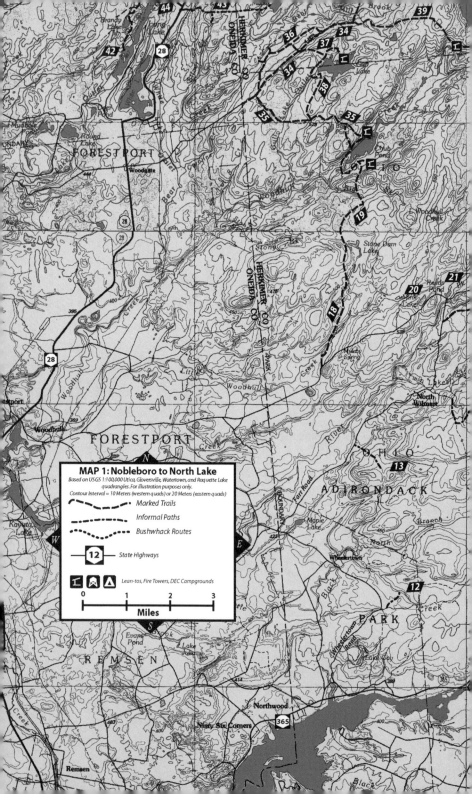

MAP 1: Nobleboro to North Lake

Based on USGS 1:100,000 Utica, Gloversville, Watertown, and Raquette Lake quadrangles. For illustration purposes only.

Contour Interval = 10 Meters (western quads) or 20 Meters (eastern quads)

--- — — --- Marked Trails

—·—·—·— Informal Paths

·········· Bushwhack Routes

12 State Highways

Lean-tos, Fire Towers, DEC Campgrounds

0   1   2   3

Miles

Continued on Map 3

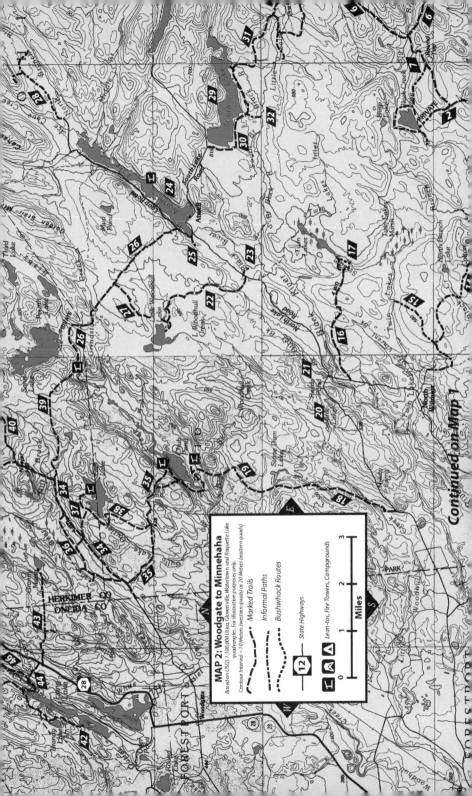

MAP 2: Woodgate to Minnehaha

Based on USGS 1:100,000 Utica, Glovesville, Watertown, and Piraquette Lake quadrangles. For illustration purposes only.

Contour Interval = 10 Meters (western quads) or 20 Meters (eastern quads)

Marked Trails

Informal Paths

Bushwhack Routes

12 State Highways

Lean-tos, Fire Towers, Campgrounds

Miles

0   1   2   3

94

103

104

104

Beach Mill
Road

M A T S O N

Huckleberry
Lake

Payne
Pond

Beaver River

Beaver River

Woodhaker
Pond

Meadow
Pond

Stony
Lake

Long
Lake

Fish
Pond

Sperryville

Stony Lake Road

Chub Lake

A D I R O N

Parsons
Pond

Chase
Lake

Hinchings
Pond

Buck
Mtn

Crooked
Lake

Pine
Grove

Sand
Pond

Little Otter
Lake

STATE FOREST
PRESERVES

Otter Creek

Mill
Trail

Pine Creek

Otter
Creek

89

88

G R

Partridgeville Road

90

Bear
Ridge

Crystal
Scoot

87

Deerlick
Pond

STATE FOREST
PRESERVE

Brantingham
Lake

Grieg

Brantingham

WD

Steam Mill Road

85

12

Campground

STATE FOREST
PRESERVES

MAP 3: Brantingham to Thendara

*Based on USGS 1:100,000 Utica, Gloversville, Watertown, and Raquette Lake
quadrangles. For illustration purposes only.
Contour Interval = 10 Meters (western quads) or 20 Meters (eastern quads)*

N

W   E

S

– – – – – –   Marked Trails

· – · – · – ·   Informal Paths

· · · · · · · ·   Bushwhack Routes

12   State Highways

⌐ 🗼 △   Lean-tos, Fire Towers, Campgrounds

0   1   2   3

Miles

Lyons
Falls

Watertown

Knowlville

Lyonsdale

Gould's
Mill

Potters
Corners

L Y O N S D A L E

Twin Sisters
Lake

Black River

Froar
Pond

Twin River

Potters
Corners

Continued on Map 2

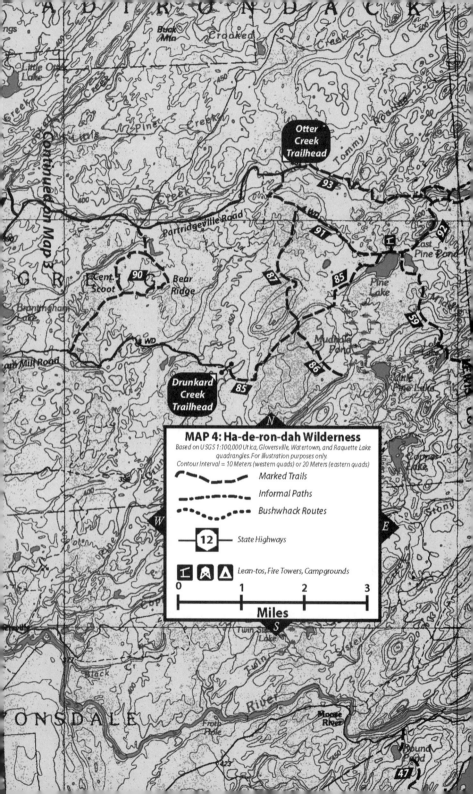

MAP 4: Ha-de-ron-dah Wilderness

Based on USGS 1:100,000 Utica, Gloversville, Watertown, and Raquette Lake quadrangles. For illustration purposes only.
Contour Interval = 10 Meters (western quads) or 20 Meters (eastern quads)

- — — — Marked Trails
- — · — · — Informal Paths
- · · · · · · Bushwhack Routes

12 State Highways

Lean-tos, Fire Towers, Campgrounds

0   1   2   3

Miles

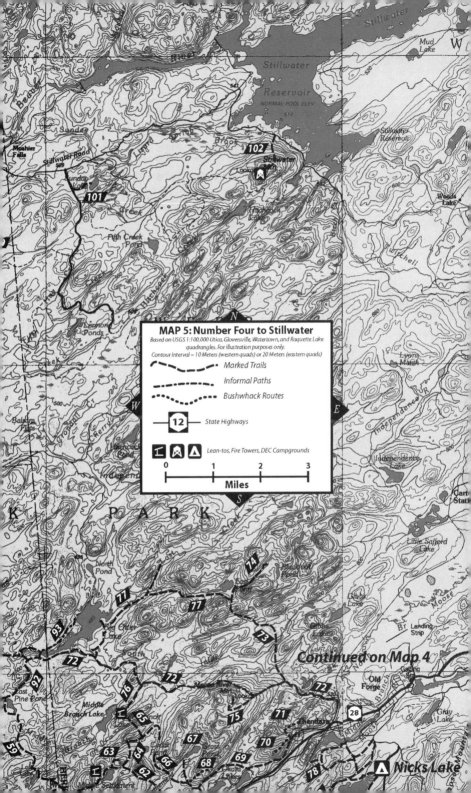

MAP 5: Number Four to Stillwater

Based on USGS 1:100,000 Utica, Gloversville, Watertown, and Raquette Lake
quadrangles. For illustration purposes only.
Contour Interval = 10 Meters (western quads) or 20 Meters (eastern quads)

— — — Marked Trails

· — · — · Informal Paths

· · · · · · Bushwhack Routes

[12] — State Highways

🛖 ⛺ ⛺ Lean-tos, Fire Towers, DEC Campgrounds

0   1   2   3

Miles

Continued on Map 4

References and Other Resources

References & Further Reading

Beetle, David H. *Up Old Forge Way and West Canada Creek*. Utica, New York: North Country Books, 1984. Reprint of 1946 and 1948 editions, printed by the Utica Observer-Dispatch, Utica, NY.

Brenan, Dan, ed. *Canoeing the Adirondacks with Nessmuk: The Adirondack Letters of George Washington Sears*. Blue Mountain Lake, New York: Adirondack Museum/ Syracuse University Press, 1962, reprinted 1993.

Dunham, Harvey L. *Adirondack French Louie: Early Life in the North Woods*. Utica, New York: North Country Books, 1953, reprinted 1996.

Grady, Joseph F. *The Adirondacks Fulton Chain – Big Moose Region: The Story of a Wilderness*. Utica, New York: North Country Books, 1933, reprinted 2002.

Graham, Frank, Jr. *The Adirondack Park: A Political History*. Syracuse, New York: Syracuse University Press, 1978, reprinted 1984.

Harter, Henry A. *Fairy Tale Railroad*. Utica, New York: North Country Books, 1979, reprinted 2001.

Herr, Charles. "The deCamp Steamer 'Fawn.'" Moose River House, 2008.

Jenkins, Jerry with Andy Keal. *The Adirondack Atlas: A Geographic Portrait of the Adirondack Park*. Syracuse, New York: Syracuse University Press/Adirondack Museum, 2004.

Kudish, Michael. *Mountain Railroads of New York State Volume One: Where Did the Tracks Go in the Western Adirondacks?* Fleischmanns, New York: Purple Mountain Press, 2005.

———. *Mountain Railroads of New York State Volume Two: Where Did the Tracks Go in the Central Adirondacks?* Fleischmanns, New York: Purple Mountain Press, 2007.

McMartin, Barbara. *Hides, Hemlocks and Adirondack History*. Utica, New York: North Country Books, 1992.

———. *The Great Forest of the Adirondacks*. Utica, New York: North Country Books, 1994, second printing 1998.

———. *The Privately Owned Adirondacks*. Canada Lake, New York: Lake View Press, 2004.

Murray, Hon. Amelia M. *Letters from the United States, Cuba and Canada, Vol. II*. London: John W. Parker and Son, 1856.

Podskoch, Martin. *Adirondack Fire Towers, Their History and Lore: The Southern Districts*. Fleischmanns, New York, 2003.

Simms, Jeptha R. *Trappers of New York, or a Biography of Nicholas Stoner & Nathaniel*

Snag at Twin Lakes

Foster; *together with Anecdotes of Other Celebrated Hunters, and Some Account of Sir William Johnson, and His Style of Living.* Albany, New York: J. Munsell, 1850.

Snyder, Charles E. "John Brown's Tract." *Papers Read before the Herkimer County Historical Society during the Years 1896, 1897 and 1898*, Citizen Publishing Company, 1899.

Storey, Mike. *Why the Adirondacks Look the Way They Do: A Natural History.* Saranac Lake, New York: Nature Knows Best Books, 2006.

Suter, H. M. "Forest Fires in the Adirondacks in 1903." United States Department of Agriculture, Bureau of Forestry, Circular No. 26, 1904.

Sylvester, Nathaniel Bartlett. *Historical Sketches of Northern New York and the Adirondack Wilderness: Including Traditions of the Indians, Early Explorers, Pioneer Settlers, Hermit Hunters, &c.* Troy, New York: William H. Young, 1877.

Thorpe, T. B. "A Visit to 'John Brown's Tract.'" *Harper's New Monthly Magazine*, July 1859.

VanValkenburgh, Norman J. *Land Acquisition for New York State: An Historical Perspective.* Arkville, New York: The Catskill Center for Conservation and Development, Inc., 1985.

Wallace, E. R. *Descriptive Guide to the Adirondacks*, Fourteenth Edition. Syracuse, New York: Bible Publishing House, 1889.

Whitford, David E. "Water Supply from the Adirondack Forest." *Annual Report of the State Engineer and Surveyor*, Wynkoop Hallenbeck Crawford Co., 1899.

Newspaper Articles

"Beach Mill Pond Only a Mirage; There's No Such Place in Lewis." *Watertown Daily Times*, May 21, 1965.

"Beach Mill Pond: Omission Is Seen Cause of Inclusion." *Watertown Daily Times*, May 22, 1965.

"Dix Has Risen Fast in State Politics." *The New York Times*, October 1, 1910.

"Measures to Prevent and Extinguish Forest Fires." *The Journal and Republican*, Lowville, May 11, 1922.

Forest Preserve Unit Management Plans

Ha-de-ron-dah Wilderness Unit Management Plan, First Five Year Revision, 1995

Independence River Wild Forest Unit Management Plan, 1986

Unit Management Plans for the Black River Wild Forest, Pratt-Northam Memorial Park, J.P. Lewis Tract Easement, John Brown Tract Easement, 1996

Other Resources

New York State Department of Environmental Conservation (Headquarters), 625 Broadway, Albany, NY 12233. Website: *www.dec.ny.gov*.

NYS DEC Herkimer Office, 225 North Main Street, Herkimer, NY 13350. Phone: (315) 866-6330.

NYS DEC Lowville Office, 7327 State Route 812, Lowville, NY 13367. Phone: (315) 376-3521.

Adirondack Mountain Club, 814 Goggins Road, Lake George, NY 12845. Phone: (518) 668-4447. Website: *www.adk.org*.

Leave No Trace Center for Outdoor Ethics, PO Box 997, Boulder, CO 80306. Phone: (800) 332-4100. Website: *www.LNT.org*.

Index

Beaver-chewed stumps in the Ha-de-ron-dah Wilderness

Barbara McMartin (1931-2005) was for over thirty years one of the Adirondacks' most active supporters. Her knowledge of the Adirondacks was comprehensive and deeply personal. Few people have written as intimately, as accurately, or with as much enthusiasm about this magnificent area. She was an avid hiker, specializing in uncovering little-used routes and forgotten places. She originated the *Discover* series and was also the author of *50 Hikes in the Adirondacks*, as well as seven histories. During her long career, she served as the vice-president of the Adirondack Mountain Club and the Association for the Protection of the Adirondacks. She chaired the Adirondack Park Centennial in 1992, and served on the DEC's Forest Preserve Advisory Committee from 1974 to 2004, the last six years as chair.

Bill Ingersoll has hiked and backpacked in the wildernesses of Montana, Wyoming, New Mexico, and California, but feels most at home in the grand forests of the Adirondacks. He became a co-author for the *Discover* series in 2000 and has now become the series' publisher. He is the author of *Snowshoe Routes: Adirondacks and Catskills*, and his articles and photos have appeared in *Adirondack Explorer, Adirondack Sports and Fitness,* and *Adirondack Life* magazines. A graduate of RIT, Ingersoll serves on the conservation committee for the Adirondack Mountain Club. You will find him exploring the North Country with his dog Lexie in all four seasons, by trail, snowshoe, and canoe.

DISCOVER
THE
SOUTHWESTERN
ADIRONDACKS

The southwestern Adirondacks are a place for nature lovers: those who want to be close to wildlife; who delight in a sphagnum bog or a pine-crowned sandy ridge; who like long, level trails or well-groomed routes for hiking; or who want to feel as if the whole forest is theirs to enjoy in solitary quiet.

The majority of the walks described in this guidebook are gentle, mirroring the gentle blue hills you see as you approach the region. The forest will seem vast and inviting, with no lack of secluded nooks to investigate. If you become seized with the curiosity to see what lies down one of those little-used trails, then this book is for you.

This edition includes descriptions of new places, enhanced descriptions of many familiar destinations, attractive photos, and newly redesigned maps to help you plan your next adventure!